# TAX CUTS AND JOBS ACT

# TAX CUTS AND JOBS ACT:

## THE COMPLETE BILL

Introduction by Patricia Cohen
Foreword by Michael Cohn

SKYHORSE PUBLISHING

First Published by the 115th US Congress in 2017.
First Skyhorse edition 2018.



Skyhorse Publishing books may be purchased in bulk at special discounts for sales promotion, corporate gifts, fund-raising, or educational purposes. Special editions can also be created to specifications. For details, contact the Special Sales Department, Skyhorse Publishing, 307 West 36th Street, 11th Floor, New York, NY 10018 or info@skyhorsepublishing.com.



Visit our website at www.skyhorsepublishing.com.

10 9 8 7 6 5 4 3 2 1

Library of Congress Cataloging-in-Publication Data is available on file.

Cover design by Brian Peterson

Print ISBN: 978-1-5107-3729-7
Ebook ISBN: 978-1-5107-3730-3

Printed in the United States of America

# CONTENTS

# FOREWORD

By Michael Cohn, editor-in-chief of AccountingToday.com

The Tax Cuts and Jobs Act moved swiftly through Congress at the end of 2017, reaching President Donald Trump's desk only days before Christmas, with little time for debate over the most far-reaching tax legislation since 1986.

The Republican-led bill passed mostly along party lines in both the House and Senate using a budget reconciliation procedure that allowed the legislation to avoid an almost certain filibuster by Senate Democrats. The House and Senate versions of the bill differed in some significant ways, including the number of individual tax brackets and a repeal of the Affordable Care Act's individual mandate, so a conference committee of lawmakers from both chambers met to reconcile the two pieces of legislation. Much of the real work of crafting the legislation and working out the compromises occurred behind closed doors, to the chagrin of Democrats, who complained they were learning about important changes in the bill from press reports and leaks from lobbyists.

Republican lawmakers agreed on a set of last-minute changes to entice a handful of reluctant GOP senators to support the legislation. Some of the changes softened several of the most controversial provisions, although the bill is still likely to provoke controversy for years to come as its impact becomes clearer. The compromise legislation that emerged from the conference committee came up before the House and Senate again for a vote in the week before Christmas. The Senate parliamentarian ruled that some of its provisions violated Senate rules, so a few were struck out, including some related to tax breaks for education. Even the name of the bill itself was challenged, so it is officially known as "An Act to provide for reconciliation pursuant to titles II and V of the concurrent resolution on the budget for fiscal year 2018." The bill then came up for one last vote before the House before it passed the final time and was signed into law just in time to meet President Trump's pledge to pass the tax overhaul before Christmas. It was the most significant legislation passed during his first year in office, and one of the most consequential for any president to sign, as it will affect nearly every American taxpayer. The repeal of the Affordable Care Act's individual mandate alone will probably have a substantial impact on the health care system and insurance market.

The bill reduces tax rates for both businesses and individuals. Many of the sharpest tax reductions are on the corporate side, where the maximum tax rate has declined from 35 percent to 21 percent. The corporate tax cuts are permanent, but the individual tax cuts are only temporary, many of them set to expire in 2025 or 2027, and in some cases even earlier, in order to keep the legislation from adding more than $1.5 trillion to the deficit over ten years. They are likely to be extended by a future Congress, but there is never any guarantee what Congress will do.

Under the original House Republican proposal, the tax plan would have reduced the number of individual tax brackets from seven to four. The Senate Republican plan kept the number of brackets at seven. In the end, the legislation retains seven tax brackets, but the maximum rate has gone down from 39.6 percent to 37 percent. The rates are now 10, 12, 22, 24, 32, 35 and 37 percent. The top rate would apply to single taxpayers with over $500,000 in income, and married couples with more than $600,000. Most people would see their tax rate go down under the plan, although many would also lose deductions or see the amount of those deductions sharply limited.

For example, the longtime deduction for state and local taxes, which has been a feature of the tax code ever since the 1913 introduction of the federal income tax, is now going to be limited to $10,000. That's a compromise, though, since the original version of the legislation from House Republicans eliminated the deduction for state and local income and sales taxes entirely. The measure was seen as punishing so-called "blue states," which traditionally vote for Democrats and rely heavily on state income tax revenue. In the end, after hearing objections from Republican lawmakers in those states, the conference committee decided to allow up to $10,000 in deductions for a combination of state and local property taxes and either income or sales taxes. Still, for taxpayers in high-tax states and cities, that may not be enough to make up for the deductions they would otherwise lose. Passage of the legislation prompted many people to scramble to pay their 2018 property taxes before the end of 2017 in states like New York and municipalities that allowed it. That way, they would be able to deduct more of their 2018 state and local income or sales taxes in 2019. The Internal Revenue Service (IRS) soon advised taxpayers, though, that prepayments would only be deductible for 2017 if the property taxes had been assessed before the end of the year.

Another popular deduction that has been scaled back under the bill is for mortgage interest. For new homes or new mortgages on a first or second home, the deduction is capped at $750,000 (or $375,000 for married taxpayers who file separately), down from $1 million. Homeowners who already have a mortgage as of December 15, 2017 can still take the full deduction of $1 million, or $500,000 for married couples who file separately.

Also on the chopping block is the deduction for alimony payments, but there's a little extra time to arrange a divorce as it only applies to divorce or separation agreements after the end of 2018. Personal casualty losses and theft losses can't be deducted either, unless they can be attributed to a disaster officially declared by the president.

Taxpayers with serious medical problems who were worried Congress might repeal the medical expense deduction can breathe a sigh of relief. The final legislation actually enhances the medical expense deduction, at least for two years, lowering the threshold for claiming the deduction to 7.5 percent of adjusted gross income for the 2017 and 2018 tax years. The threshold used to be 10 percent, meaning the taxpayer's medical expenses had to be at least 10 percent of their income. Thanks to the change, more taxpayers with high medical expenses should be able to qualify, albeit temporarily.

To make up for the lost deductions for taxpayers who traditionally itemize, the bill nearly doubles the standard deduction, from $6,350 to $12,000 for single taxpayers, from $12,700 to $24,000 for couples, and from $9,350 to $18,000 for heads of households. The doubling of the standard deduction is expected to cause more people to stop itemizing deductions, hence the concept of tax simplification. But that could be a problem for many charities that depend on contributions and the tax deductions associated with them. While the tax reform law does retain the deduction for charitable contributions, it's expected to mainly benefit individual taxpayers whose total itemized deductions exceed the new standard deduction level of $12,000, or $24,000 for couples.

The tax reform law gets rid of personal exemptions, including for dependents such as children and aged parents, along with the personal exemption phaseout. Personal exemptions of $4,050 had been allowed for each family member. This may wipe out the benefit of the standard deduction for many families. On the other hand, the new law doubles the Child Tax Credit from $1,000 to $2,000 for each child. Up to $1,400 would be refundable in 2018, so even parents who don't earn enough to pay income taxes could qualify for the tax credit. The credit starts to phase out for couples who earn more than $400,000, and single parents who earn more than $200,000. A new $500 temporary tax credit until 2025 for non-child dependents offers some aid to people caring for elderly parents, children over seventeen years of age, and adult children with disabilities.

Congress decided to use a different measure of inflation in the income cutoffs for tax brackets, which may put many taxpayers in higher tax brackets in the years ahead, even if their salaries don't go up as much. The measure, known as "chained consumer price index," or "chained CPI" for short, tends to state the rate of inflation lower than the traditional consumer price index. Each year, the IRS adjusts the income levels for the tax brackets and many other tax items based on inflation.

The alternative minimum tax (AMT), which was expected to be repealed under the new tax reform law, is actually going to stay, at least for individual taxpayers, but with some modifications. The AMT is a supplemental income tax required in addition to regular income tax for some who have exemptions or special circumstances allowing for lower payments of standard income tax. The exemption amount is going up to $109,400 for married couples filing jointly, and $70,300 for singles and others, through 2025. The AMT is also going to apply just to incomes over $1 million for joint filers and $500,000 for singles and other filers. In contrast, the corporate version of the AMT for businesses has been completely repealed.

Repeal of the estate tax, often derided as the "death tax," has been a long-cherished goal of Republicans. While the original proposal was to gradually do away with the estate tax, the conference committee followed the Senate's lead and opted to double both the estate and gift tax exclusion for people who die or make gifts after December 31, 2017 and before January 1, 2026. That means married couples can now inherit up to $20 million (or $22.4 million indexed for inflation), while single taxpayers can receive up to $10 million (or around $11.2 million indexed for inflation) without facing estate or gift taxes.

Many students had reason to be thankful for some alterations to the original legislation. Graduate students won't be subject to taxes on tuition waivers after some last-minute changes in the conference committee. The final legislation also keeps the deduction on student loan interest. There are even some expansions in tax breaks for section

529 education savings plans and ABLE accounts. The 529 plans have traditionally been used to save money for college, but can now apply to elementary and secondary schools as well. "Qualified higher education expenses" now include tuition at an elementary or secondary public, private, or religious school. However, the Senate parliamentarian said no to permitting 529 plans to be used for home schooling. The assets from 529 plans can now be rolled over to ABLE savings accounts, which benefit people with disabilities. The final legislation left out some of the proposals in the House bill that would have combined the American Opportunity Tax Credit (AOTC) with the Hope Scholarship Credit and Lifetime Learning Credit into an enhanced AOTC, and repealed the exclusion on interest on US savings bonds used for higher education, so all those tax breaks are still available.

School teachers can continue to deduct up to $250 in classroom supplies they pay for out of pocket. The House version of the tax bill had eliminated the longstanding deduction, while the Senate version doubled it to $500, but the conference committee decided in the end to keep it at $250.

Those who are saving for retirement can also rest easier, as the law mostly keeps the existing tax breaks for 401(k) accounts and individual retirement accounts, despite some proposals to eliminate the ability to have 401(k) contributions taken out on a pre-tax basis. There are a few changes, though, like elimination of the ability to recharacterize Roth IRA contributions as regular IRA contributions when undoing a Roth conversion.

That just covers the individual side of the tax code. On the business side, there are plenty of changes in the tax law, starting with the dramatic and "permanent" reduction of the top corporate tax rate from 35 down to 21 percent and some tax breaks for pass-through businesses too. Businesses will be able to fully and immediately expense the cost of equipment they buy and place in service between September 27, 2017 and January 1, 2023, instead of needing to depreciate it over time. The so-called "bonus depreciation" tax break increases from 50 percent to 100 percent of the property placed in service between those dates. It also now applies to the purchase of used property, not just new equipment. Starting in 2023, the tax break starts to phase out.

A related tax break involves expensing under Section 179 of the tax code. The dollar limitation for Section 179 expensing has increased under the new tax law to $1 million, while the phase-out threshold or investment limitation has increased to $2.5 million. More types of property can now be included within Section 179 expenses, such as some depreciable tangible personal property used to provide lodging. On the other hand, there are limitations now on net operating losses, restricting them to 80 percent of a business's taxable income and eliminating most carrybacks of losses for previous tax years.

One of the goals of the 21 percent maximum corporate tax rate is to put the United States more in line with other industrialized countries and bring more jobs and profits back from abroad. Most large multinational corporations don't pay anywhere close to the old maximum 35 percent, but with the new lower tax rate, the hope is they will be less likely to move their tax address to low-tax countries like Ireland and the Cayman Islands while deferring taxes on the profits they hold abroad. The new tax law moves the United States to what's known as a "territorial tax system," instead of a worldwide tax system that taxes companies on their foreign profits once they're brought back to the United States. The Tax Cuts and Jobs Act aims to encourage companies to "repatriate" the trillions of dollars estimated to be held offshore, taxing them at a reduced rate of 15.5 percent for cash assets and 8 percent for noncash or illiquid assets. The tax bill also repeals the corporate AMT of 20 percent, enabling companies to reduce their effective tax rate further.

Pass-through businesses, such as partnerships, S corporations, limited liability companies, and sole proprietorships, which have traditionally paid their taxes at individual tax rates, also get some new rules under the tax law. Their rates don't fall as low as the corporate tax rate because Congress wanted to set up "guardrails" to keep individual taxpayers from simply reclassifying all their income as business income. House and Senate Republicans differed in how their versions of the bill treated pass-through business income. The conference committee mostly went with the Senate approach, but with some changes. The final legislation gives business owners a 20 percent deduction on their business income, reducing their effective marginal tax rate to a maximum of 29.6 percent, but with limits starting at $315,000 for married couples, or half that amount for single people. There are also limitations for some professional service providers such as accountants, lawyers, and doctors on treating their compensation income as profits to qualify for the lower rate. In other words, accountants who will have the burden of making sense of the new tax laws for their clients won't get as much benefit, aside from charging for all the extra work.

The carried interest tax break used by hedge fund managers and private equity firm partners that President Trump pledged to eliminate during his campaign survived thanks to Congress and lobbyists, albeit with the holding period for long-term capital gains extended to three years to qualify for the lower capital gains tax rate.

Incentives for renewable energy sources haven't changed as much as feared. The original House version of the tax bill would have gotten rid of the tax credit for plug-in electric vehicles and scaled back tax incentives for energy efficient homes, but the Senate bill largely kept those tax breaks intact along with the Investment Tax Credit and Production Tax Credit on which the energy industry relies. The final bill also lets companies offset up to 80 percent of taxes on their foreign transactions with renewable energy tax credits until 2025. But the final bill continues to worry some producers of wind and solar energy because of a provision called BEAT, short for Base Erosion and Anti-Abuse Tax. BEAT kicks in if they make 3 percent of their deductible payments to a foreign affiliate, or 2 percent for banks. Renewable energy producers worry the BEAT provision could reduce the incentives for tax equity financing they receive from banks and other sources.

For the fossil fuel industry, the Senate added a controversial provision opening the Arctic National Wildlife Refuge to oil drilling.

All in all, the Tax Cuts and Jobs Act holds plenty of uncertainty for taxpayers. While many can look forward to tax breaks in the next few years, it's up to Congress to decide whether to extend the tax cuts for individuals beyond 2025 and make them as permanent as the corporate tax cut, at the risk of adding trillions more dollars to the national debt. Much of the work of clarifying the hastily written legislation and spelling out the exact regulations, as well as authoritative guidance, will fall to the IRS, an agency that has suffered a series of budget cuts and staff reductions in recent years and will now have to scramble to put the law into practice over the course of 2018. Congress will likely need to produce a follow-up technical corrections bill to fix drafting errors and close unintentional loopholes, as was necessary after previous tax cut legislation. But with Democrats feeling sidelined by Republicans' insistence on passing the bill without meaningful input from the other side of the aisle, the two parties may not be able to agree on a technical corrections bill, leaving the Tax Cuts and Jobs Act in its present form as the law of the land.

# INTRODUCTION

by Patricia Cohen, an economics and tax policy reporter for the *New York Times*

The Republicans' hurried passage of a costly and contentious tax bill in the final weeks of 2017 ushers in a sweeping overhaul that will touch the lives of minimum-wage workers and multimillionaires, and affect businesses with kitchen-table headquarters and those with corporate boardrooms.

The new law, signed by President Donald Trump in the Oval Office on December 22, 2017 contains more than what he described as a "great, big, beautiful" Christmas present of a tax cut. This important political and legislative victory for Republicans also presages a further revamping of the social contract between Americans and their government, and a ratcheting up of bitter partisan fighting.

Tax legislation is always messy, complicated, and politically fraught. Yet even by those standards, the 2017 rewrite broke new ground. Battered by criticism from the president, the public, and irate donors for failing to follow through on other policy initiatives, the Republican leadership in Congress decided to push through a major tax plan at breakneck speed, with virtually no public debate and no input from Democrats.

Votes were scheduled before Congress's own scorekeepers finished their estimates of the legislation's economic, budgetary, and distributional effects. And although the bill is the most comprehensive rewrite of the tax code in three decades, even Republican lawmakers acknowledged they had little time to read it and were unfamiliar with many details. Such circumstances are what make the publication of the law in its entirety all the more pressing.

In the end, Republican supporters argued that the benefits outweighed the drawbacks. The whole process took roughly seven weeks, a rebuke to critics who complained of a do-nothing Congress. President Trump marketed the bill as economic "rocket fuel" that would propel the economy to unaccustomed growth and prosperity. Businesses would use their sizable tax windfalls to take risks, invest, and hire, proponents argued, and consumers would spend more. The promises echoed those made by trickle-down theorists who believe that giving more money to people at the very top of the income ladder will eventually flow down to those on rungs lower down.

Dramatic reductions in taxes for corporations and other businesses in the final plan were given top priority and elicited widespread applause from chief executives and trade associations. The act transformed the way global profits are taxed in an effort to persuade companies to keep operations in the United States and reduce their reliance on foreign tax havens. Changes to the individual side that increased the standard deduction and eliminated breaks will simplify filing for more Americans. In the beginning, a majority of taxpayers will see a modest, temporary tax cut. The largest and longest-lasting rewards go to the richest households. This group pays the most money in taxes, but has also reaped the largest pre-tax benefits in recent decades.

The hasty passage, though, came at a cost that extends beyond the $1.5 trillion price tag over ten years. It also meant slapdash legislative language that invites creative tax dodging, an unusual level of secrecy, and insufficient time to analyze the impact of untested provisions.

For years, both Democrats and Republicans have railed against the tax system's deep flaws and undertook attempts at repairs. The code as a whole was needlessly complex, and in the context of a globalized economy, many provisions affecting businesses were outdated. Although most companies paid less than the nominal corporate rate of 35 percent, multinationals complained that they were at a disadvantage relative to foreign competitors. Some of the international provisions had the perverse effect of incentivizing companies to locate headquarters and other operations abroad. And the ability to delay paying taxes on global profits that had not been repatriated encouraged companies like Apple, Amazon, Pfizer, and others to keep nearly $3 trillion in foreign earnings off their US books and out of the Internal Revenue Service's reach. Wily accountants and tax lawyers had figured more and more ways to shelter income from tax collectors. Loopholes and special interest breaks generated inefficiencies and undermined confidence in the system's fundamental fairness.

Although control of the White House and Congress shifted hands over the years, majorities in both parties continued to embrace several reform guideposts: reduce the corporate rate in exchange for gutting industry-specific tax breaks; employ a bipartisan approach to ensure long-term predictability; don't increase the deficit; simplify the code and eliminate notorious tax avoidance provisions. As presidential candidates, both Hillary Clinton and Donald Trump, for example, had promised to get rid of the so-called "carried interest" deduction, which permits hedge fund, real estate, and private equity managers to reclassify what are essentially management fees as investment income in order to pay a sharply reduced tax.

By the time the bill passed in the House of Representatives and the Senate, though, several of these goals were abandoned. The carried interest deduction remained essentially intact. Some of the new provisions expire. And the deficit is estimated to balloon by more than $1 trillion over ten years according to Congress' nonpartisan Joint Committee on Taxation. Still, Republican lawmakers, including impassioned deficit hawks who vowed to "never, never, ever" add a single penny to the nation's debt load, ultimately rallied around the plan.

Among the highlights on the individual side:

- The new law maintains seven tax brackets, but lowers the highest from 39.6 percent to 37 percent. Over time, some people will find themselves shifting more rapidly than expected to a higher tax bracket because the inflation measure will be switched to one that slows the pace of price increases.
- The standard deduction for singles will increase from $6,350 to $12,000 and from $12,700 to $24,000 for couples. This is likely to shrink the share of households that itemize their taxes from 30 percent to roughly 6 percent. Personal exemptions, worth $4,050 for each person claimed, and a boon to larger families, will be eliminated. The decline in itemized deductions may cause charitable contributions to decline.
- The alternative minimum tax remains, but with a higher exemption level.
- The child tax credit doubles to $2,000; a larger refundable portion will allow more lower-income families to benefit even if they don't owe any taxes.
- Families who put money into tax-free education savings accounts known as 529s will be able to use those funds to pay for K–12 education, in addition to college.
- The deduction for state and local taxes—whether for property, sales, or income—was capped at $10,000. High tax states, like liberal-leaning New York and California, will be hit the hardest.
- The penalty for not having health insurance, a feature of the Affordable Care Act intended to keep the system solvent, was eliminated. Taxpayers will be able to deduct medical expenses that exceed 7.5 percent of their income, instead of the current 10 percent.
- The deduction on mortgage interest will be capped at $750,000 worth of debt, down from $1 million. The deductibility of home equity loans was eliminated.

- The estate tax, which under current law applies to the top 0.2 percent of Americans with individual estates worth more than $5.49 million, will in the future apply only to individual estates valued at more than $11.2 million ($22.4 million for couples).

As for the business side of the ledger:

- The corporate tax will be cut from 35 percent to 21 percent.
- Also slated for a tax cut are other businesses like proprietorships, partnerships, and closely held corporations that pass along profits to their owners or shareholders, who are then taxed at ordinary rates. Pass-through earnings up to $157,500 for individuals and $315,000 for couples will now get a 20 percent discount. The measure applies to small enterprises like corner newsstands and self-employed house painters as well as global giants like Cargill, Georgia-Pacific (a Koch Industries subsidiary), and the National Football League. More than 95 percent of the nation's businesses are characterized as pass-throughs, but most of the money they earn—nearly 70 percent—goes to people in the top 1 percent.
- The new plan eliminates the corporate alternative minimum tax, allows full expensing for five years, and caps business interest deductions at 30 percent.
- Some of the most radical changes can be found in the international provisions. The United States is shifting away from what is known as a worldwide system—where corporate profits are taxed no matter where they are earned—to a territorial one, in which only earnings generated within its own borders are taxed. The new law also imposes a mandatory one-time tax on unrepatriated profits—15.5 percent on cash and 8 percent on non-liquid assets—that American multinationals racked up overseas.

The clearest winners are businesses and wealthy Americans, who own the most stock and receive the lion's share of gains in dividends and stock prices that flow from the corporate cuts. Middle-class Americans get small tax reductions in the early years, but most of those breaks are scheduled to expire in 2025. By the end of the ten-year window, most households with a yearly income of $75,000 or less will end up with a tax increase. Those who earn more can continue to look forward to additional tax cuts. In 2027, the top 1 percent will corral 83 percent of the tax benefits that year, according to the nonpartisan Tax Policy Center.

Lowering the tax rate most for the highest-income Americans makes the tax code less progressive. There will also be a significant redistribution from middle-income households to million-dollar ones compared to what would have occurred under the existing law. Estimates by the Joint Committee on Taxation show that by 2027, households with annual incomes between $40,000 to $75,000 would lose a total of $8.4 billion, while those earning $1 million or more would gain $8.5 billion. (The estimates include the loss of health insurance subsidies to lower-income Americans who are unlikely to sign up for insurance once the Affordable Care Act's mandate is repealed.) At the same time, the doubling of the estate tax exemption allows the first $22 million of a family estate to escape any tax at all. Such measures will continue to widen the inequality gap.

Because of the legislation's scope and ambition, the mammoth tax reform of 1986 has become a frequent reference point. But a comparison of the two bills ends up highlighting important differences much more starkly than similarities.

First, the 1986 reform bill was notable for its bipartisanship. Although Democrats controlled the House of Representatives and Republicans controlled the White House then, the groundbreaking effort on taxes rested on several earlier bipartisan initiatives that enabled both sides to slowly build up trust over a period of several years. In 1981, for example, they agreed on deep across-the-board cuts in personal marginal rates, followed by significant deficit reduction in 1982. In 1983, the Democratic House Speaker Tip O'Neill and President Ronald

Reagan collaborated to rescue Social Security from bankruptcy, and Democratic Senator Bill Bradley of New Jersey co-sponsored a tax bill.

In contrast, Republicans in 2017 froze out Democrats. Out-of-favor constituencies and large liberal urban centers were ignored or punished. At one point in the process, Democratic Senator Claire McCaskill of Missouri tweeted that the only reason she had a list of proposed amendments was that a lobbyist—and not her Republican colleagues—had shared it. By opting for a slim majority vote, Republican leaders utilized a mechanism known as budget reconciliation that enabled them to sidestep the threat of a Democratic filibuster. But that process meant adhering to certain budgetary restrictions that ended up driving the negotiations, as well as certain time limits that undermined the law's long-term sustainability.

Second, the authors of the 1986 reform were intent on simplifying the code and eliminating opportunities for tax avoidance by exploiting rate differences. One of the features they were proudest of was a uniform tax rate on income regardless of whether it came from a paycheck or investments. It marked a brief period when long-term capital gains were taxed at the same rate as salaries. The rationale was contained in a 1984 Treasury Department report: "A tax that places significantly different burdens on taxpayers in similar economic circumstances is not fair. For example, if two similar families have the same income, they should ordinarily pay roughly the same amount of income tax, regardless of the sources or uses of that income."*

The 2017 act moves in the opposite direction, varying rates even more and basing them on novel characteristics, such as organizational structure and occupation. For the first time since the income tax was adopted, wage and salary earners' income will be taxed at a different rate than the income of people who are self-employed or organized as partnerships and S corporations.

---

* Tax Reform report of the Treasury Department to President Ronald Reagan, November 1984

And while some special tax breaks were eliminated, others were inserted that favor particular industries, such as craft beer and wine producers, private equity, oil and gas pipeline managers, and commercial real estate. Such special treatment is a testament to the abiding influence of lobbyists and wealthy donors.

Finally, the 1986 legislation was the culmination of a long process that aired, scrutinized, and debated competing ideas, provisions, and legislative language. President Reagan's Treasury Department issued two in-depth reports, for example, while Congress held extensive hearings.

The rush and secrecy that characterized the 2017 effort was so pronounced that even some Republican supporters criticized the proceedings. Hearings were scarce and the Treasury Department produced no full-blown assessment. Only after repeated criticisms did the agency issue a vague, one-page analysis in the final days that was based on a raft of unspecified future policy changes and an unusually optimistic estimate that the economy would grow 2.9 percent over the next decade.

Ultimately the White House and Republican congressional leaders simply eschewed traditional forecasts and models. They declared that the economic hurricane unleashed by the tax cuts would make up for its hefty cost and spur growth far beyond the 2.1 percent that the US economy had averaged since the financial crisis—although virtually no independent analyses, including the one done by Congress's Joint Committee on Taxation, supported those claims.

In December 2017, the nation's central bank, the Federal Reserve, for instance, estimated overall real growth at 2.5 percent in 2018, 2.1 percent in 2019, and 1.8 percent over the longer run. On Wall Street, the consensus forecasts did not stray far from that mark. Analysts mostly viewed the tax plan as functioning like a sugar rush, providing a burst of economic momentum in the first two years, but petering out after that.

Conservative and liberal economists agree that large tax cuts don't pay for themselves through economic growth and that cuts financed by deficits do more harm than good in the long run because they reduce savings and push up interest rates. Tax breaks can provide incentives to invest, but businesses are more swayed by technological advances and demand for their goods or services. And when the economy is operating close to full employment, as a jobless rate near 4 percent would suggest, the impact tax cuts have is more limited.

Some critics argue that the $1.5 trillion being spent on the tax plan would do more to boost growth if it were put to other uses, such as invested in roads and bridges, communications technology, education, health care, or research and development.

The bill's high cost and the staggering deficits do, however, pave the way for another important Republican goal: spending cuts. Party leaders have long made clear their desire to rollback the social spending of the New Deal and the Great Society and shrink the safety net. Drastically reducing federal revenues is one way to do it. As the tax bill was hurtling its way through Congress, Republican leaders pointed to entitlements like Medicare, Medicaid, and Social Security, in addition to other programs designed to aid poor and elderly Americans, as the main reason the nation's debt load was reaching an unmanageable level. House Speaker Paul Ryan of Wisconsin talked of tackling the major entitlement programs in the next session while President Trump promised "to go into welfare reform."

The tax plan begins to take a step in that direction. Eliminating the federal penalty for failing to have health insurance will result in 13 million fewer people with coverage, according to the Congressional Budget Office, and a 10 percent rise in insurance premiums.

On a local scale, capping the deduction of state and local taxes is another way of pressuring high-tax states to curb their spending.

Regardless of what follows, though, one sector that is guaranteed to flourish as a result of the new legislation is tax preparation, as accountants and tax lawyers work to understand all the new provisions, and then figure out ways to comply, exploit, or circumvent them.

115TH CONGRESS
*1st Session*

HOUSE OF REPRESENTATIVES

REPORT
115—___

# TAX CUTS AND JOBS ACT

________, 2017.—Ordered to be printed

Mr. Brady of Texas, from the committee of conference, submitted the following

## CONFERENCE REPORT

[To accompany H.R. 1]

The committee of conference on the disagreeing votes of the two Houses on the amendment of the Senate to the bill (H.R. 1), to provide for reconciliation pursuant to titles II and V of the concurrent resolution on the budget for fiscal year 2018, having met, after full and free conference, have agreed to recommend and do recommend to their respective Houses as follows:

That the House recede from its disagreement to the amendment of the Senate and agree to the same with an amendment as follows:

In lieu of the matter proposed to be inserted by the Senate amendment, insert the following:

And the Senate agree to the same.

# TITLE I

**SEC. 11000. SHORT TITLE, ETC.**

(a) SHORT TITLE.—This title may be cited as the "Tax Cuts and Jobs Act".

(b) AMENDMENT OF 1986 CODE.—Except as otherwise expressly provided, whenever in this title an amendment or repeal is expressed in terms of an amendment to, or repeal of, a section or other provision, the reference shall be considered to be made to a section or other provision of the Internal Revenue Code of 1986.

## Subtitle A—Individual Tax Reform

### PART I—TAX RATE REFORM

**SEC. 11001. MODIFICATION OF RATES.**

(a) IN GENERAL.—Section 1 is amended by adding at the end the following new subsection:

"(j) MODIFICATIONS FOR TAXABLE YEARS 2018 THROUGH 2025.—

"(1) IN GENERAL.—In the case of a taxable year beginning after December 31, 2017, and before January 1, 2026—

"(A) subsection (i) shall not apply, and

"(B) this section (other than subsection (i)) shall be applied as provided in paragraphs (2) through (6).

"(2) RATE TABLES.—

"(A) MARRIED INDIVIDUALS FILING JOINT RETURNS AND SURVIVING SPOUSES.—The following table shall be applied in lieu of the table contained in subsection (a):

| **"If taxable income is:** | **The tax is:** |
|---|---|
| Not over $19,050 | 10% of taxable income. |
| Over $19,050 but not over $77,400 | $1,905, plus 12% of the excess over $19,050. |
| Over $77,400 but not over $165,000 | $8,907, plus 22% of the excess over $77,400. |
| Over $165,000 but not over $315,000 | $28,179, plus 24% of the excess over $165,000. |
| Over $315,000 but not over $400,000 | $64,179, plus 32% of the excess over $315,000. |
| Over $400,000 but not over $600,000 | $91,379, plus 35% of the excess over $400,000. |
| Over $600,000 | $161,379, plus 37% of the excess over $600,000. |

"(B) HEADS OF HOUSEHOLDS.—The following table shall be applied in lieu of the table contained in subsection (b):

| **"If taxable income is:** | **The tax is:** |
|---|---|
| Not over $13,600 | 10% of taxable income. |
| Over $13,600 but not over $51,800 | $1,360, plus 12% of the excess over $13,600. |
| Over $51,800 but not over $82,500 | $5,944, plus 22% of the excess over $51,800. |
| Over $82,500 but not over $157,500 | $12,698, plus 24% of the excess over $82,500. |
| Over $157,500 but not over $200,000 | $30,698, plus 32% of the excess over $157,500. |
| Over $200,000 but not over $500,000 | $44,298, plus 35% of the excess |

| "If taxable income is: | The tax is: |
|---|---|
| Over $500,000 | $149,298, plus 37% of the excess over $500,000. |

"(C) UNMARRIED INDIVIDUALS OTHER THAN SURVIVING SPOUSES AND HEADS OF HOUSEHOLDS.—The following table shall be applied in lieu of the table contained in subsection (c):

| "If taxable income is: | The tax is: |
|---|---|
| Not over $9,525 | 10% of taxable income. |
| Over $9,525 but not over $38,700 | $952.50, plus 12% of the excess over $9,525. |
| Over $38,700 but not over $82,500 | $4,453.50, plus 22% of the excess over $38,700. |
| Over $82,500 but not over $157,500 | $14,089.50, plus 24% of the excess over $82,500. |
| Over $157,500 but not over $200,000 | $32,089.50, plus 32% of the excess over $157,500. |
| Over $200,000 but not over $500,000 | $45,689.50, plus 35% of the excess over $200,000. |
| Over $500,000 | $150,689.50, plus 37% of the excess over $500,000. |

"(D) MARRIED INDIVIDUALS FILING SEPARATE RETURNS.—The following table shall be applied in lieu of the table contained in subsection (d):

| "If taxable income is: | The tax is: |
|---|---|
| Not over $9,525 | 10% of taxable income. |
| Over $9,525 but not over $38,700 | $952.50, plus 12% of the excess over $9,525. |
| Over $38,700 but not over $82,500 | $4,453.50, plus 22% of the excess over $38,700. |
| Over $82,500 but not over $157,500 | $14,089.50, plus 24% of the excess over $82,500. |
| Over $157,500 but not over $200,000 | $32,089.50, plus 32% of the excess over $157,500. |

| "If taxable income is: | The tax is: |
| --- | --- |
| Over $200,000 but not over $300,000 | $45,689.50, plus 35% of the excess over $200,000. |
| Over $300,000 | $80,689.50, plus 37% of the excess over $300,000. |

"(E) ESTATES AND TRUSTS.—The following table shall be applied in lieu of the table contained in subsection (e):

| "If taxable income is: | The tax is: |
| --- | --- |
| Not over $2,550 | 10% of taxable income. |
| Over $2,550 but not over $9,150 | $255, plus 24% of the excess over $2,550. |
| Over $9,150 but not over $12,500 | $1,839, plus 35% of the excess over $9,150. |
| Over $12,500 | $3,011.50, plus 37% of the excess over $12,500. |

"(F) REFERENCES TO RATE TABLES.—Any reference in this title to a rate of tax under subsection (c) shall be treated as a reference to the corresponding rate bracket under subparagraph (C) of this paragraph, except that the reference in section 3402(q)(1) to the third lowest rate of tax applicable under subsection (c) shall be treated as a reference to the fourth lowest rate of tax under subparagraph (C).

"(3) ADJUSTMENTS.—

"(A) NO ADJUSTMENT IN 2018.—The tables contained in paragraph (2) shall apply without adjustment for taxable years beginning after December 31, 2017, and before January 1, 2019.

"(B) SUBSEQUENT YEARS.—For taxable years beginning after December 31, 2018, the Secretary shall prescribe tables which shall apply in lieu of the tables contained in paragraph (2) in the same manner as under paragraphs (1) and (2) of subsection (f) (applied without regard to clauses (i) and (ii) of subsection (f)(2)(A)), except that in prescribing such tables—

"(i) subsection (f)(3) shall be applied by substituting 'calendar year 2017' for 'calendar year 2016' in subparagraph (A)(ii) thereof,

"(ii) subsection (f)(7)(B) shall apply to any unmarried individual other than a surviving spouse or head of household, and

"(iii) subsection (f)(8) shall not apply.

"(4) SPECIAL RULES FOR CERTAIN CHILDREN WITH UNEARNED INCOME.—

"(A) IN GENERAL.—In the case of a child to whom subsection (g) applies for the taxable year, the rules of subparagraphs (B) and (C) shall apply in lieu of the rule under subsection (g)(1).

"(B) MODIFICATIONS TO APPLICABLE RATE BRACKETS.—In determining the amount of tax imposed by this section for the taxable year on a child described in subparagraph (A), the income tax table otherwise applicable under this subsection to the child shall be applied with the following modifications:

"(i) 24-PERCENT BRACKET.—The maximum taxable income which is taxed at a rate below 24 percent shall not be more than the sum of—

"(I) the earned taxable income of such child, plus

"(II) the minimum taxable income for the 24-percent bracket in the table under paragraph (2)(E) (as adjusted under paragraph (3)) for the taxable year.

"(ii) 35-PERCENT BRACKET.—The maximum taxable income which is taxed at a rate below 35 percent shall not be more than the sum of—

"(I) the earned taxable income of such child, plus

"(II) the minimum taxable income for the 35-percent bracket in the table under paragraph (2)(E) (as adjusted under paragraph (3)) for the taxable year.

"(iii) 37-PERCENT BRACKET.—The maximum taxable income which is taxed at a rate below 37 percent shall not be more than the sum of—

"(I) the earned taxable income of such child, plus

"(II) the minimum taxable income for the 37-percent bracket in the table under paragraph (2)(E) (as adjusted under paragraph (3)) for the taxable year.

"(C) COORDINATION WITH CAPITAL GAINS RATES.—For purposes of applying section 1(h) (after the modifications under paragraph (5)(A))—

"(i) the maximum zero rate amount shall not be more than the sum of—

"(I) the earned taxable income of such child, plus

"(II) the amount in effect under paragraph (5)(B)(i)(IV) for the taxable year, and

"(ii) the maximum 15-percent rate amount shall not be more than the sum of—

"(I) the earned taxable income of such child, plus

"(II) the amount in effect under paragraph (5)(B)(ii)(IV) for the taxable year.

"(D) EARNED TAXABLE INCOME.—For purposes of this paragraph, the term 'earned taxable income' means, with respect to any child for any taxable year, the taxable income of such child reduced (but not below zero) by the net unearned income (as defined in subsection (g)(4)) of such child.

"(5) APPLICATION OF CURRENT INCOME TAX BRACKETS TO CAPITAL GAINS BRACKETS.—

"(A) IN GENERAL.—Section 1(h)(1) shall be applied—

"(i) by substituting 'below the maximum zero rate amount' for 'which would (without regard to this paragraph) be taxed at a rate below 25 percent' in subparagraph (B)(i), and

"(ii) by substituting 'below the maximum 15-percent rate amount' for 'which would (without regard to this paragraph) be taxed at a rate below 39.6 percent' in subparagraph (C)(ii)(I).

"(B) MAXIMUM AMOUNTS DEFINED.—For purposes of applying section 1(h) with the modifications described in subparagraph (A)—

"(i) MAXIMUM ZERO RATE AMOUNT.—The maximum zero rate amount shall be—

"(I) in the case of a joint return or surviving spouse, $77,200,

"(II) in the case of an individual who is a head of household (as defined in section 2(b)), $51,700,

"(III) in the case of any other individual (other than an estate or trust), an amount equal to ½ of the amount in effect for the taxable year under subclause (I), and

"(IV) in the case of an estate or trust, $2,600.

"(ii) MAXIMUM 15-PERCENT RATE AMOUNT.—The maximum 15-percent rate amount shall be—

"(I) in the case of a joint return or surviving spouse, $479,000 (½ such amount in the case of a married individual filing a separate return),

"(II) in the case of an individual who is the head of a household (as defined in section 2(b)), $452,400,

"(III) in the case of any other individual (other than an estate or trust), $425,800, and

"(IV) in the case of an estate or trust, $12,700.

"(C) INFLATION ADJUSTMENT.—In the case of any taxable year beginning after 2018, each of the dollar amounts in clauses (i) and (ii) of subparagraph (B) shall be increased by an amount equal to—

"(i) such dollar amount, multiplied by

"(ii) the cost-of-living adjustment determined under subsection (f)(3) for the calendar year in which the taxable year begins, determined by substituting 'calendar year 2017' for 'calendar year 2016' in subparagraph (A)(ii) thereof.

If any increase under this subparagraph is not a multiple of $50, such increase shall be rounded to the next lowest multiple of $50.

"(6) SECTION 15 NOT TO APPLY.—Section 15 shall not apply to any change in a rate of tax by reason of this subsection.".

(b) DUE DILIGENCE TAX PREPARER REQUIREMENT WITH RESPECT TO HEAD OF HOUSEHOLD FILING STATUS.—Subsection (g) of section 6695 is amended to read as follows:

"(g) FAILURE TO BE DILIGENT IN DETERMINING ELIGIBILITY FOR CERTAIN TAX BENEFITS.—Any person who is a tax return preparer with respect to any return or claim for refund who fails to comply with due diligence requirements imposed by the Secretary by regulations with respect to determining—

"(1) eligibility to file as a head of household (as defined in section 2(b)) on the return, or

"(2) eligibility for, or the amount of, the credit allowable by section 24, 25A(a)(1), or 32,

shall pay a penalty of $500 for each such failure.".

(c) EFFECTIVE DATE.—The amendments made by this section shall apply to taxable years beginning after December 31, 2017.

**SEC. 11002. INFLATION ADJUSTMENTS BASED ON CHAINED CPI.**

(a) IN GENERAL.—Subsection (f) of section 1 is amended by striking paragraph (3) and by inserting after paragraph (2) the following new paragraph:

"(3) COST-OF-LIVING ADJUSTMENT.—For purposes of this subsection—

"(A) IN GENERAL.—The cost-of-living adjustment for any calendar year is the percentage (if any) by which—

"(i) the C-CPI-U for the preceding calendar year, exceeds

"(ii) the CPI for calendar year 2016, multiplied by the amount determined under subparagraph (B).

"(B) AMOUNT DETERMINED.—The amount determined under this clause is the amount obtained by dividing—

"(i) the C-CPI-U for calendar year 2016, by

"(ii) the CPI for calendar year 2016.

"(C) SPECIAL RULE FOR ADJUSTMENTS WITH A BASE YEAR AFTER 2016.—For purposes of any provision of this title which provides for the substitution of a year after 2016 for '2016' in subparagraph (A)(ii), subparagraph (A) shall be applied by substituting 'the C-CPI-U for calendar year 2016' for 'the CPI for calendar year 2016' and all that follows in clause (ii) thereof.".

(b) C-CPI-U.—Subsection (f) of section 1 is amended by striking paragraph (7), by redesignating paragraph (6) as paragraph (7), and by inserting after paragraph (5) the following new paragraph:

"(6) C-CPI-U.—For purposes of this subsection—

"(A) IN GENERAL.—The term 'C-CPI-U' means the Chained Consumer Price Index for All Urban Consumers (as published by the Bureau of Labor Statistics of the Department of Labor). The values of the Chained Consumer Price Index for All Urban Consumers taken into account for purposes of determining the cost-of-living adjustment for any calendar year under this subsection shall be the latest values so published as of the date on which such Bureau publishes the initial value of the Chained Consumer Price Index for All Urban Consumers for the month of August for the preceding calendar year.

"(B) DETERMINATION FOR CALENDAR YEAR.—The C-CPI-U for any calendar year is the average of the C-CPI-U as of the close of the 12-month period ending on August 31 of such calendar year.".

(c) APPLICATION TO PERMANENT TAX TABLES.—

(1) IN GENERAL.—Section 1(f)(2)(A) is amended to read as follows:

"(A) except as provided in paragraph (8), by increasing the minimum and maximum dollar amounts for each bracket for which a tax is imposed under such table by the cost-of-living adjustment for such calendar year, determined—

"(i) except as provided in clause (ii), by substituting '1992' for '2016' in paragraph (3)(A)(ii), and "(ii) in the case of adjustments to the dollar amounts at which the 36 percent rate bracket begins or at which the 39.6 percent rate bracket begins, by substituting '1993' for '2016' in paragraph (3)(A)(ii),".

(2) CONFORMING AMENDMENTS.—Section 1(i) is amended—

(A) by striking "for '1992' in subparagraph (B)" in paragraph (1)(C) and inserting "for '2016' in subparagraph (A)(ii)", and

(B) by striking "subsection (f)(3)(B) shall be applied by substituting '2012' for '1992' " in paragraph (3)(C) and inserting "subsection (f)(3)(A)(ii) shall be applied by substituting '2012' for '2016' ".

(d) APPLICATION TO OTHER INTERNAL REVENUE CODE OF 1986 PROVISIONS.—

(1) The following sections are each amended by striking "for 'calendar year 1992' in subparagraph (B)" and inserting "for 'calendar year 2016' in subparagraph (A)(ii)":

(A) Section 23(h)(2).

(B) Paragraphs (1)(A)(ii) and (2)(A)(ii) of section 25A(h).

(C) Section 25B(b)(3)(B).

(D) Subsection (b)(2)(B)(ii)(II), and clauses (i) and (ii) of subsection (j)(1)(B), of section 32.

(E) Section 36B(f)(2)(B)(ii)(II).

(F) Section 41(e)(5)(C)(i).

(G) Subsections (e)(3)(D)(ii) and (h)(3)(H)(i)(II) of section 42.

(H) Section 45R(d)(3)(B)(ii).

(I) Section 55(d)(4)(A)(ii).

(J) Section 62(d)(3)(B).

(K) Section 63(c)(4)(B).

(L) Section 125(i)(2)(B).

(M) Section 135(b)(2)(B)(ii).

(N) Section 137(f)(2).

(O) Section 146(d)(2)(B).

(P) Section 147(c)(2)(H)(ii).

(Q) Section 151(d)(4)(B).

(R) Section 179(b)(6)(A)(ii).

(S) Subsections (b)(5)(C)(i)(II) and (g)(8)(B) of section 219.

(T) Section 220(g)(2).

(U) Section 221(f)(1)(B).

(V) Section 223(g)(1)(B).

(W) Section 408A(c)(3)(D)(ii).

(X) Section 430(c)(7)(D)(vii)(II).

(Y) Section 512(d)(2)(B).

(Z) Section 513(h)(2)(C)(ii).

(AA) Section 831(b)(2)(D)(ii).

(BB) Section 877A(a)(3)(B)(i)(II).

(CC) Section 2010(c)(3)(B)(ii).

(DD) Section 2032A(a)(3)(B).

(EE) Section 2503(b)(2)(B).

(FF) Section 4261(e)(4)(A)(ii).

(GG) Section 5000A(c)(3)(D)(ii).

(HH) Section 6323(i)(4)(B).

(II) Section 6334(g)(1)(B).

(JJ) Section 6601(j)(3)(B).

(KK) Section 6651(i)(1).

(LL) Section 6652(c)(7)(A).

(MM) Section 6695(h)(1).

(NN) Section 6698(e)(1).

(OO) Section 6699(e)(1).

(PP) Section 6721(f)(1).

(QQ) Section 6722(f)(1).

(RR) Section 7345(f)(2).

(SS) Section 7430(c)(1).

(TT) Section 9831(d)(2)(D)(ii)(II).

(2) Sections 41(e)(5)(C)(ii) and 68(b)(2)(B) are each amended—

(A) by striking "1(f)(3)(B)" and inserting "1(f)(3)(A)(ii)", and

(B) by striking "1992" and inserting "2016".

(3) Section 42(h)(6)(G) is amended—

(A) by striking "for 'calendar year 1987'" in clause (i)(II) and inserting "for 'calendar year 2016' in subparagraph (A)(ii) thereof", and

(B) by striking "if the CPI for any calendar year" and all that follows in clause (ii) and inserting "if the C-CPI-U for any calendar year (as defined in section 1(f)(6)) exceeds the C-CPI-U for the preceding calendar year by more than 5 percent, the C-CPI-U for the base calendar year shall be increased such that such excess shall never be taken into account under clause (i). In the case of a base calendar year before 2017, the C-CPI-U for such year shall be determined by multiplying the CPI for such year by the amount determined under section 1(f)(3)(B).".

(4) Section 59(j)(2)(B) is amended by striking "for '1992' in subparagraph (B)" and inserting "for '2016' in subparagraph (A)(ii)".

(5) Section 132(f)(6)(A)(ii) is amended by striking "for 'calendar year 1992' " and inserting "for 'calendar year 2016' in subparagraph (A)(ii) thereof".

(6) Section 162(o)(3) is amended by striking "adjusted for changes in the Consumer Price Index (as defined in section 1(f)(5)) since 1991" and inserting "adjusted by increasing any such amount under the 1991 agreement by an amount equal to—

"(A) such amount, multiplied by

"(B) the cost-of-living adjustment determined under section 1(f)(3) for the calendar year in which the taxable year begins, by substituting 'calendar year 1990' for 'calendar year 2016' in subparagraph (A)(ii) thereof".

(7) So much of clause (ii) of section 213(d)(10)(B) as precedes the last sentence is amended to read as follows:

"(ii) MEDICAL CARE COST ADJUSTMENT.—For purposes of clause (i), the medical care cost adjustment for any calendar year is the percentage (if any) by which—

"(I) the medical care component of the C-CPI-U (as defined in section

1(f)(6)) for August of the preceding calendar year, exceeds

"(II) such component of the CPI (as defined in section 1(f)(4)) for August of 1996, multiplied by the amount determined under section 1(f)(3)(B).".

(8) Subparagraph (B) of section 280F(d)(7) is amended to read as follows:

"(B) AUTOMOBILE PRICE INFLATION ADJUSTMENT.—For purposes of this paragraph—

"(i) IN GENERAL.—The automobile price inflation adjustment for any calendar year is the percentage (if any) by which—

"(I) the C-CPI-U automobile component for October of the preceding calendar year, exceeds

"(II) the automobile component of the CPI (as defined in section 1(f)(4)) for October of 1987, multiplied by the amount determined under 1(f)(3)(B).

"(ii) C-CPI-U AUTOMOBILE COMPONENT.—The term 'C-CPI-U automobile component' means the automobile component of the Chained Consumer Price Index for All Urban Consumers (as described in section 1(f)(6)).".

(9) Section 911(b)(2)(D)(ii)(II) is amended by striking "for '1992' in subparagraph (B)" and inserting "for '2016' in subparagraph (A)(ii)".

(10) Paragraph (2) of section 1274A(d) is amended to read as follows:

"(2) ADJUSTMENT FOR INFLATION.—In the case of any debt instrument arising out of a sale or exchange during any calendar year after 1989, each dollar amount contained in the preceding provisions of this section shall be increased by an amount equal to—

"(A) such amount, multiplied by

"(B) the cost-of-living adjustment determined under section 1(f)(3) for the calendar year in which the taxable year begins, by substituting 'calendar year 1988' for 'calendar year 2016' in subparagraph (A)(ii) thereof.

Any increase under the preceding sentence shall be rounded to the nearest multiple of $100 (or, if such increase is a multiple of $50, such increase shall be increased to the nearest multiple of $100).".

(11) Section 4161(b)(2)(C)(i)(II) is amended by striking "for '1992' in subparagraph (B)" and inserting "for '2016' in subparagraph (A)(ii)".

(12) Section 4980I(b)(3)(C)(v)(II) is amended by striking "for '1992' in subparagraph (B)" and inserting "for '2016' in subparagraph (A)(ii)".

(13) Section 6039F(d) is amended by striking "subparagraph (B) thereof shall be applied by substituting '1995' for '1992'" and inserting "subparagraph (A)(ii) thereof shall be applied by substituting '1995' for '2016'".

(14) Section 7872(g)(5) is amended to read as follows:

"(5) ADJUSTMENT OF LIMIT FOR INFLATION.—In the case of any loan made during any calendar year after 1986, the dollar amount in paragraph (2) shall be increased by an amount equal to—

"(A) such amount, multiplied by

"(B) the cost-of-living adjustment determined under section 1(f)(3) for the calendar year in which the taxable year begins, by substituting 'calendar year 1985' for 'calendar year 2016' in subparagraph (A)(ii) thereof.

Any increase under the preceding sentence shall be rounded to the nearest multiple of $100 (or, if such increase is a multiple of $50, such increase shall be increased to the nearest multiple of $100).''.

(e) EFFECTIVE DATE.—The amendments made by this section shall apply to taxable years beginning after December 31, 2017.

## PART II—DEDUCTION FOR QUALIFIED BUSINESS INCOME OF PASS-THRU ENTITIES

### SEC. 11011. DEDUCTION FOR QUALIFIED BUSINESS INCOME.

(a) IN GENERAL.—Part VI of subchapter B of chapter 1 is amended by adding at the end the following new section:

**"SEC. 199A. QUALIFIED BUSINESS INCOME.**

"(a) IN GENERAL.—In the case of a taxpayer other than a corporation, there shall be allowed as a deduction for any taxable year an amount equal to the sum of—

"(1) the lesser of—

"(A) the combined qualified business income amount of the taxpayer, or

"(B) an amount equal to 20 percent of the excess (if any) of—

"(i) the taxable income of the taxpayer for the taxable year, over

"(ii) the sum of any net capital gain (as defined in section 1(h)), plus the aggregate amount of the qualified cooperative dividends, of the taxpayer for the taxable year, plus

"(2) the lesser of—

"(A) 20 percent of the aggregate amount of the qualified cooperative dividends of the taxpayer for the taxable year, or

"(B) taxable income (reduced by the net capital gain (as so defined)) of the taxpayer for the taxable year.

The amount determined under the preceding sentence shall not exceed the taxable income (reduced by the net capital gain (as so defined)) of the taxpayer for the taxable year.

"(b) COMBINED QUALIFIED BUSINESS INCOME AMOUNT.—For purposes of this section—

"(1) IN GENERAL.—The term 'combined qualified business income amount' means, with respect to any taxable year, an amount equal to—

"(A) the sum of the amounts determined under paragraph (2) for each qualified trade or business carried on by the taxpayer, plus

"(B) 20 percent of the aggregate amount of the qualified REIT dividends and qualified publicly traded partnership income of the taxpayer for the taxable year.

"(2) DETERMINATION OF DEDUCTIBLE AMOUNT FOR EACH TRADE OR BUSINESS.—The amount determined under this paragraph with respect to any qualified trade or business is the lesser of—

"(A) 20 percent of the taxpayer's qualified business income with respect to the qualified trade or business, or

"(B) the greater of—

"(i) 50 percent of the W–2 wages with respect to the qualified trade or business, or

"(ii) the sum of 25 percent of the W–2 wages with respect to the qualified trade or business, plus 2.5 percent of the unadjusted basis immediately after acquisition of all qualified property.

"(3) MODIFICATIONS TO LIMIT BASED ON TAXABLE INCOME.—

"(A) EXCEPTION FROM LIMIT.—In the case of any taxpayer whose taxable income for the taxable year does not exceed the threshold amount, paragraph (2) shall be applied without regard to subparagraph (B).

"(B) PHASE-IN OF LIMIT FOR CERTAIN TAXPAYERS.—

"(i) IN GENERAL.—If—

"(I) the taxable income of a taxpayer for any taxable year exceeds the threshold amount, but does not exceed the sum of the threshold amount plus $50,000 ($100,000 in the case of a joint return), and

"(II) the amount determined under paragraph (2)(B) (determined without regard to this subparagraph) with respect to any qualified trade or business carried on by the taxpayer is less than the amount determined under paragraph (2)(A) with respect such trade or business,

then paragraph (2) shall be applied with respect to such trade or business without regard to subparagraph (B) thereof and by reducing the amount determined under subparagraph (A) thereof by the amount determined under clause (ii).

"(ii) AMOUNT OF REDUCTION.—The amount determined under this subparagraph is the amount which bears the same ratio to the excess amount as—

"(I) the amount by which the taxpayer's taxable income for the taxable year exceeds the threshold amount, bears to

"(II) $50,000 ($100,000 in the case of a joint return).

"(iii) EXCESS AMOUNT.—For purposes of clause (ii), the excess amount is the excess of—

"(I) the amount determined under paragraph (2)(A) (determined without regard to this paragraph), over

"(II) the amount determined under paragraph (2)(B) (determined without regard to this paragraph).

"(4) WAGES, ETC.—

"(A) IN GENERAL.—The term 'W–2 wages' means, with respect to any person for any taxable year of such person, the amounts described in paragraphs (3) and (8) of section

6051(a) paid by such person with respect to employment of employees by such person during the calendar year ending during such taxable year.

"(B) LIMITATION TO WAGES ATTRIBUTABLE TO QUALIFIED BUSINESS INCOME.—Such term shall not include any amount which is not properly allocable to qualified business income for purposes of subsection (c)(1).

"(C) RETURN REQUIREMENT.—Such term shall not include any amount which is not properly included in a return filed with the Social Security Administration on or before the 60th day after the due date (including extensions) for such return.

"(5) ACQUISITIONS, DISPOSITIONS, AND SHORT TAXABLE YEARS.—The Secretary shall provide for the application of this subsection in cases of a short taxable year or where the taxpayer acquires, or disposes of, the major portion of a trade or business or the major portion of a separate unit of a trade or business during the taxable year.

"(6) QUALIFIED PROPERTY.—For purposes of this section:

"(A) IN GENERAL.—The term 'qualified property' means, with respect to any qualified trade or business for a taxable year, tangible property of a character subject to the allowance for depreciation under section 167—

"(i) which is held by, and available for use in, the qualified trade or business at the close of the taxable year,

"(ii) which is used at any point during the taxable year in the production of qualified business income, and

"(iii) the depreciable period for which has not ended before the close of the taxable year.

"(B) DEPRECIABLE PERIOD.—The term 'depreciable period' means, with respect to qualified property of a taxpayer, the period beginning on the date the property was first placed in service by the taxpayer and ending on the later of—

"(i) the date that is 10 years after such date, or

"(ii) the last day of the last full year in the applicable recovery period that would apply to the property under section

168 (determined without regard to subsection (g) thereof).

"(c) QUALIFIED BUSINESS INCOME.—For purposes of this section—

"(1) IN GENERAL.—The term 'qualified business income' means, for any taxable year, the net amount of qualified items of income, gain, deduction, and loss with respect to any qualified trade or business of the taxpayer. Such term shall not include any qualified REIT dividends, qualified cooperative dividends, or qualified publicly traded partnership income.

"(2) CARRYOVER OF LOSSES.—If the net amount of qualified income, gain, deduction, and loss with respect to qualified trades or businesses of the taxpayer for any taxable year is less than zero, such amount shall be treated as a loss from a qualified trade or business in the succeeding taxable year.

"(3) QUALIFIED ITEMS OF INCOME, GAIN, DEDUCTION, AND LOSS.—For purposes of this subsection—

"(A) IN GENERAL.—The term 'qualified items of income, gain, deduction, and loss' means items of income, gain, deduction, and loss to the extent such items are—

"(i) effectively connected with the conduct of a trade or business within the United States (within the meaning of section 864(c), determined by substituting 'qualified trade or business (within the meaning of section 199A)' for 'nonresident alien individual or a foreign corporation' or for 'a foreign corporation' each place it appears), and

"(ii) included or allowed in determining taxable income for the taxable year.

"(B) EXCEPTIONS.—The following investment items shall not be taken into account as a qualified item of income, gain, deduction, or loss:

"(i) Any item of short-term capital gain, short-term capital loss, long-term capital gain, or long-term capital loss.

"(ii) Any dividend, income equivalent to a dividend, or payment in lieu of dividends described in section 954(c)(1)(G).

"(iii) Any interest income other than interest income which is properly allocable to a trade or business.

"(iv) Any item of gain or loss described in subparagraph (C) or (D) of section 954(c)(1) (applied by substituting 'qualified trade or business' for 'controlled foreign corporation').

"(v) Any item of income, gain, deduction, or loss taken into account under section 954(c)(1)(F) (determined without regard to clause (ii) thereof and other than items attributable to notional principal contracts entered into in transactions qualifying under section 1221(a)(7)).

"(vi) Any amount received from an annuity which is not received in connection with the trade or business.

"(vii) Any item of deduction or loss properly allocable to an amount described in any of the preceding clauses.

"(4) TREATMENT OF REASONABLE COMPENSATION AND GUARANTEED PAYMENTS.—Qualified business income shall not include—

"(A) reasonable compensation paid to the taxpayer by any qualified trade or business of the taxpayer for services rendered with respect to the trade or business,

"(B) any guaranteed payment described in section 707(c) paid to a partner for services rendered with respect to the trade or business, and

"(C) to the extent provided in regulations, any payment described in section 707(a) to a partner for services rendered with respect to the trade or business.

"(d) QUALIFIED TRADE OR BUSINESS.—For purposes of this section—

"(1) IN GENERAL.—The term 'qualified trade or business' means any trade or business other than—

"(A) a specified service trade or business, or

"(B) the trade or business of performing services as an employee.

"(2) SPECIFIED SERVICE TRADE OR BUSINESS.—The term 'specified service trade or business' means any trade or business—

"(A) which is described in section 1202(e)(3)(A) (applied without regard to the words 'engineering, architecture,') or which would be so described if the term 'employees or owners' were substituted for 'employees' therein, or

"(B) which involves the performance of services that consist of investing and investment management, trading, or dealing in securities (as defined in section 475(c)(2)), partnership interests, or commodities (as defined in section 475(e)(2)).

"(3) EXCEPTION FOR SPECIFIED SERVICE BUSINESSES BASED ON TAXPAYER'S INCOME.—

"(A) IN GENERAL.—If, for any taxable year, the taxable income of any taxpayer is less than the sum of the threshold amount plus $50,000 ($100,000 in the case of a joint return), then—

"(i) any specified service trade or business of the taxpayer shall not fail to be treated as a qualified trade or business due to paragraph (1)(A), but

"(ii) only the applicable percentage of qualified items of income, gain, deduction, or loss, and the W–2 wages and the unadjusted basis immediately after acquisition of qualified property, of the taxpayer allocable to such specified service trade or business shall be taken into account in computing the qualified business income, W–2 wages, and the unadjusted basis immediately after acquisition of qualified property of the taxpayer for the taxable year for purposes of applying this section.

"(B) APPLICABLE PERCENTAGE.—For purposes of subparagraph (A), the term 'applicable percentage' means, with respect to any taxable year, 100 percent reduced (not below zero) by the percentage equal to the ratio of—

"(i) the taxable income of the taxpayer for the taxable year in excess of the threshold amount, bears to

"(ii) $50,000 ($100,000 in the case of a joint return).

"(e) OTHER DEFINITIONS.—For purposes of this section—

"(1) TAXABLE INCOME.—Taxable income shall be computed without regard to the deduction allowable under this section.

"(2) THRESHOLD AMOUNT.—

"(A) IN GENERAL.—The term 'threshold amount' means $157,500 (200 percent of such amount in the case of a joint return).

"(B) INFLATION ADJUSTMENT.—In the case of any taxable year beginning after 2018, the dollar amount in subparagraph (A) shall be increased by an amount equal to—

"(i) such dollar amount, multiplied by

"(ii) the cost-of-living adjustment determined under section 1(f)(3) for the calendar year in which the taxable year begins, determined by substituting 'calendar year 2017' for 'calendar year 2016' in subparagraph (A)(ii) thereof.

The amount of any increase under the preceding sentence shall be rounded as provided in section 1(f)(7).

"(3) QUALIFIED REIT DIVIDEND.—The term 'qualified REIT dividend' means any dividend from a real estate investment trust received during the taxable year which—

"(A) is not a capital gain dividend, as defined in section 857(b)(3), and

"(B) is not qualified dividend income, as defined in section 1(h)(11).

"(4) QUALIFIED COOPERATIVE DIVIDEND.—The term 'qualified cooperative dividend' means any patronage dividend (as defined in section 1388(a)), any per-unit retain allocation (as defined in section 1388(f)), and any qualified written notice of allocation (as defined in section 1388(c)), or any similar amount received from an organization described in subparagraph (B)(ii), which—

"(A) is includible in gross income, and

"(B) is received from—

"(i) an organization or corporation described in section 501(c)(12) or 1381(a), or

"(ii) an organization which is governed under this title by the rules applicable to cooperatives under this title before the enactment of subchapter T.

"(5) QUALIFIED PUBLICLY TRADED PARTNERSHIP INCOME.—The term 'qualified publicly traded partnership income' means, with respect to any qualified trade or business of a taxpayer, the sum of—

"(A) the net amount of such taxpayer's allocable share of each qualified item of income, gain, deduction, and loss (as defined in subsection (c)(3) and determined after the application of subsection (c)(4)) from a publicly traded partnership (as defined in section 7704(a)) which is not treated as a corporation under section 7704(c), plus

"(B) any gain recognized by such taxpayer upon disposition of its interest in such partnership to the extent such gain is treated as an amount realized from the sale or exchange of property other than a capital asset under section 751(a).

"(f) SPECIAL RULES.—

"(1) APPLICATION TO PARTNERSHIPS AND S CORPORATIONS.—

"(A) IN GENERAL.—In the case of a partnership or S corporation—

"(i) this section shall be applied at the partner or shareholder level,

"(ii) each partner or shareholder shall take into account such person's allocable share of each qualified item of income, gain, deduction, and loss, and

"(iii) each partner or shareholder shall be treated for purposes of subsection (b) as having W–2 wages and unadjusted basis immediately after acquisition of qualified property for the taxable year in an amount equal to such person's allocable share of the W–2 wages and the unadjusted basis immediately after acquisition of qualified property of the partnership or S corporation for the taxable year (as determined under regulations prescribed by the Secretary).

For purposes of clause (iii), a partner's or shareholder's allocable share of W–2 wages shall be determined in the same manner as the partner's or shareholder's allocable share of wage expenses. For purposes of such clause, partner's or shareholder's allocable share of the unadjusted basis immediately after acquisition of qualified property shall be determined in the same manner as the partner's or shareholder's allocable share of depreciation. For purposes of this subparagraph, in the case of an S corporation, an allocable share shall be the shareholder's pro rata share of an item.

"(B) APPLICATION TO TRUSTS AND ESTATES.—Rules similar to the rules under section 199(d)(1)(B)(i) (as in effect on December 1, 2017) for the apportionment of W–2 wages shall apply to the apportionment of W–2 wages and the apportionment of unadjusted basis immediately after acquisition of qualified property under this section.

"(C) TREATMENT OF TRADES OR BUSINESS IN PUERTO RICO.—

"(i) IN GENERAL.—In the case of any taxpayer with qualified business income from sources within the commonwealth of Puerto Rico, if all such income is taxable under section 1 for such taxable year, then for purposes of determining the qualified business income of such taxpayer for such taxable year, the term 'United States' shall include the Commonwealth of Puerto Rico.

"(ii) SPECIAL RULE FOR APPLYING LIMIT.—In the case of any taxpayer described in clause (i), the determination of W–2 wages of such taxpayer with respect to any qualified trade or business conducted in Puerto Rico shall be made without regard to any exclusion under section 3401(a)(8) for remuneration paid for services in Puerto Rico.

"(2) COORDINATION WITH MINIMUM TAX.—For purposes of determining alternative minimum taxable income under section 55, qualified business income shall be determined without regard to any adjustments under sections 56 through 59.

"(3) DEDUCTION LIMITED TO INCOME TAXES.—The deduction under subsection (a) shall only be allowed for purposes of this chapter.

"(4) REGULATIONS.—The Secretary shall prescribe such regulations as are necessary to carry out the purposes of this section, including regulations—

"(A) for requiring or restricting the allocation of items and wages under this section and such reporting requirements as the Secretary determines appropriate, and

"(B) for the application of this section in the case of tiered entities.

"(g) DEDUCTION ALLOWED TO SPECIFIED AGRICULTURAL OR HORTICULTURAL COOPERATIVES.—

"(1) IN GENERAL.—In the case of any taxable year of a specified agricultural or horticultural cooperative beginning after December 31, 2017, there shall be allowed a deduction in an amount equal to the lesser of—

"(A) 20 percent of the excess (if any) of—

"(i) the gross income of a specified agricultural or horticultural cooperative, over "(ii) the qualified cooperative dividends (as defined in subsection (e)(4)) paid during the taxable year for the taxable year, or

"(B) the greater of—

"(i) 50 percent of the W–2 wages of the cooperative with respect to its trade or business, or

"(ii) the sum of 25 percent of the W–2 wages of the cooperative with respect to its trade or business, plus 2.5 percent of the unadjusted basis immediately after acquisition of all qualified property of the cooperative.

"(2) LIMITATION.—The amount determined under paragraph (1) shall not exceed the taxable income of the specified agricultural or horticultural for the taxable year.

"(3) SPECIFIED AGRICULTURAL OR HORTICULTURAL COOPERATIVE.—For purposes of this subsection, the term 'specified agricultural or horticultural cooperative' means an organization to which part I of subchapter T applies which is engaged in—

"(A) the manufacturing, production, growth, or extraction in whole or significant part of any agricultural or horticultural product,

"(B) the marketing of agricultural or horticultural products which its patrons have so manufactured, produced, grown, or extracted, or

"(C) the provision of supplies, equipment, or services to farmers or to organizations described in subparagraph (A) or (B).

"(h) ANTI-ABUSE RULES.—The Secretary shall—

"(1) apply rules similar to the rules under section 179(d)(2) in order to prevent the manipulation of the depreciable period of qualified property using transactions between related parties, and

"(2) prescribe rules for determining the unadjusted basis immediately after acquisition of qualified property acquired in like-kind exchanges or involuntary conversions.

"(i) TERMINATION.—This section shall not apply to taxable years beginning after December 31, 2025.".

(b) TREATMENT OF DEDUCTION IN COMPUTING ADJUSTED GROSS AND TAXABLE INCOME.—

(1) DEDUCTION NOT ALLOWED IN COMPUTING ADJUSTED GROSS INCOME.—Section 62(a) is amended by adding at the end the following new sentence:

"The deduction allowed by section 199A shall not be treated as a deduction described in any of the preceding paragraphs of this subsection.".

(2) DEDUCTION ALLOWED TO NON-ITEMIZERS.—Section 63(b) is amended by striking "and" at the end of paragraph (1), by striking the period at the end of paragraph (2) and inserting ", and", and by adding at the end the following new paragraph:

"(3) the deduction provided in section 199A.".

(3) DEDUCTION ALLOWED TO ITEMIZERS WITHOUT LIMITS ON ITEMIZED DEDUCTIONS.—Section 63(d) is amended by striking "and" at the end of paragraph (1), by striking the period at the end of paragraph (2) and inserting ", and", and by adding at the end the following new paragraph:

"(3) the deduction provided in section 199A.".

(4) CONFORMING AMENDMENT.—Section 3402(m)(1) is amended by inserting "and the estimated deduction allowed under section 199A" after "chapter 1".

(c) ACCURACY-RELATED PENALTY ON DETERMINATION OF APPLICABLE PERCENTAGE.—Section 6662(d)(1) is amended by inserting at the end the following new subparagraph:

"(C) SPECIAL RULE FOR TAXPAYERS CLAIMING SECTION 199A DEDUCTION.—In the case of any taxpayer who claims the deduction allowed under section 199A for the taxable year, subparagraph (A) shall be applied by substituting '5 percent' for '10 percent'.".

(d) CONFORMING AMENDMENTS.—

(1) Section 172(d) is amended by adding at the end the following new paragraph:

"(8) QUALIFIED BUSINESS INCOME DEDUCTION.—The deduction under section 199A shall not be allowed.".

(2) Section 246(b)(1) is amended by inserting "199A," before "243(a)(1)".

(3) Section 613(a) is amended by inserting "and without the deduction under section 199A" after "and without the deduction under section 199".

(4) Section 613A(d)(1) is amended by redesignating subparagraphs (C), (D), and (E) as subparagraphs (D), (E), and (F), respectively, and by inserting after subparagraph (B), the following new subparagraph:

"(C) any deduction allowable under section 199A,".

(5) Section 170(b)(2)(D) is amended by striking "and" in clause (iv), by striking the period at the end of clause (v), and by adding at the end the following new clause:

"(vi) section 199A(g).".

(6) The table of sections for part VI of subchapter B of chapter 1 is amended by inserting at the end the following new item:

"Sec. 199A. Qualified business income.".

(e) EFFECTIVE DATE.—The amendments made by this section shall apply to taxable years beginning after December 31, 2017.

**SEC. 11012. LIMITATION ON LOSSES FOR TAXPAYERS OTHER THAN CORPORATIONS.**

(a) IN GENERAL.—Section 461 is amended by adding at the end the following new subsection:

"(l) LIMITATION ON EXCESS BUSINESS LOSSES OF NONCORPORATE TAXPAYERS.—

"(1) LIMITATION.—In the case of taxable year of a taxpayer other than a corporation beginning after December 31, 2017, and before January 1, 2026—

"(A) subsection (j) (relating to limitation on excess farm losses of certain taxpayers) shall not apply, and

"(B) any excess business loss of the taxpayer for the taxable year shall not be allowed.

"(2) DISALLOWED LOSS CARRYOVER.—Any loss which is disallowed under paragraph (1) shall be treated as a net operating loss carryover to the following taxable year under section 172.

"(3) EXCESS BUSINESS LOSS.—For purposes of this subsection—

"(A) IN GENERAL.—The term 'excess business loss' means the excess (if any) of—

"(i) the aggregate deductions of the taxpayer for the taxable year which are attributable to trades or businesses of such taxpayer (determined without regard to whether or not such deductions are disallowed for such taxable year under paragraph (1)), over

"(ii) the sum of—

"(I) the aggregate gross income or gain of such taxpayer for the taxable year which is attributable to such trades or businesses, plus

"(II) $250,000 (200 percent of such amount in the case of a joint return).

"(B) ADJUSTMENT FOR INFLATION.—In the case of any taxable year beginning after December 31, 2018, the $250,000 amount in subparagraph (A)(ii)(II) shall be increased by an amount equal to—

"(i) such dollar amount, multiplied by

"(ii) the cost-of-living adjustment determined under section 1(f)(3) for the calendar year in which the taxable year begins, determined by substituting '2017' for '2016' in subparagraph (A)(ii) thereof.

If any amount as increased under the preceding sentence is not a multiple of $1,000, such amount shall be rounded to the nearest multiple of $1,000.

"(4) APPLICATION OF SUBSECTION IN CASE OF PARTNERSHIPS AND S CORPORATIONS.—In the case of a partnership or S corporation—

"(A) this subsection shall be applied at the partner or shareholder level, and

"(B) each partner's or shareholder's allocable share of the items of income, gain, deduction, or loss of the partnership or S corporation for any taxable year from trades or businesses attributable to the partnership or S corporation shall be taken into account by the partner or shareholder in applying this subsection to the taxable year of such partner or shareholder with or within which the taxable year of the partnership or S corporation ends.

For purposes of this paragraph, in the case of an S corporation, an allocable share shall be the shareholder's pro rata share of an item.

"(5) ADDITIONAL REPORTING.—The Secretary shall prescribe such additional reporting requirements as the Secretary determines necessary to carry out the purposes of this subsection.

"(6) COORDINATION WITH SECTION 469.—This subsection shall be applied after the application of section 469.".

(b) EFFECTIVE DATE.—The amendments made by this section shall apply to taxable years beginning after December 31, 2017.

## PART III—TAX BENEFITS FOR FAMILIES AND INDIVIDUALS

### SEC. 11021. INCREASE IN STANDARD DEDUCTION.

(a) IN GENERAL.—Subsection (c) of section 63 is amended by adding at the end the following new paragraph:

"(7) SPECIAL RULES FOR TAXABLE YEARS 2018 THROUGH 2025.—In the case of a taxable year beginning after December 31, 2017, and before January 1, 2026—

"(A) INCREASE IN STANDARD DEDUCTION.—Paragraph (2) shall be applied—

"(i) by substituting '$18,000' for '$4,400' in subparagraph (B), and

"(ii) by substituting '$12,000' for '$3,000' in subparagraph (C).

"(B) ADJUSTMENT FOR INFLATION.—

"(i) IN GENERAL.—Paragraph (4) shall not apply to the dollar amounts contained in paragraphs (2)(B) and (2)(C).

"(ii) ADJUSTMENT OF INCREASED AMOUNTS.—In the case of a taxable year beginning after 2018, the $18,000 and $12,000 amounts in subparagraph (A) shall each be increased by an amount equal to—

"(I) such dollar amount, multiplied by

"(II) the cost-of-living adjustment determined under section 1(f)(3) for the calendar year in which the taxable year begins, determined by substituting '2017' for '2016' in subparagraph (A)(ii) thereof.

If any increase under this clause is not a multiple of $50, such increase shall be rounded to the next lowest multiple of $50.''.

(b) EFFECTIVE DATE.—The amendment made by this section shall apply to taxable years beginning after December 31, 2017.

**SEC. 11022. INCREASE IN AND MODIFICATION OF CHILD TAX CREDIT.**

(a) IN GENERAL.—Section 24 is amended by adding at the end the following new subsection:

"(h) SPECIAL RULES FOR TAXABLE YEARS 2018 THROUGH 2025.—

"(1) IN GENERAL.—In the case of a taxable year beginning after December 31, 2017, and before January 1, 2026, this section shall be applied as provided in paragraphs (2) through (7).

"(2) CREDIT AMOUNT.—Subsection (a) shall be applied by substituting '$2,000' for '$1,000'.

"(3) LIMITATION.—In lieu of the amount determined under subsection (b)(2), the threshold amount shall be $400,000 in the case of a joint return ($200,000 in any other case).

"(4) PARTIAL CREDIT ALLOWED FOR CERTAIN OTHER DEPENDENTS.—

"(A) IN GENERAL.—The credit determined under subsection (a) (after the application of paragraph (2)) shall be increased by $500 for each dependent of the taxpayer (as defined in section 152) other than a qualifying child described in subsection (c).

"(B) EXCEPTION FOR CERTAIN NONCITIZENS.—Subparagraph (A) shall not apply with respect to any individual who would not be a dependent if subparagraph (A) of section 152(b)(3) were applied without regard to all that follows 'resident of the United States'.

"(C) CERTAIN QUALIFYING CHILDREN.—In the case of any qualifying child with respect to whom a credit is not allowed under this section by reason of paragraph (7), such child shall be treated as a dependent to whom subparagraph (A) applies.

"(5) MAXIMUM AMOUNT OF REFUNDABLE CREDIT.—

"(A) IN GENERAL.—The amount determined under subsection (d)(1)(A) with respect to any qualifying child shall not exceed $1,400, and such subsection shall be applied without regard to paragraph (4) of this subsection.

"(B) ADJUSTMENT FOR INFLATION.—In the case of a taxable year beginning after 2018, the $1,400 amount in subparagraph (A) shall be increased by an amount equal to—

"(i) such dollar amount, multiplied by

"(ii) the cost-of-living adjustment determined under section 1(f)(3) for the calendar year in which the taxable year begins, determined by substituting '2017' for '2016' in subparagraph (A)(ii) thereof.

If any increase under this clause is not a multiple of $100, such increase shall be rounded to the next lowest multiple of $100.

"(6) EARNED INCOME THRESHOLD FOR REFUNDABLE CREDIT.—Subsection (d)(1)(B)(i) shall be applied by substituting '$2,500' for '$3,000'.

"(7) SOCIAL SECURITY NUMBER REQUIRED.—No credit shall be allowed under this section to a taxpayer with respect to any qualifying child unless the taxpayer includes the social security number of such child on the return of tax for the taxable year. For purposes of the preceding sentence, the term 'social security number' means a social security number issued to an individual by the Social Security Administration, but only if the social security number is issued—

"(A) to a citizen of the United States or pursuant to subclause (I) (or that portion of subclause (III) that relates to subclause (I)) of section 205(c)(2)(B)(i) of the Social Security Act, and

"(B) before the due date for such return.".

(b) EFFECTIVE DATE.—The amendment made by this section shall apply to taxable years beginning after December 31, 2017.

**SEC. 11023. INCREASED LIMITATION FOR CERTAIN CHARITABLE CONTRIBUTIONS.**

(a) IN GENERAL.—Section 170(b)(1) is amended by redesignating subparagraph (G) as subparagraph (H) and by inserting after subparagraph (F) the following new subparagraph:

"(G) INCREASED LIMITATION FOR CASH CONTRIBUTIONS.—

"(i) IN GENERAL.—In the case of any contribution of cash to an organization described in subparagraph (A), the total amount of such contributions which may be taken into account under subsection (a) for any taxable year beginning after December 31, 2017, and before January 1, 2026, shall not exceed 60 percent of the taxpayer's contribution base for such year.

"(ii) CARRYOVER.—If the aggregate amount of contributions described in clause (i) exceeds the applicable limitation under clause (i) for any taxable year described in such clause, such excess shall be treated (in a manner consistent with the rules of subsection (d)(1)) as a charitable contribution to which clause (i) applies in each of the 5 succeeding years in order of time.

"(iii) COORDINATION WITH SUBPARAGRAPHS (A) AND (B).—

"(I) IN GENERAL.—Contributions taken into account under this subparagraph shall not be taken into account under subparagraph (A).

"(II) LIMITATION REDUCTION.—For each taxable year described in clause (i), and each taxable year to which any contribution under this subparagraph is carried over under clause (ii), subparagraph (A) shall be applied by reducing (but not below zero) the contribution limitation allowed for the taxable year under such subparagraph by the aggregate contributions allowed under this subparagraph for such taxable year, and subparagraph (B) shall be applied by treating any reference to subparagraph (A) as a reference to both subparagraph (A) and this subparagraph.".

(b) EFFECTIVE DATE.—The amendment made by this section shall apply to contributions in taxable years beginning after December 31, 2017.

**SEC. 11024. INCREASED CONTRIBUTIONS TO ABLE ACCOUNTS.**

(a) INCREASE IN LIMITATION FOR CONTRIBUTIONS FROM COMPENSATION OF INDIVIDUALS WITH DISABILITIES.—

(1) IN GENERAL.—Section 529A(b)(2)(B) is amended to read as follows:

"(B) except in the case of contributions under subsection (c)(1)(C), if such contribution to an ABLE account would result in aggregate contributions from all contributors to the ABLE account for the taxable year exceeding the sum of—

"(i) the amount in effect under section 2503(b) for the calendar year in which the taxable year begins, plus

"(ii) in the case of any contribution by a designated beneficiary described in paragraph (7) before January 1, 2026, the lesser of—

"(I) compensation (as defined by section 219(f)(1)) includible in the designated beneficiary's gross income for the taxable year, or

"(II) an amount equal to the poverty line for a one-person household, as determined for the calendar year preceding the calendar year in which the taxable year begins.".

(2) RESPONSIBILITY FOR CONTRIBUTION LIMITATION.—Paragraph (2) of section 529A(b) is amended by adding at the end the following: "A des-

ignated beneficiary (or a person acting on behalf of such beneficiary) shall maintain adequate records for purposes of ensuring, and shall be responsible for ensuring, that the requirements of subparagraph (B)(ii) are met."

(3) ELIGIBLE DESIGNATED BENEFICIARY.—Section 529A(b) is amended by adding at the end the following:

"(7) SPECIAL RULES RELATED TO CONTRIBUTION LIMIT.—For purposes of paragraph (2)(B)(ii)—

"(A) DESIGNATED BENEFICIARY.—A designated beneficiary described in this paragraph is an employee (including an employee within the meaning of section 401(c)) with respect to whom—

"(i) no contribution is made for the taxable year to a defined contribution plan (within the meaning of section 414(i)) with respect to which the requirements of section 401(a) or 403(a) are met,

"(ii) no contribution is made for the taxable year to an annuity contract described in section 403(b), and "(iii) no contribution is made for the taxable year to an eligible deferred compensation plan described in section 457(b).

"(B) POVERTY LINE.—The term 'poverty line' has the meaning given such term by section 673 of the Community Services Block Grant Act (42 U.S.C. 9902).".

(b) ALLOWANCE OF SAVER'S CREDIT FOR ABLE CONTRIBUTIONS BY ACCOUNT HOLDER.—Section 25B(d)(1) is amended by striking "and" at the end of subparagraph (B)(ii), by striking the period at the end of subparagraph (C) and inserting ", and", and by inserting at the end the following:

"(D) the amount of contributions made before January 1, 2026, by such individual to the ABLE account (within the meaning of section 529A) of which such individual is the designated beneficiary.".

(c) EFFECTIVE DATE.—The amendments made by this section shall apply to taxable years beginning after the date of the enactment of this Act.

**SEC. 11025. ROLLOVERS TO ABLE PROGRAMS FROM 529 PROGRAMS.**

(a) IN GENERAL.—Clause (i) of section 529(c)(3)(C) is amended by striking "or" at the end of subclause (I), by striking the period at the end of subclause (II) and inserting ", or", and by adding at the end the following:

"(III) before January 1, 2026, to an ABLE account (as defined in section 529A(e)(6)) of the designated beneficiary or a member of the family of the designated beneficiary.

Subclause (III) shall not apply to so much of a distribution which, when added to all other contributions made to the ABLE account for the taxable year, exceeds the limitation under section 529A(b)(2)(B)(i).".

(b) EFFECTIVE DATE.—The amendments made by this section shall apply to distributions after the date of the enactment of this Act.

**SEC. 11026. TREATMENT OF CERTAIN INDIVIDUALS PERFORMING SERVICES IN THE SINAI PENINSULA OF EGYPT.**

(a) IN GENERAL.—For purposes of the following provisions of the Internal Revenue Code of 1986, with respect to the applicable period, a qualified hazardous duty area shall be treated in the same manner as if it were a combat zone (as determined under section 112 of such Code):

(1) Section 2(a)(3) (relating to special rule where deceased spouse was in missing status).

(2) Section 112 (relating to the exclusion of certain combat pay of members of the Armed Forces).

(3) Section 692 (relating to income taxes of members of Armed Forces on death).

(4) Section 2201 (relating to members of the Armed Forces dying in combat zone or by reason of combat-zone-incurred wounds, etc.).

(5) Section 3401(a)(1) (defining wages relating to combat pay for members of the Armed Forces).

(6) Section 4253(d) (relating to the taxation of phone service originating from a combat zone from members of the Armed Forces).

(7) Section 6013(f)(1) (relating to joint return where individual is in missing status).

(8) Section 7508 (relating to time for performing certain acts postponed by reason of service in combat zone).

(b) QUALIFIED HAZARDOUS DUTY AREA.—For purposes of this section, the term "qualified hazardous duty area" means the Sinai Peninsula of Egypt, if as of the date of the enactment of this section any member of the Armed Forces of the United States is entitled to special pay under section 310 of title 37, United States Code (relating to special pay; duty subject to hostile fire or imminent danger), for services performed in such location. Such term includes such location only during the period such entitlement is in effect.

(c) APPLICABLE PERIOD.—

(1) IN GENERAL.—Except as provided in paragraph (2), the applicable period is—

(A) the portion of the first taxable year ending after June 9, 2015, which begins on such date, and

(B) any subsequent taxable year beginning before January 1, 2026.

(2) WITHHOLDING.—In the case of subsection (a)(5), the applicable period is—

(A) the portion of the first taxable year ending after the date of the enactment of this Act which begins on such date, and

(B) any subsequent taxable year beginning before January 1, 2026.

(d) EFFECTIVE DATE.—

(1) IN GENERAL.—Except as provided in paragraph (2), the provisions of this section shall take effect on June 9, 2015.

(2) WITHHOLDING.—Subsection (a)(5) shall apply to remuneration paid after the date of the enactment of this Act.

**SEC. 11027. TEMPORARY REDUCTION IN MEDICAL EXPENSE DEDUCTION FLOOR.**

(a) IN GENERAL.—Subsection (f) of section 213 is amended to read as follows:

"(f) SPECIAL RULES FOR 2013 THROUGH 2018.—In the case of any taxable year—

"(1) beginning after December 31, 2012, and ending before January 1, 2017, in the case of a taxpayer if such taxpayer or such taxpayer's spouse has attained age 65 before the close of such taxable year, and

"(2) beginning after December 31, 2016, and ending before January 1, 2019, in the case of any taxpayer,

subsection (a) shall be applied with respect to a taxpayer by substituting '7.5 percent' for '10 percent'.".

(b) MINIMUM TAX PREFERENCE NOT TO APPLY.—Section 56(b)(1)(B) is amended by adding at the end the following new sentence:"This subparagraph shall not apply to taxable years beginning after December 31, 2016, and ending before January 1, 2019".

(c) EFFECTIVE DATE.—The amendment made by this section shall apply to taxable years beginning after December 31, 2016.

**SEC. 11028. RELIEF FOR 2016 DISASTER AREAS.**

(a) IN GENERAL.—For purposes of this section, the term "2016 disaster area" means any area with respect to which a major disaster has been declared by the President under section 401 of the Robert T. Stafford Disaster Relief and Emergency Assistance Act during calendar year 2016.

(b) SPECIAL RULES FOR USE OF RETIREMENT FUNDS WITH RESPECT TO AREAS DAMAGED BY 2016 DISASTERS.—

(1) TAX-FAVORED WITHDRAWALS FROM RETIREMENT PLANS.—

(A) IN GENERAL.—Section 72(t) of the Internal Revenue Code of 1986 shall not apply to any qualified 2016 disaster distribution.

(B) AGGREGATE DOLLAR LIMITATION.—

(i) IN GENERAL.—For purposes of this subsection, the aggregate amount of distributions received by an individual which may be treated as qualified 2016 disaster distributions for any taxable year shall not exceed the excess (if any) of—

(I) $100,000, over

(II) the aggregate amounts treated as qualified 2016 disaster distributions received by such individual for all prior taxable years.

(ii) TREATMENT OF PLAN DISTRIBUTIONS.—If a distribution to an individual would (without regard to clause (i)) be a qualified 2016 disaster distribution, a plan shall not be treated as violating any requirement of this title merely because the plan treats such distribution as a qualified 2016 disaster distribution, unless the aggregate amount of such distributions from all plans maintained by the employer (and any member of any controlled group which includes the employer) to such individual exceeds $100,000.

(iii) CONTROLLED GROUP.—For purposes of clause (ii), the term "controlled group" means any group treated as a single employer under subsection (b), (c), (m), or (o) of section 414 of the Internal Revenue Code of 1986.

(C) AMOUNT DISTRIBUTED MAY BE REPAID.—

(i) IN GENERAL.—Any individual who receives a qualified 2016 disaster distribution may, at any time during the 3-year period beginning on the day after the date on which such distribution was received, make one or more contributions in an aggregate amount not to exceed the amount of such distribution to an eligible retirement plan of which such individual is a beneficiary and to which a rollover contribution of such distribution could be made under section 402(c), 403(a)(4), 403(b)(8), 408(d)(3), or 457(e)(16) of the Internal Revenue Code of 1986, as the case may be.

(ii) TREATMENT OF REPAYMENTS OF DISTRIBUTIONS FROM ELIGIBLE RETIREMENT PLANS OTHER THAN IRAS.—For purposes of the Internal Revenue Code of 1986, if a contribution is made pursuant to clause (i) with respect to a qualified 2016 disaster distribution from an eligible retirement plan other than an individual retirement plan, then the taxpayer shall, to the extent of the amount of the contribution, be treated as having received the qualified 2016 disaster distribution in an eligible rollover distribution (as defined in section 402(c)(4) of the Internal Revenue Code of 1986) and as having transferred the amount to the eligible retirement plan in a direct trustee to trustee transfer within 60 days of the distribution.

(iii) TREATMENT OF REPAYMENTS FOR DISTRIBUTIONS FROM IRAS.—For purposes of the Internal Revenue Code of 1986, if a contribution is made pursuant to clause (i) with respect to a qualified 2016 disaster distribution from an individual retirement plan (as defined by section 7701(a)(37) of the Internal Revenue Code of 1986), then, to the extent of the amount of the contribution, the qualified 2016 disaster distribution shall be treated as a distribution described in section 408(d)(3) of such Code and as having been transferred to the eligible retirement plan in a direct trustee to trustee transfer within 60 days of the distribution.

(D) DEFINITIONS.—For purposes of this paragraph—

(i) QUALIFIED 2016 DISASTER DISTRIBUTION.—Except as provided in subparagraph (B), the term "qualified 2016 disaster distribution" means any distribution from an eligible retirement plan made on or after January 1, 2016, and before January 1, 2018, to an individual whose principal place of abode at any time during calendar year 2016 was located in a disaster area described in subsection (a) and who has sustained an economic loss by reason of the events giving rise to the Presidential declaration described in subsection (a) which was applicable to such area.

(ii) ELIGIBLE RETIREMENT PLAN.—The term "eligible retirement plan" shall have the meaning given such term by section 402(c)(8)(B) of the Internal Revenue Code of 1986.

(E) INCOME INCLUSION SPREAD OVER 3-YEAR PERIOD.—

(i) IN GENERAL.—In the case of any qualified 2016 disaster distribution, unless the taxpayer elects not to have this subparagraph apply for any taxable year, any amount required to be included in gross income for such taxable year shall be so included ratably over the 3-taxable-year period beginning with such taxable year.

(ii) SPECIAL RULE.—For purposes of clause (i), rules similar to the rules of subparagraph (E) of section 408A(d)(3) of the Internal Revenue Code of 1986 shall apply.

(F) SPECIAL RULES.—

(i) EXEMPTION OF DISTRIBUTIONS FROM TRUSTEE TO TRUSTEE TRANSFER AND WITHHOLDING RULES.—For purposes of sections 401(a)(31), 402(f), and 3405 of the Internal Revenue Code of 1986, qualified 2016 disaster distribution shall not be treated as eligible rollover distributions.

(ii) QUALIFIED 2016 DISASTER DISTRIBUTIONS TREATED AS MEETING PLAN DISTRIBUTION REQUIREMENTS.—For purposes of the Internal Revenue Code of 1986, a qualified 2016 disaster distribution shall be treated as meeting the requirements of sections 401(k)(2)(B)(i), 403(b)(7)(A)(ii), 403(b)(11), and

457(d)(1)(A) of the Internal Revenue Code of 1986.

(2) PROVISIONS RELATING TO PLAN AMENDMENTS.—

(A) IN GENERAL.—If this paragraph applies to any amendment to any plan or annuity contract, such plan or contract shall be treated as being operated in accordance with the terms of the plan during the period described in subparagraph (B)(ii)(I).

(B) AMENDMENTS TO WHICH SUBSECTION APPLIES.—

(i) IN GENERAL.—This paragraph shall apply to any amendment to any plan or annuity contract which is made—

(I) pursuant to any provision of this section, or pursuant to any regulation under any provision of this section, and

(II) on or before the last day of the first plan year beginning on or after January 1, 2018, or such later date as the Secretary prescribes.

In the case of a governmental plan (as defined in section 414(d) of the Internal Revenue Code of 1986), subclause (II) shall be applied by substituting the date which is 2 years after the date otherwise applied under subclause (II).

(ii) CONDITIONS.—This paragraph shall not apply to any amendment to a plan or contract unless such amendment applies retroactively for such period, and shall not apply to any such amendment unless the plan or contract is operated as if such amendment were in effect during the period—

(I) beginning on the date that this section or the regulation described in clause (i)(I) takes effect (or in the case of a plan or contract amendment not required by this section or such regulation, the effective date specified by the plan), and

(II) ending on the date described in clause (i)(II) (or, if earlier, the date the plan or contract amendment is adopted).

(c) SPECIAL RULES FOR PERSONAL CASUALTY LOSSES RELATED TO 2016 MAJOR DISASTER.—

(1) IN GENERAL.—If an individual has a net disaster loss for any taxable year beginning after December 31, 2015, and before January 1, 2018—

(A) the amount determined under section 165(h)(2)(A)(ii) of the Internal Revenue Code of 1986 shall be equal to the sum of—

(i) such net disaster loss, and

(ii) so much of the excess referred to in the matter preceding clause (i) of section 165(h)(2)(A) of such Code (reduced by the amount in clause (i) of this subparagraph) as exceeds 10 percent of the adjusted gross income of the individual,

(B) section 165(h)(1) of such Code shall be applied by substituting "$500" for "$500 ($100 for taxable years beginning after December 31, 2009)",

(C) the standard deduction determined under section 63(c) of such Code shall be increased by the net disaster loss, and

(D) section 56(b)(1)(E) of such Code shall not apply to so much of the standard deduction as is attributable to the increase under subparagraph (C) of this paragraph.

(2) NET DISASTER LOSS.—For purposes of this subsection, the term "net disaster loss" means the excess of qualified disaster-related personal casualty losses over personal casualty gains (as defined in section 165(h)(3)(A) of the Internal Revenue Code of 1986).

(3) QUALIFIED DISASTER-RELATED PERSONAL CASUALTY LOSSES.—For purposes of this paragraph, the term "qualified disaster-related personal casualty losses" means losses described in section 165(c)(3) of the Internal Revenue Code of 1986 which arise in a disaster area described in subsection (a) on or after January 1, 2016, and which are attributable to the events giving rise to the Presidential declaration described in subsection (a) which was applicable to such area.

## PART IV—EDUCATION

### SEC. 11031. TREATMENT OF STUDENT LOANS DISCHARGED ON ACCOUNT OF DEATH OR DISABILITY.

(a) IN GENERAL.—Section 108(f) is amended by adding at the end the following new paragraph:

"(5) DISCHARGES ON ACCOUNT OF DEATH OR DISABILITY.—

"(A) IN GENERAL.—In the case of an individual, gross income does not include any amount which (but for this subsection) would be includible in gross income for such taxable year by reasons of the discharge (in whole or in part) of any loan described in subparagraph (B) after December 31, 2017, and before January 1, 2026, if such discharge was—

"(i) pursuant to subsection (a) or (d) of section 437 of the Higher Education Act of 1965 or the parallel benefit under part D of title IV of such Act (relating to the repayment of loan liability),

"(ii) pursuant to section 464(c)(1)(F) of such Act, or

"(iii) otherwise discharged on account of the death or total and permanent disability of the student.

"(B) LOANS DESCRIBED.—A loan is described in this subparagraph if such loan is—

"(i) a student loan (as defined in paragraph (2)), or

"(ii) a private education loan (as defined in section 140(7) of the Consumer Credit Protection Act (15 U.S.C. 1650(7)))."

(b) EFFECTIVE DATE.—The amendment made by this section shall apply to discharges of indebtedness after December 31, 2017.

**SEC. 11032. 529 ACCOUNT FUNDING FOR ELEMENTARY AND SECONDARY EDUCATION.**

(a) IN GENERAL.—

(1) IN GENERAL.—Section 529(c) is amended by adding at the end the following new paragraph:

"(7) TREATMENT OF ELEMENTARY AND SECONDARY TUITION.—Any reference in this subsection to the term 'qualified higher education expense' shall include a reference to—

"(A) expenses for tuition in connection with enrollment or attendance at an elementary or secondary public, private, or religious school, and

"(B) expenses for—

"(i) curriculum and curricular materials,

"(ii) books or other instructional materials,

"(iii) online educational materials,

"(iv) tuition for tutoring or educational classes outside of the home (but only if the tutor or instructor is not related (within the meaning of section 152(d)(2)) to the student),

"(v) dual enrollment in an institution of higher education, and

"(vi) educational therapies for students with disabilities,

in connection with a homeschool (whether treated as a homeschool or a private school for purposes of applicable State law).".

(2) LIMITATION.—Section 529(e)(3)(A) is amended by adding at the end the following: "The amount of cash distributions from all qualified tuition programs described in subsection (b)(1)(A)(ii) with respect to a beneficiary during any taxable year shall, in the aggregate, include not more than $10,000 in expenses described in subsection (c)(7) incurred during the taxable year.".

(b) EFFECTIVE DATE.—The amendments made by this section shall apply to distributions made after December 31, 2017.

## PART V—DEDUCTIONS AND EXCLUSIONS

### SEC. 11041. SUSPENSION OF DEDUCTION FOR PERSONAL EXEMPTIONS.

(a) IN GENERAL.—Subsection (d) of section 151 is amended—

(1) by striking "In the case of" in paragraph (4) and inserting "Except as provided in paragraph (5), in the case of", and

(2) by adding at the end the following new paragraph:

"(5) SPECIAL RULES FOR TAXABLE YEARS 2018 THROUGH 2025.—In the case of a taxable year beginning after December 31, 2017, and before January 1, 2026—

"(A) EXEMPTION AMOUNT.—The term 'exemption amount' means zero.

"(B) REFERENCES.—For purposes of any other provision of this title, the reduction of the exemption amount to zero under subparagraph (A) shall not be taken into account in determining whether a deduction is allowed or allowable, or whether a taxpayer is entitled to a deduction, under this section.".

(b) APPLICATION TO ESTATES AND TRUSTS.—Section 642(b)(2)(C) is amended by adding at the end the following new clause:

"(iii) YEARS WHEN PERSONAL EXEMPTION AMOUNT IS ZERO.—

"(I) IN GENERAL.—In the case of any taxable year in which the exemption amount under section 151(d) is zero, clause (i) shall be applied by substituting '$4,150' for 'the exemption amount under section 151(d)'.

"(II) INFLATION ADJUSTMENT.—In the case of any taxable year beginning in a calendar year after 2018, the $4,150 amount in subparagraph (A) shall be increased in the same manner as provided in section 6334(d)(4)(C).".

(c) MODIFICATION OF WAGE WITHHOLDING RULES.—

(1) IN GENERAL.—Section 3402(a)(2) is amended by striking "means the amount" and all that follows and inserting "means the amount by which the wages exceed the taxpayer's withholding allowance, prorated to the payroll period.".

(2) CONFORMING AMENDMENTS.—

(A) Section 3401 is amended by striking subsection (e).

(B) Paragraphs (1) and (2) of section 3402(f) are amended to read as follows:

"(1) IN GENERAL.—Under rules determined by the Secretary, an employee receiving wages shall on any day be entitled to a withholding allowance determined based on—

"(A) whether the employee is an individual for whom a deduction is allowable with respect to another taxpayer under section 151;

"(B) if the employee is married, whether the employee's spouse is entitled to an allowance, or would be so entitled if such spouse were an employee receiving wages, under subparagraph (A) or (D), but only if such spouse does not have in effect a withholding allowance certificate claiming such allowance;

"(C) the number of individuals with respect to whom, on the basis of facts existing at the beginning of such day, there may reasonably be expected to be allowable a credit under section 24(a) for the taxable year under subtitle A in respect of which amounts deducted and withheld under this chapter in the calendar year in which such day falls are allowed as a credit;

"(D) any additional amounts to which the employee elects to take into account under subsection (m), but only if the employee's spouse does not have in effect a withholding allowance certificate making such an election;

"(E) the standard deduction allowable to such employee (one-half of such standard deduction in the case of an employee who is married (as determined under section 7703) and whose spouse is an employee receiving wages subject to withholding); and

"(F) whether the employee has withholding allowance certificates in effect with respect to more than 1 employer.

"(2) ALLOWANCE CERTIFICATES.—

"(A) ON COMMENCEMENT OF EMPLOYMENT.—On or before the date of the commencement of employment with an employer, the employee shall furnish the employer with a signed withholding allowance certificate relating to the withholding allowance claimed by the employee, which shall in no event exceed the amount to which the employee is entitled.

"(B) CHANGE OF STATUS.—If, on any day during the calendar year, an employee's withholding allowance is in excess of the withholding allowance to which the employee would be entitled had the employee submitted a true and accurate withholding allowance certificate to the employer on that day, the employee shall within 10 days thereafter furnish the employer with a new withholding allowance certificate. If, on any day during the calendar year, an employee's withholding allowance is greater than the withholding allowance claimed, the employee may furnish the employer with a new withholding allowance certificate relating to the withholding allowance to which the employee is so entitled, which shall in no event exceed the amount to which the employee is entitled on such day.

"(C) CHANGE OF STATUS WHICH AFFECTS NEXT CALENDAR YEAR.—If on any day during the calendar year the withholding allowance to which the employee will be, or may reasonably be expected to be, entitled at the beginning of the employee's next taxable year under subtitle A is different from the allowance to which the employee is entitled on such day, the employee shall, in such cases and at such times as the Secretary shall by regulations prescribe, furnish the employer with a withholding allowance certificate relating to the withholding allowance which the employee claims with respect to such next taxable year, which shall in no event exceed the withholding allowance to which the employee will be, or may reasonably be expected to be, so entitled.".

(C) Subsections (b)(1), (b)(2), (f)(3), (f)(4), (f)(5), (f)(7) (including the heading thereof), (g)(4), (l)(1), (l)(2), and (n) of section 3402 are each amended by striking "exemption" each place it appears and inserting "allowance".

(D) The heading of section 3402(f) is amended by striking "EXEMPTIONS" and inserting "ALLOWANCE".

(E) Section 3402(m) is amended by striking "additional withholding allowances or additional reductions in withholding under this subsection. In determining the number of additional withholding allowances" and inserting "an additional withholding allowance or additional reductions in withholding under this subsection. In determining the additional withholding allowance".

(F) Paragraphs (3) and (4) of section 3405(a) (and the heading for such paragraph (4)) are each amended by striking "exemption" each place it appears and inserting "allowance".

(G) Section 3405(a)(4) is amended by striking "shall be determined" and all that follows through "3 withholding exemptions" and inserting "shall be determined under rules prescribed by the Secretary".

(d) EXCEPTION FOR DETERMINING PROPERTY EXEMPT FROM LEVY.—Section 6334(d) is amended by adding at the end the following new paragraph:

"(4) YEARS WHEN PERSONAL EXEMPTION AMOUNT IS ZERO.—

"(A) IN GENERAL.—In the case of any taxable year in which the exemption amount under section 151(d) is zero, paragraph (2) shall not apply and for purposes of paragraph (1) the term 'exempt amount' means an amount equal to—

"(i) the sum of the amount determined under subparagraph (B) and the standard deduction, divided by

"(ii) 52.

"(B) AMOUNT DETERMINED.—For purposes of subparagraph (A), the amount determined under this subparagraph is $4,150 multiplied by the number of the taxpayer's dependents for the taxable year in which the levy occurs.

"(C) Inflation adjustment.—In the case of any taxable year beginning in a calendar year after 2018, the $4,150 amount in subparagraph (B) shall be increased by an amount equal to—

"(i) such dollar amount, multiplied by

"(ii) the cost-of-living adjustment determined under section 1(f)(3) for the calendar year in which the taxable year begins, determined by substituting '2017' for '2016' in subparagraph (A)(ii) thereof.

If any increase determined under the preceding sentence is not a multiple of $100, such increase shall be rounded to the next lowest multiple of $100.

"(D) Verified statement.—Unless the taxpayer submits to the Secretary a written and properly verified statement specifying the facts necessary to determine the proper amount under subparagraph (A), subparagraph (A) shall be applied as if the taxpayer were a married individual filing a separate return with no dependents.".

(e) PERSONS REQUIRED TO MAKE RETURNS OF INCOME.—Section 6012 is amended by adding at the end the following new subsection:

"(f) SPECIAL RULE FOR TAXABLE YEARS 2018 THROUGH 2025.—In the case of a taxable year beginning after December 31, 2017, and before January 1, 2026, subsection (a)(1) shall not apply, and every individual who has gross income for the taxable year shall be required to make returns with respect to income taxes under subtitle A, except that a return shall not be required of—

"(1) an individual who is not married (determined by applying section 7703) and who has gross income for the taxable year which does not exceed the standard deduction applicable to such individual for such taxable year under section 63, or

"(2) an individual entitled to make a joint return if—

"(A) the gross income of such individual, when combined with the gross income of such individual's spouse, for the taxable year does not exceed the standard deduction which would be applicable to the taxpayer for such taxable year under section 63 if such individual and such individual's spouse made a joint return,

"(B) such individual and such individual's spouse have the same household as their home at the close of the taxable year,

"(C) such individual's spouse does not make a separate return, and

"(D) neither such individual nor such individual's spouse is an individual described in section 63(c)(5) who has income (other than earned income) in excess of the amount in effect under section 63(c)(5)(A).".

(f) EFFECTIVE DATE.—

(1) IN GENERAL.—Except as provided in paragraph (2), the amendments made by this section shall apply to taxable years beginning after December 31, 2017.

(2) WAGE WITHHOLDING.—The Secretary of the Treasury may administer section 3402 for taxable years beginning before January 1, 2019, without regard to the amendments made by subsections (a) and (c).

**SEC. 11042. LIMITATION ON DEDUCTION FOR STATE AND LOCAL, ETC. TAXES.**

(a) IN GENERAL.—Subsection (b) of section 164 is amended by adding at the end the following new paragraph:

"(6) LIMITATION ON INDIVIDUAL DEDUCTIONS FOR TAXABLE YEARS 2018 THROUGH 2025.—In the case of an individual and a taxable year beginning after December 31, 2017, and before January 1, 2026—

"(A) foreign real property taxes shall not be taken into account under subsection (a)(1), and

"(B) the aggregate amount of taxes taken into account under paragraphs (1), (2), and (3) of subsection (a) and paragraph (5) of this subsection for any taxable year shall not exceed $10,000 ($5,000 in the case of a married individual filing a separate return).

The preceding sentence shall not apply to any foreign taxes described in subsection (a)(3) or to any taxes described in paragraph (1) and (2) of subsection (a) which are paid or accrued in carrying on a trade or business or an activity described in section 212. For purposes of subparagraph (B), an amount paid in a taxable year beginning before January 1, 2018, with respect to a State or local income tax imposed for a taxable year beginning after December 31, 2017, shall be treated as paid on the last day of the taxable year for which such tax is so imposed.".

(b) EFFECTIVE DATE.—The amendment made by this section shall apply to taxable years beginning after December 31, 2016.

**SEC. 11043. LIMITATION ON DEDUCTION FOR QUALIFIED RESIDENCE INTEREST.**

(a) IN GENERAL.—Section 163(h)(3) is amended by adding at the end the following new subparagraph:

"(F) SPECIAL RULES FOR TAXABLE YEARS 2018 THROUGH 2025.—

"(i) IN GENERAL.—In the case of taxable years beginning after December 31, 2017, and before January 1, 2026—

"(I) DISALLOWANCE OF HOME EQUITY INDEBTEDNESS INTEREST.—Subparagraph (A)(ii) shall not apply.

"(II) LIMITATION ON ACQUISITION INDEBTEDNESS.—Subparagraph (B)(ii) shall be applied by substituting '$750,000 ($375,000' for '$1,000,000 ($500,000'.

"(III) TREATMENT OF INDEBTEDNESS INCURRED ON OR BEFORE DECEMBER 15, 2017.—Subclause (II) shall not apply to any indebtedness incurred on or before December 15, 2017, and, in applying such subclause to any indebtedness incurred after such date, the limitation under such subclause shall be reduced (but not below zero) by the amount of any indebtedness incurred on or before December 15, 2017, which is treated as acquisition indebtedness for purposes of this subsection for the taxable year.

"(IV) BINDING CONTRACT EXCEPTION.—In the case of a taxpayer who enters into a written binding contract before December 15, 2017, to close on the purchase of a principal residence before January 1, 2018, and who purchases such residence before April 1, 2018, subclause (III) shall be applied by substituting 'April 1, 2018' for 'December 15, 2017'.

"(ii) TREATMENT OF LIMITATION IN TAXABLE YEARS AFTER DECEMBER 31, 2025.—In the case of taxable years beginning after December 31, 2025, the limitation under subparagraph (B)(ii) shall be applied to the aggregate amount of indebtedness of the taxpayer described in subparagraph (B)(i) without regard to the taxable year in which the indebtedness was incurred.

"(iii) TREATMENT OF REFINANCINGS OF INDEBTEDNESS.—

"(I) IN GENERAL.—In the case of any indebtedness which is incurred to refinance indebtedness, such refinanced indebtedness shall be treated for purposes of clause (i)(III) as incurred on the date that the original indebtedness was incurred to the extent the amount of the indebtedness resulting from such refinancing does not exceed the amount of the refinanced indebtedness.

"(II) LIMITATION ON PERIOD OF REFINANCING.—Subclause (I) shall not apply to any indebtedness after the expiration of the term of the original indebtedness or, if the principal of such original indebtedness is not amortized over its term, the expiration of the term of the 1st refinancing of such indebtedness (or if earlier, the date which is 30 years after the date of such 1st refinancing).

"(iv) COORDINATION WITH EXCLUSION OF INCOME FROM DISCHARGE OF INDEBTEDNESS.—Section 108(h)(2) shall be applied without regard to this subparagraph.".

(b) EFFECTIVE DATE.—The amendments made by this section shall apply to taxable years beginning after December 31, 2017.

**SEC. 11044. MODIFICATION OF DEDUCTION FOR PERSONAL CASUALTY LOSSES.**

(a) IN GENERAL.—Subsection (h) of section 165 is amended by adding at the end the following new paragraph:

"(5) LIMITATION FOR TAXABLE YEARS 2018 THROUGH 2025.—

"(A) IN GENERAL.—In the case of an individual, except as provided in subparagraph (B), any personal casualty loss which (but for this paragraph) would be deductible in a taxable year beginning after December 31, 2017, and before January 1, 2026, shall be allowed as a deduction under subsection (a) only to the extent it is attributable to a Federally declared disaster (as defined in subsection (i)(5)).

"(B) EXCEPTION RELATED TO PERSONAL CASUALTY GAINS.—If a taxpayer has personal casualty gains for any taxable year to which subparagraph (A) applies—

"(i) subparagraph (A) shall not apply to the portion of the personal casualty loss not attributable to a Federally declared disaster (as so defined) to the extent such loss does not exceed such gains, and

"(ii) in applying paragraph (2) for purposes of subparagraph (A) to the portion of personal casualty loss which is so attributable to such a disaster, the amount of personal casualty gains taken into account under paragraph (2)(A) shall be reduced by the portion of such gains taken into account under clause (i).".

(b) EFFECTIVE DATE.—The amendment made by this section shall apply to losses incurred in taxable years beginning after December 31, 2017.

**SEC. 11045. SUSPENSION OF MISCELLANEOUS ITEMIZED DEDUCTIONS.**

(a) IN GENERAL.—Section 67 is amended by adding at the end the following new subsection:

"(g) SUSPENSION FOR TAXABLE YEARS 2018 THROUGH 2025.—Notwithstanding subsection (a), no miscellaneous itemized deduction shall be allowed for any taxable year beginning after December 31, 2017, and before January 1, 2026.".

(b) EFFECTIVE DATE.—The amendment made by this section shall apply to taxable years beginning after December 31, 2017.

**SEC. 11046. SUSPENSION OF OVERALL LIMITATION ON ITEMIZED DEDUCTIONS.**

(a) IN GENERAL.—Section 68 is amended by adding at the end the following new subsection:

"(f) SECTION NOT TO APPLY.—This section shall not apply to any taxable year beginning after December 31, 2017, and before January 1, 2026.".

(b) EFFECTIVE DATE.—The amendments made by this section shall apply to taxable years beginning after December 31, 2017.

**SEC. 11047. SUSPENSION OF EXCLUSION FOR QUALIFIED BICYCLE COMMUTING REIMBURSEMENT.**

(a) IN GENERAL.—Section 132(f) is amended by

"(8) SUSPENSION OF QUALIFIED BICYCLE COMMUTING REIMBURSEMENT EXCLUSION.—Paragraph (1)(D) shall not apply to any taxable year beginning after December 31, 2017, and before January 1, 2026.".

(b) EFFECTIVE DATE.—The amendment made by this section shall apply to taxable years beginning after December 31, 2017.

**SEC. 11048. SUSPENSION OF EXCLUSION FOR QUALIFIED MOVING EXPENSE REIMBURSEMENT.**

(a) IN GENERAL.—Section 132(g) is amended—

(1) by striking "For purposes of this section, the term" and inserting "For purposes of this section—

"(1) IN GENERAL.—The term", and

(2) by adding at the end the following new paragraph:

"(2) SUSPENSION FOR TAXABLE YEARS 2018 THROUGH 2025.—Except in the case of a member of the Armed Forces of the United States on active duty who moves pursuant to a military order and incident to a permanent change of station, subsection (a)(6) shall not apply to any taxable year beginning after December 31, 2017, and before January 1, 2026.".

(b) EFFECTIVE DATE.—The amendments made by this section shall apply to taxable years beginning after December 31, 2017.

**SEC. 11049. SUSPENSION OF DEDUCTION FOR MOVING EXPENSES.**

(a) IN GENERAL.—Section 217 is amended by adding at the end the following new subsection:

"(k) SUSPENSION OF DEDUCTION FOR TAXABLE YEARS 2018 THROUGH 2025.—Except in the case of an individual to whom subsection (g) applies, this section shall not apply to any taxable year beginning after December 31, 2017, and before January 1, 2026.".

(b) EFFECTIVE DATE.—The amendment made by this section shall apply to taxable years beginning after December 31, 2017.

**SEC. 11050. LIMITATION ON WAGERING LOSSES.**

(a) IN GENERAL.—Section 165(d) is amended by adding at the end the following: "For purposes of the preceding sentence, in the case of taxable years beginning after December 31, 2017, and before January 1, 2026, the term 'losses from wagering transactions' includes any deduction otherwise allowable under this chapter incurred in carrying on any wagering transaction.".

(b) EFFECTIVE DATE.—The amendment made by this section shall apply to taxable years beginning after December 31, 2017.

**SEC. 11051. REPEAL OF DEDUCTION FOR ALIMONY PAYMENTS.**

(a) IN GENERAL.—Part VII of subchapter B is amended by striking by striking section 215 (and by striking the item relating to such section in the table of sections for such subpart).

(b) CONFORMING AMENDMENTS.—

(1) CORRESPONDING REPEAL OF PROVISIONS PROVIDING FOR INCLUSION OF ALIMONY IN GROSS INCOME.—

(A) Subsection (a) of section 61 is amended by striking paragraph (8) and by redesignating paragraphs (9) through (15) as paragraphs (8) through (14), respectively.

(B) Part II of subchapter B of chapter 1 is amended by striking section 71 (and by striking the item relating to such section in the table of sections for such part).

(C) Subpart F of part I of subchapter J of chapter 1 is amended by striking section 682 (and by striking the item relating to such section in the table of sections for such subpart).

(2) RELATED TO REPEAL OF SECTION 215.—

(A) Section 62(a) is amended by striking paragraph (10).

(B) Section 3402(m)(1) is amended by striking "(other than paragraph (10) thereof)".

(C) Section 6724(d)(3) is amended by striking subparagraph (C) and by redesignating subparagraph (D) as subparagraph (C).

(3) RELATED TO REPEAL OF SECTION 71.—

(A) Section 121(d)(3) is amended—

(i) by striking "(as defined in section 71(b)(2))" in subparagraph (B), and

(ii) by adding at the end the following new subparagraph:

"(C) DIVORCE OR SEPARATION INSTRUMENT.—For purposes of this paragraph, the term 'divorce or separation instrument' means—

"(i) a decree of divorce or separate maintenance or a written instrument incident to such a decree,

"(ii) a written separation agreement, or

"(iii) a decree (not described in clause (i)) requiring a spouse to make payments for the support or maintenance of the other spouse.".

(B) Section 152(d)(5) is amended to read as follows:

"(5) SPECIAL RULES FOR SUPPORT.—

"(A) IN GENERAL.—For purposes of this subsection—

"(i) payments to a spouse of alimony or separate maintenance payments shall not be treated as a payment by the payor spouse for the support of any dependent, and

"(ii) in the case of the remarriage of a parent, support of a child received from the parent's spouse shall be treated as received from the parent.

"(B) ALIMONY OR SEPARATE MAINTENANCE PAYMENT.—For purposes of subparagraph (A), the term 'alimony or separate maintenance payment' means any payment in cash if—

"(i) such payment is received by (or on behalf of) a spouse under a divorce or separation instrument (as defined in section 121(d)(3)(C)), "(ii) in the case of an individual legally separated from the individual's spouse under a decree of divorce or of separate maintenance, the payee spouse and the payor spouse are not members of the same household at the time such payment is made, and

"(iii) there is no liability to make any such payment for any period after the death of the payee spouse and there is no liability to make any payment (in cash or property) as a substitute for such payments after the death of the payee spouse.".

(C) Section 219(f)(1) is amended by striking the third sentence.

(D) Section 220(f)(7) is amended by striking "subparagraph (A) of section 71(b)(2)" and inserting "clause (i) of section 121(d)(3)(C)".

(E) Section 223(f)(7) is amended by striking "subparagraph (A) of section 71(b)(2)" and inserting "clause (i) of section 121(d)(3)(C)".

(F) Section 382(l)(3)(B)(iii) is amended by striking "section 71(b)(2)" and inserting "section 121(d)(3)(C)".

(G) Section 408(d)(6) is amended by striking "subparagraph (A) of section 71(b)(2)" and inserting "clause (i) of section 121(d)(3)(C)".

(4) ADDITIONAL CONFORMING AMENDMENTS.—Section 7701(a)(17) is amended—

(A) by striking "sections 682 and 2516" and inserting "section 2516", and

(B) by striking "such sections" each place it appears and inserting "such section".

(c) EFFECTIVE DATE.—The amendments made by this section shall apply to—

(1) any divorce or separation instrument (as defined in section 71(b)(2) of the Internal Revenue Code of 1986 as in effect before the date of the enactment of this Act) executed after December 31, 2018, and

(2) any divorce or separation instrument (as so defined) executed on or before such date and modified after such date if the modification expressly provides that the amendments made by this section apply to such modification.

## PART VI—INCREASE IN ESTATE AND GIFT TAX EXEMPTION

### SEC. 11061. INCREASE IN ESTATE AND GIFT TAX EXEMPTION.

(a) In General.—Section 2010(c)(3) is amended by adding at the end the following new subparagraph:

"(C) Increase in basic exclusion amount.—In the case of estates of decedents dying or gifts made after December 31, 2017, and before January 1, 2026, subparagraph (A) shall be applied by substituting '$10,000,000' for '$5,000,000'.".

(b) Conforming Amendment.—Subsection (g) of section 2001 is amended to read as follows:

"(g) Modifications to Tax Payable.—

"(1) Modifications to gift tax payable to reflect different tax rates.—For purposes of applying subsection (b)(2) with respect to 1 or more gifts, the rates of tax under subsection (c) in effect at the decedent's death shall, in lieu of the rates of tax in effect at the time of such gifts, be used both to compute—

"(A) the tax imposed by chapter 12 with respect to such gifts, and

"(B) the credit allowed against such tax

"(i) the applicable credit amount under section 2505(a)(1), and

"(ii) the sum of the amounts allowed as a credit for all preceding periods under section 2505(a)(2).

"(2) MODIFICATIONS TO ESTATE TAX PAYABLE TO REFLECT DIFFERENT BASIC EXCLUSION AMOUNTS.—The Secretary shall prescribe such regulations as may be necessary or appropriate to carry out this section with respect to any difference between—

"(A) the basic exclusion amount under section 2010(c)(3) applicable at the time of the decedent's death, and

"(B) the basic exclusion amount under such section applicable with respect to any gifts made by the decedent.".

(c) EFFECTIVE DATE.—The amendments made by this section shall apply to estates of decedents dying and gifts made after December 31, 2017.

## PART VII—EXTENSION OF TIME LIMIT FOR CONTESTING IRS LEVY

### SEC. 11071. EXTENSION OF TIME LIMIT FOR CONTESTING IRS LEVY.

(a) EXTENSION OF TIME FOR RETURN OF PROPERTY SUBJECT TO LEVY.—Subsection (b) of section 6343 is amended by striking "9 months" and inserting "2 years".

(b) PERIOD OF LIMITATION ON SUITS.—Subsection (c) of section 6532 is amended—

(1) by striking "9 months" in paragraph (1) and inserting "2 years", and

(2) by striking "9-month" in paragraph (2) and inserting "2-year".

(c) EFFECTIVE DATE.—The amendments made by this section shall apply to—

(1) levies made after the date of the enactment of this Act, and

(2) levies made on or before such date if the 9-month period has not expired under section 6343(b) of the Internal Revenue Code of 1986 (without regard to this section) as of such date.

## PART VIII—INDIVIDUAL MANDATE

### SEC. 11081. ELIMINATION OF SHARED RESPONSIBILITY PAYMENT FOR INDIVIDUALS FAILING TO MAINTAIN MINIMUM ESSENTIAL COVERAGE.

(1) in paragraph (2)(B)(iii), by striking "2.5 percent" and inserting "Zero percent", and

(2) in paragraph (3)—

(A) by striking "$695" in subparagraph (A) and inserting "$0", and

(B) by striking subparagraph (D).

(b) EFFECTIVE DATE.—The amendments made by this section shall apply to months beginning after December 31, 2018.

## Subtitle B—Alternative Minimum Tax

### SEC. 12001. REPEAL OF TAX FOR CORPORATIONS.

(a) IN GENERAL.—Section 55(a) is amended by striking "There" and inserting "In the case of a taxpayer other than a corporation, there".

(b) CONFORMING AMENDMENTS.—

(1) Section 38(c)(6) is amended by adding at the end the following new subparagraph:

"(E) CORPORATIONS.—In the case of a corporation, this subsection shall be applied by treating the corporation as having a tentative minimum tax of zero.".

(2) Section 53(d)(2) is amended by inserting ", except that in the case of a corporation, the ten-

tative minimum tax shall be treated as zero" before the period at the end.

(3)(A) Section 55(b)(1) is amended to read as follows:

"(1) AMOUNT OF TENTATIVE TAX.—

"(A) IN GENERAL.—The tentative minimum tax for the taxable year is the sum of—

"(i) 26 percent of so much of the taxable excess as does not exceed $175,000, plus

"(ii) 28 percent of so much of the taxable excess as exceeds $175,000.

The amount determined under the preceding sentence shall be reduced by the alternative minimum tax foreign tax credit for the taxable year.

"(B) TAXABLE EXCESS.—For purposes of this subsection, the term 'taxable excess' means so much of the alternative minimum taxable income for the taxable year as exceeds the exemption amount.

"(C) MARRIED INDIVIDUAL FILING SEPARATE RETURN.—In the case of a married individual filing a separate return, subparagraph (A) shall be applied by substituting 50 percent of the dollar amount otherwise applicable under clause (i) and clause (ii) thereof. For purposes of the preceding sentence, marital status shall be determined under section 7703.".

(B) Section 55(b)(3) is amended by striking "paragraph (1)(A)(i)" and inserting "paragraph (1)(A)".

(C) Section 59(a) is amended—

(i) by striking "subparagraph (A)(i) or (B)(i) of section 55(b)(1) (whichever applies) in lieu of the highest rate of tax specified in section 1 or 11 (whichever applies)" in paragraph (1)(C) and inserting "section 55(b)(1) in lieu of the highest rate of tax specified in section 1", and

(ii) in paragraph (2), by striking "means" and all that follows and inserting "means the amount determined under the first sentence of section 55(b)(1)(A).".

(D) Section 897(a)(2)(A) is amended by striking "section 55(b)(1)(A)" and inserting "section 55(b)(1)".

(E) Section 911(f) is amended—

(i) in paragraph (1)(B)—

(I) by striking "section 55(b)(1)(A)(ii)" and inserting "section 55(b)(1)(B)", and

(II) by striking "section 55(b)(1)(A)(i)" and inserting "section 55(b)(1)(A)", and

(ii) in paragraph (2)(B), by striking "section 55(b)(1)(A)(ii)" each place it appears and inserting "section 55(b)(1)(B)".

(4) Section 55(c)(1) is amended by striking ", the section 936 credit allowable under section 27(b), and the Puerto Rico economic activity credit under section 30A".

(5) Section 55(d), as amended by section 11002, is amended—

(A) by striking paragraph (2) and redesignating paragraphs (3) and (4) as paragraphs (2) and (3), respectively,

(B) in paragraph (2) (as so redesignated), by inserting "and" at the end of subparagraph (B), by striking ", and" at the end of subparagraph (C) and inserting a period, and by striking subparagraph (D), and

(C) in paragraph (3) (as so redesignated)—

(i) by striking "(b)(1)(A)(i)" in subparagraph (B)(i) and inserting "(b)(1)(A)", and

(ii) by striking "paragraph (3)" in subparagraph (B)(iii) and inserting "paragraph (2)".

(6) Section 55 is amended by striking subsection (e).

(7) Section 56(b)(2) is amended by striking subparagraph (C) and by redesignating subparagraph (D) as subparagraph (C).

(8)(A) Section 56 is amended by striking subsections (c) and (g).

(B) Section 847 is amended by striking the last sentence of paragraph (9).

(C) Section 848 is amended by striking subsection (i).

(9) Section 58(a) is amended by striking paragraph (3) and redesignating paragraph (4) as paragraph (3).

(10) Section 59 is amended by striking subsections (b) and (f).

(11) Section 11(d) is amended by striking "the taxes imposed by subsection (a) and section 55" and inserting "the tax imposed by subsection (a)".

(12) Section 12 is amended by striking paragraph (7).

(13) Section 168(k) is amended by striking paragraph (4).

(14) Section 882(a)(1) is amended by striking ", 55,".

(15) Section 962(a)(1) is amended by striking "sections 11 and 55" and inserting "section 11".

(16) Section 1561(a) is amended—

(A) by inserting "and" at the end of paragraph (1), by striking ", and" at the end of paragraph (2) and inserting a period, and by striking paragraph (3), and

(B) by striking the last sentence.

(17) Section 6425(c)(1)(A) is amended to read as follows:

"(A) the tax imposed by section 11 or 1201(a), or subchapter L of chapter 1, whichever is applicable, over".

(18) Section 6655(e)(2) is amended by striking "and alternative minimum taxable income" each place it appears in subparagraphs (A) and (B)(i).

(19) Section 6655(g)(1)(A) is amended by inserting "plus" at the end of clause (i), by striking

clause (ii), and by redesignating clause (iii) as clause (ii).

(c) EFFECTIVE DATE.—The amendments made by this section shall apply to taxable years beginning after December 31, 2017.

**SEC. 12002. CREDIT FOR PRIOR YEAR MINIMUM TAX LIABILITY OF CORPORATIONS.**

(a) CREDITS TREATED AS REFUNDABLE.—Section 53 is amended by adding at the end the following new subsection:

"(e) PORTION OF CREDIT TREATED AS REFUNDABLE.—

"(1) IN GENERAL.—In the case of any taxable year of a corporation beginning in 2018, 2019, 2020, or 2021, the limitation under subsection (c) shall be increased by the AMT refundable credit amount for such year.

"(2) AMT REFUNDABLE CREDIT AMOUNT.—For purposes of paragraph (1), the AMT refundable credit amount is an amount equal to 50 percent (100 percent in the case of a taxable year beginning in 2021) of the excess (if any) of—

"(A) the minimum tax credit determined under subsection (b) for the taxable year, over

"(B) the minimum tax credit allowed under subsection (a) for such year (before the application of this subsection for such year).

"(3) CREDIT REFUNDABLE.—For purposes of this title (other than this section), the credit allowed by reason of this subsection shall be treated as a credit allowed under subpart C (and not this subpart).

"(4) SHORT TAXABLE YEARS.—In the case of any taxable year of less than 365 days, the AMT refundable credit amount determined under paragraph (2) with respect to such taxable year shall be the amount which bears the same ratio to such amount determined without regard to this paragraph as the number of days in such taxable year bears to 365.".

(b) TREATMENT OF REFERENCES.—Section 53(d) is amended by adding at the end the following new paragraph:

"(3) AMT TERM REFERENCES.—In the case of a corporation, any references in this subsection to section 55, 56, or 57 shall be treated as a reference to such section as in effect before the amendments made by Tax Cuts and Jobs Act.".

(c) CONFORMING AMENDMENT.—Section 1374(b)(3)(B) is amended by striking the last sentence thereof.

(d) EFFECTIVE DATE.—

(1) IN GENERAL.—The amendments made by this section shall apply to taxable years beginning after December 31, 2017.

(2) CONFORMING AMENDMENT.—The amendment made by subsection (c) shall apply to taxable years beginning after December 31, 2021.

**SEC. 12003. INCREASED EXEMPTION FOR INDIVIDUALS.**

(a) IN GENERAL.—Section 55(d), as amended by the preceding provisions of this Act, is amended by adding at the end the following new paragraph:

"(4) SPECIAL RULE FOR TAXABLE YEARS BEGINNING AFTER 2017 AND BEFORE 2026.—

"(A) IN GENERAL.—In the case of any taxable year beginning after December 31, 2017, and before January 1, 2026—

"(i) paragraph (1) shall be applied—

"(I) by substituting '$109,400' for '$78,750' in subparagraph (A), and

"(II) by substituting '$70,300' for '$50,600' in subparagraph (B), and

"(ii) paragraph (2) shall be applied—

"(I) by substituting '$1,000,000' for '$150,000' in subparagraph (A),

"(II) by substituting '50 percent of the dollar amount applicable under subparagraph (A)' for '$112,500' in subparagraph (B), and

"(III) in the case of a taxpayer described in paragraph (1)(D), without regard to the substitution under subclause (I).

"(B) INFLATION ADJUSTMENT.—

"(i) IN GENERAL.—In the case of any taxable year beginning in a calendar year after 2018, the amounts described in clause (ii) shall each be increased by an amount equal to—

"(I) such dollar amount, multiplied by

"(II) the cost-of-living adjustment determined under section 1(f)(3) for the calendar year in which the taxable year begins, determined by substituting 'calendar year 2017' for 'calendar year 2016' in subparagraph (A)(ii) thereof.

"(ii) AMOUNTS DESCRIBED.—The amounts described in this clause are the $109,400 amount in subparagraph (A)(i)(I), the $70,300 amount in subparagraph (A)(i)(II), and the $1,000,000 amount in subparagraph (A)(ii)(I).

"(iii) ROUNDING.—Any increased amount determined under clause (i) shall be rounded to the nearest multiple of $100.

"(iv) COORDINATION WITH CURRENT ADJUSTMENTS.—In the case of any taxable year to which subparagraph (A) applies, no adjustment shall be made under paragraph (3) to any of the numbers which are substituted under subparagraph (A) and adjusted under this subparagraph.".

(b) EFFECTIVE DATE.—The amendments made by this section shall apply to taxable years beginning after December 31, 2017.

# Subtitle C—Business-related Provisions

## PART I—CORPORATE PROVISIONS

### SEC. 13001. 21-PERCENT CORPORATE TAX RATE.

(a) In General.—Subsection (b) of section 11 is amended to read as follows:

"(b) Amount of Tax.—The amount of the tax imposed by subsection (a) shall be 21 percent of taxable income.".

(b) Conforming Amendments.—

(1) The following sections are each amended by striking "section 11(b)(1)" and inserting "section 11(b)":

(A) Section 280C(c)(3)(B)(ii)(II).

(B) Paragraphs (2)(B) and (6)(A)(ii) of section 860E(e).

(C) Section 7874(e)(1)(B).

(2)(A) Part I of subchapter P of chapter 1 is amended by striking section 1201 (and by striking the item relating to such section in the table of sections for such part).

(B) Section 12 is amended by striking paragraphs (4) and (6), and by redesignating paragraph (5) as paragraph (4).

(C) Section 453A(c)(3) is amended by striking "or 1201 (whichever is appropriate)".

(D) Section 527(b) is amended—

(i) by striking paragraph (2), and

(ii) by striking all that precedes "is hereby imposed" and inserting:

"(b) TAX IMPOSED.—A tax".

(E) Sections 594(a) is amended by striking "taxes imposed by section 11 or 1201(a)" and inserting "tax imposed by section 11".

(F) Section 691(c)(4) is amended by striking "1201,".

(G) Section 801(a) is amended—

(i) by striking paragraph (2), and

(ii) by striking all that precedes "is hereby imposed" and inserting:

"(a) TAX IMPOSED.—A tax".

(H) Section 831(e) is amended by striking paragraph (1) and by redesignating paragraphs (2) and (3) as paragraphs (1) and (2), respectively.

(I) Sections 832(c)(5) and 834(b)(1)(D) are each amended by striking "sec. 1201 and following,".

(J) Section 852(b)(3)(A) is amended by striking "section 1201(a)" and inserting "section 11(b)".

(K) Section 857(b)(3) is amended—

(i) by striking subparagraph (A) and redesignating subparagraphs (B) through (F) as subparagraphs (A) through (E), respectively,

(ii) in subparagraph (C), as so redesignated—

(I) by striking "subparagraph (A)(ii)" in clause (i) thereof and inserting "paragraph (1)",

(II) by striking "the tax imposed by subparagraph (A)(ii)" in clauses (ii) and (iv) thereof and inserting "the tax imposed by paragraph (1) on undistributed capital gain",

(iii) in subparagraph (E), as so redesignated, by striking "subparagraph (B) or (D)" and inserting "subparagraph (A) or (C)", and

(iv) by adding at the end the following new subparagraph:

"(F) UNDISTRIBUTED CAPITAL GAIN.—For purposes of this paragraph, the term 'undistributed capital gain' means the excess of the net capital gain over the deduction for dividends paid (as defined in section 561) determined with reference to capital gain dividends only.''.

(L) Section 882(a)(1), as amended by section 12001, is further amended by striking ''or 1201(a)''.

(M) Section 904(b) is amended—

(i) by striking ''or 1201(a)'' in paragraph (2)(C),

(ii) by striking paragraph (3)(D) and inserting the following:

''(D) CAPITAL GAIN RATE DIFFERENTIAL.—There is a capital gain rate differential for any year if subsection (h) of section 1 applies to such taxable year.'', and

(iii) by striking paragraph (3)(E) and inserting the following:

''(E) RATE DIFFERENTIAL PORTION.—The rate differential portion of foreign source net capital gain, net capital gain, or the excess of net capital gain from sources within the United States over net capital gain, as the case may be, is the same proportion of such amount as—

''(i) the excess of—

''(I) the highest rate of tax set forth in subsection (a), (b), (c), (d), or

(e) of section 1 (whichever applies), over

"(II) the alternative rate of tax determined under section 1(h), bears to

"(ii) that rate referred to in subclause (I).".

(N) Section 1374(b) is amended by striking paragraph (4).

(O) Section 1381(b) is amended by striking "taxes imposed by section 11 or 1201" and inserting "tax imposed by section 11".

(P) Sections 6425(c)(1)(A), as amended by section 12001, and 6655(g)(1)(A)(i) are each amended by striking "or 1201(a),".

(Q) Section 7518(g)(6)(A) is amended by striking "or 1201(a)".

(3)(A) Section 1445(e)(1) is amended—

(i) by striking "35 percent" and inserting "the highest rate of tax in effect for the taxable year under section 11(b)", and

(ii) by striking "of the gain" and inserting "multiplied by the gain".

(B) Section 1445(e)(2) is amended by striking "35 percent of the amount" and inserting "the highest rate of tax in effect for the taxable year under section 11(b) multiplied by the amount".

(C) Section 1445(e)(6) is amended—

(i) by striking "35 percent" and inserting "the highest rate of tax in effect for the taxable year under section 11(b)", and

(ii) by striking "of the amount" and inserting "multiplied by the amount".

(D) Section 1446(b)(2)(B) is amended by striking "section 11(b)(1)" and inserting "section 11(b)".

(4) Section 852(b)(1) is amended by striking the last sentence.

(5)(A) Part I of subchapter B of chapter 5 is amended by striking section 1551 (and by striking the item relating to such section in the table of sections for such part).

(B) Section 535(c)(5) is amended to read as follows:

"(5) CROSS REFERENCE.—For limitation on credit provided in paragraph (2) or (3) in the case of certain controlled corporations, see section 1561.".

(6)(A) Section 1561, as amended by section 12001, is amended to read as follows:

**"SEC. 1561. LIMITATION ON ACCUMULATED EARNINGS CREDIT IN THE CASE OF CERTAIN CONTROLLED CORPORATIONS.**

"(a) IN GENERAL.—The component members of a controlled group of corporations on a December 31 shall, for their taxable years which include such December 31, be limited for purposes of this subtitle to one $250,000 ($150,000 if any component member is a corporation described in section 535(c)(2)(B)) amount for purposes of computing the accumulated earnings credit under section 535(c)(2) and (3). Such amount shall be divided equally among the component members of such group on such December 31 unless the Secretary prescribes regulations permitting an unequal allocation of such amount.

"(b) CERTAIN SHORT TAXABLE YEARS.—If a corporation has a short taxable year which does not include a December 31 and is a component member of a controlled group of corporations with respect to such taxable year, then for purposes of this subtitle, the amount to be used in computing the accumulated earnings credit under section 535(c)(2) and (3) of such corporation for such taxable year shall be the amount specified in subsection (a) with respect to such group, divided by the number of corporations which are component members of such group on the last day of such taxable year. For purposes of the preceding sentence, section 1563(b) shall be applied as if such last day were substituted for December 31.".

(B) The table of sections for part II of subchapter B of chapter 5 is amended by striking the item relating to section 1561 and inserting the following new item:

"Sec. 1561. Limitation on accumulated earnings credit in the case of certain controlled corporations.".

(7) Section 7518(g)(6)(A) is amended—

(A) by striking "With respect to the portion" and inserting "In the case of a taxpayer other than a corporation, with respect to the portion", and

(B) by striking "(34 percent in the case of a corporation)".

(c) EFFECTIVE DATE.—

(1) IN GENERAL.—Except as otherwise provided in this subsection, the amendments made by subsections (a) and (b) shall apply to taxable years beginning after December 31, 2017.

(2) WITHHOLDING.—The amendments made by subsection (b)(3) shall apply to distributions made after December 31, 2017.

(3) CERTAIN TRANSFERS.—The amendments made by subsection (b)(6) shall apply to transfers made after December 31, 2017.

(d) NORMALIZATION REQUIREMENTS.—

(1) IN GENERAL.—A normalization method of accounting shall not be treated as being used with respect to any public utility property for purposes of section 167 or 168 of the Internal Revenue Code of 1986 if the taxpayer, in computing its cost of service for ratemaking purposes and reflecting operating results in its regulated books of account, reduces the excess tax reserve more rapidly or to a greater extent than such reserve would be reduced under the average rate assumption method.

(2) ALTERNATIVE METHOD FOR CERTAIN TAXPAYERS.—If, as of the first day of the taxable year that includes the date of enactment of this Act—

(A) the taxpayer was required by a regulatory agency to compute depreciation for public utility property on the basis of an average life or composite rate method, and

(B) the taxpayer's books and underlying records did not contain the vintage account data necessary to apply the average rate assumption method,

the taxpayer will be treated as using a normalization method of accounting if, with respect to such jurisdiction, the taxpayer uses the alternative method for public utility property that is subject to the regulatory authority of that jurisdiction.

(3) DEFINITIONS.—For purposes of this subsection—

(A) EXCESS TAX RESERVE.—The term "excess tax reserve" means the excess of—

(i) the reserve for deferred taxes (as described in section 168(i)(9)(A)(ii) of the Internal Revenue Code of 1986) as of the day before the corporate rate reductions provided in the amendments made by this section take effect, over

(ii) the amount which would be the balance in such reserve if the amount of such reserve were determined by assuming that the corporate rate reductions provided in this Act were in effect for all prior periods.

(B) AVERAGE RATE ASSUMPTION METHOD.—The average rate assumption method is the method under which the excess in the reserve for deferred taxes is reduced over the remaining lives of the property as used in its regulated books of account which gave rise to the reserve for deferred taxes. Under such method, during the time period in which the timing differences for the property reverse, the amount of the adjustment to the reserve for the deferred taxes is calculated by multiplying—

(i) the ratio of the aggregate deferred taxes for the property to the aggregate timing differences for the property as of the beginning of the period in question, by

(ii) the amount of the timing differences which reverse during such period.

(C) ALTERNATIVE METHOD.—The "alternative method" is the method in which the taxpayer—

(i) computes the excess tax reserve on all public utility property included in the plant account on the basis of the weighted average life or composite rate used to compute depreciation for regulatory purposes, and

(ii) reduces the excess tax reserve ratably over the remaining regulatory life of the property.

(4) TAX INCREASED FOR NORMALIZATION VIOLATION.—If, for any taxable year ending after the date of the enactment of this Act, the taxpayer does

not use a normalization method of accounting for the corporate rate reductions provided in the amendments made by this section—

(A) the taxpayer's tax for the taxable year shall be increased by the amount by which it reduces its excess tax reserve more rapidly than permitted under a normalization method of accounting, and

(B) such taxpayer shall not be treated as using a normalization method of accounting for purposes of subsections (f)(2) and (i)(9)(C) of section 168 of the Internal Revenue Code of 1986.

**SEC. 13002. REDUCTION IN DIVIDEND RECEIVED DEDUCTIONS TO REFLECT LOWER CORPORATE INCOME TAX RATES.**

(a) DIVIDENDS RECEIVED BY CORPORATIONS.—

(1) IN GENERAL.—Section 243(a)(1) is amended by striking "70 percent" and inserting "50 percent".

(2) DIVIDENDS FROM 20-PERCENT OWNED CORPORATIONS.—Section 243(c)(1) is amended—

(A) by striking "80 percent" and inserting "65 percent", and

(B) by striking "70 percent" and inserting "50 percent".

(3) CONFORMING AMENDMENT.—The heading for section 243(c) is amended by striking "RETENTION OF 80-PERCENT DIVIDEND RECEIVED DEDUCTION" and inserting "INCREASED PERCENTAGE".

(b) DIVIDENDS RECEIVED FROM FSC.—Section 245(c)(1)(B) is amended—

(1) by striking "70 percent" and inserting "50 percent", and

(2) by striking "80 percent" and inserting "65 percent".

(c) LIMITATION ON AGGREGATE AMOUNT OF DEDUCTIONS.—Section 246(b)(3) is amended—

(1) by striking "80 percent" in subparagraph (A) and inserting "65 percent", and

(2) by striking "70 percent" in subparagraph (B) and inserting "50 percent".

(d) REDUCTION IN DEDUCTION WHERE PORTFOLIO STOCK IS DEBT-FINANCED.—Section 246A(a)(1) is amended—

(1) by striking "70 percent" and inserting "50 percent", and

(2) by striking "80 percent" and inserting "65 percent".

(e) INCOME FROM SOURCES WITHIN THE UNITED STATES.—Section 861(a)(2) is amended—

(1) by striking "100/70th" and inserting "100/50th" in subparagraph (B), and

(2) in the flush sentence at the end—

(A) by striking "100/80th" and inserting "100/65th", and

(B) by striking "100/70th" and inserting "100/50th".

(f) EFFECTIVE DATE.—The amendments made by this section shall apply to taxable years beginning after December 31, 2017.

## PART II—SMALL BUSINESS REFORMS

### SEC. 13101. MODIFICATIONS OF RULES FOR EXPENSING DEPRECIABLE BUSINESS ASSETS.

(a) INCREASE IN LIMITATION.—

(1) DOLLAR LIMITATION.—Section 179(b)(1) is amended by striking "$500,000" and inserting "$1,000,000".

(2) REDUCTION IN LIMITATION.—Section 179(b)(2) is amended by striking "$2,000,000" and inserting "$2,500,000".

(3) INFLATION ADJUSTMENTS.—

(A) IN GENERAL.—Subparagraph (A) of section 179(b)(6), as amended by section 11002(d), is amended—

(i) by striking "2015" and inserting "2018", and

(ii) in clause (ii), by striking "calendar year 2014" and inserting "calendar year 2017".

(B) SPORT UTILITY VEHICLES.—Section 179(b)(6) is amended—

(i) in subparagraph (A), by striking "paragraphs (1) and (2)" and inserting "paragraphs (1), (2), and (5)(A)", and

(ii) in subparagraph (B), by inserting "($100 in the case of any increase in the amount under paragraph (5)(A))" after "$10,000".

(b) Section 179 Property To Include Qualified Real Property.—

(1) IN GENERAL.—Subparagraph (B) of section 179(d)(1) is amended to read as follows:

"(B) which is—

"(i) section 1245 property (as defined in section 1245(a)(3)), or "(ii) at the election of the taxpayer, qualified real property (as defined in subsection (f)), and".

(2) QUALIFIED REAL PROPERTY DEFINED.—Subsection (f) of section 179 is amended to read as follows:

"(f) QUALIFIED REAL PROPERTY.—For purposes of this section, the term 'qualified real property' means—

"(1) any qualified improvement property described in section 168(e)(6), and

"(2) any of the following improvements to nonresidential real property placed in service after the date such property was first placed in service:

"(A) Roofs.

"(B) Heating, ventilation, and air-conditioning property.

"(C) Fire protection and alarm systems.

"(D) Security systems.".

(c) REPEAL OF EXCLUSION FOR CERTAIN PROPERTY.—The last sentence of section 179(d)(1) is amended by inserting "(other than paragraph (2) thereof)" after "section 50(b)".

(d) EFFECTIVE DATE.—The amendments made by this section shall apply to property placed in service in taxable years beginning after December 31, 2017.

**SEC. 13102. SMALL BUSINESS ACCOUNTING METHOD REFORM AND SIMPLIFICATION.**

(a) MODIFICATION OF LIMITATION ON CASH METHOD OF ACCOUNTING.—

(1) INCREASED LIMITATION.—So much of section 448(c) as precedes paragraph (2) is amended to read as follows:

"(c) GROSS RECEIPTS TEST.—For purposes of this section—

"(1) IN GENERAL.—A corporation or partnership meets the gross receipts test of this subsection for any taxable year if the average annual gross receipts of such entity for the 3-taxable-year period ending with the taxable year which precedes such taxable year does not exceed $25,000,000.".

(2) APPLICATION OF EXCEPTION ON ANNUAL BASIS.—Section 448(b)(3) is amended to read as follows:

"(3) ENTITIES WHICH MEET GROSS RECEIPTS TEST.—Paragraphs (1) and (2) of subsection (a) shall not apply to any corporation or partnership for any taxable year if such entity (or any predecessor) meets the gross receipts test of subsection (c) for such taxable year.".

(3) INFLATION ADJUSTMENT.—Section 448(c) is amended by adding at the end the following new paragraph:

"(4) ADJUSTMENT FOR INFLATION.—In the case of any taxable year beginning after December 31, 2018, the dollar amount in paragraph (1) shall be increased by an amount equal to—

"(A) such dollar amount, multiplied by

"(B) the cost-of-living adjustment determined under section 1(f)(3) for the calendar year in which the taxable year begins, by substituting 'calendar year 2017' for 'calendar year 2016' in subparagraph (A)(ii) thereof.

If any amount as increased under the preceding sentence is not a multiple of $1,000,000, such amount shall be rounded to the nearest multiple of $1,000,000.".

(4) COORDINATION WITH SECTION 481.—Section 448(d)(7) is amended to read as follows:

"(7) COORDINATION WITH SECTION 481.—Any change in method of accounting made pursuant to this section shall be treated for purposes of section 481 as initiated by the taxpayer and made with the consent of the Secretary.".

(5) APPLICATION OF EXCEPTION TO CORPORATIONS ENGAGED IN FARMING.—

(A) IN GENERAL.—Section 447(c) is amended—

(i) by inserting "for any taxable year" after "not being a corporation" in the matter preceding paragraph (1), and

(ii) by amending paragraph (2) to read as follows:

"(2) a corporation which meets the gross receipts test of section 448(c) for such taxable year.".

(B) COORDINATION WITH SECTION 481.—Section 447(f) is amended to read as follows:

"(f) COORDINATION WITH SECTION 481.—Any change in method of accounting made pursuant to this section shall be treated for purposes of section 481 as initiated by the taxpayer and made with the consent of the Secretary.".

(C) CONFORMING AMENDMENTS.—Section 447 is amended—

(i) by striking subsections (d), (e), (h), and (i), and

(ii) by redesignating subsections (f) and (g) (as amended by subparagraph (B)) as subsections (d) and (e), respectively.

(b) EXEMPTION FROM UNICAP REQUIREMENTS.—

(1) IN GENERAL.—Section 263A is amended by redesignating subsection (i) as subsection (j) and by inserting after subsection (h) the following new subsection:

"(i) EXEMPTION FOR CERTAIN SMALL BUSINESSES.—

"(1) IN GENERAL.—In the case of any taxpayer (other than a tax shelter prohibited from using the cash receipts and disbursements method of accounting under section 448(a)(3)) which meets the gross receipts test of section 448(c) for any taxable year, this section shall not apply with respect to such taxpayer for such taxable year.

"(2) APPLICATION OF GROSS RECEIPTS TEST TO INDIVIDUALS, ETC.— In the case of any taxpayer which is not a corporation or a partnership, the gross receipts test of section 448(c) shall be applied in the same manner as if each trade or business of such taxpayer were a corporation or partnership.

"(3) COORDINATION WITH SECTION 481.—Any change in method of accounting made pursuant to this subsection shall be treated for purposes of section 481 as initiated by the taxpayer and made with the consent of the Secretary.".

(2) CONFORMING AMENDMENT.—Section 263A(b)(2) is amended to read as follows:

"(2) PROPERTY ACQUIRED FOR RESALE.—Real or personal property described in section 1221(a)(1) which is acquired by the taxpayer for resale.".

(c) EXEMPTION FROM INVENTORIES.—Section 471 is amended by redesignating subsection (c) as subsection (d) and by inserting after subsection (b) the following new subsection:

"(c) EXEMPTION FOR CERTAIN SMALL BUSINESSES.—

"(1) IN GENERAL.—In the case of any taxpayer (other than a tax shelter prohibited from using the cash receipts and disbursements method of accounting under section 448(a)(3)) which meets the gross receipts test of section 448(c) for any taxable year—

"(A) subsection (a) shall not apply with respect to such taxpayer for such taxable year, and

"(B) the taxpayer's method of accounting for inventory for such taxable year shall not be treated as failing to clearly reflect income if such method either—

"(i) treats inventory as non-incidental materials and supplies, or "(ii) conforms to such taxpayer's method of accounting reflected in an applicable financial statement of the taxpayer with respect to such taxable year or, if the taxpayer does not have any applicable financial statement with respect to such taxable year, the books and records of the taxpayer prepared in accordance with the taxpayer's accounting procedures.

"(2) APPLICABLE FINANCIAL STATEMENT.—For purposes of this subsection, the term 'applicable financial statement' has the meaning given the term in section 451(b)(3).

"(3) APPLICATION OF GROSS RECEIPTS TEST TO INDIVIDUALS, ETC.—In the case of any taxpayer which is not a corporation or a partnership, the gross receipts test of section 448(c) shall be applied in the same manner as if each trade or business of such taxpayer were a corporation or partnership.

"(4) COORDINATION WITH SECTION 481.—Any change in method of accounting made pursuant to this subsection shall be treated for purposes of section 481 as initiated by the taxpayer and made with the consent of the Secretary.".

(d) Exemption From Percentage Completion for Long-term Contracts.—

(1) In general.—Section 460(e)(1)(B) is amended—

(A) by inserting "(other than a tax shelter prohibited from using the cash receipts and disbursements method of accounting under section 448(a)(3))" after "taxpayer" in the matter preceding clause (i), and

(B) by amending clause (ii) to read as follows:

"(ii) who meets the gross receipts test of section 448(c) for the taxable year in which such contract is entered into.".

(2) Conforming amendments.—Section 460(e) is amended by striking paragraphs (2) and (3), by redesignating paragraphs (4), (5), and (6) as paragraphs (3), (4), and (5), respectively, and by inserting after paragraph (1) the following new paragraph:

"(2) Rules related to gross receipts test.—

"(A) Application of gross receipts test to individuals, etc.— For purposes of paragraph (1)(B)(ii), in the case of any taxpayer which is not a corporation or a partnership, the gross receipts test of section 448(c) shall be applied in the same manner as if each trade or business of such taxpayer were a corporation or partnership.

"(B) COORDINATION WITH SECTION 481.—Any change in method of accounting made pursuant to paragraph (1)(B)(ii) shall be treated as initiated by the taxpayer and made with the consent of the Secretary. Such change shall be effected on a cut-off basis for all similarly classified contracts entered into on or after the year of change.".

(e) EFFECTIVE DATE.—

(1) IN GENERAL.—Except as otherwise provided in this subsection, the amendments made by this section shall apply to taxable years beginning after December 31, 2017.

(2) PRESERVATION OF SUSPENSE ACCOUNT RULES WITH RESPECT TO ANY EXISTING SUSPENSE ACCOUNTS.—So much of the amendments made by subsection (a)(5)(C) as relate to section 447(i) of the Internal Revenue Code of 1986 shall not apply with respect to any suspense account established

under such section before the date of the enactment of this Act.

(3) EXEMPTION FROM PERCENTAGE COMPLETION FOR LONG-TERM CONTRACTS.—The amendments made by subsection (d) shall apply to contracts entered into after December 31, 2017, in taxable years ending after such date.

## PART III—COST RECOVERY AND ACCOUNTING METHODS

### Subpart A—Cost Recovery

#### SEC. 13201. TEMPORARY 100-PERCENT EXPENSING FOR CERTAIN BUSINESS ASSETS.

(a) INCREASED EXPENSING.—

(1) IN GENERAL.—Section 168(k) is amended—

(A) in paragraph (1)(A), by striking "50 percent" and inserting "the applicable percentage", and

(B) in paragraph (5)(A)(i), by striking "50 percent" and inserting "the applicable percentage".

(2) APPLICABLE PERCENTAGE.—Paragraph (6) of section 168(k) is amended to read as follows:

"(6) APPLICABLE PERCENTAGE.—For purposes of this subsection—

"(A) IN GENERAL.—Except as otherwise provided in this paragraph, the term 'applicable percentage' means—

"(i) in the case of property placed in service after September 27, 2017, and before January 1, 2023, 100 percent,

"(ii) in the case of property placed in service after December 31, 2022, and before January 1, 2024, 80 percent,

"(iii) in the case of property placed in service after December 31, 2023, and before January 1, 2025, 60 percent,

"(iv) in the case of property placed in service after December 31, 2024, and before January 1, 2026, 40 percent, and

"(v) in the case of property placed in service after December 31, 2025, and before January 1, 2027, 20 percent.

"(B) RULE FOR PROPERTY WITH LONGER PRODUCTION PERIODS.—In the case of property described in subparagraph (B) or (C) of paragraph (2), the term 'applicable percentage' means—

"(i) in the case of property placed in service after September 27, 2017, and before January 1, 2024, 100 percent,

"(ii) in the case of property placed in service after December 31, 2023, and before January 1, 2025, 80 percent,

"(iii) in the case of property placed in service after December 31, 2024, and before January 1, 2026, 60 percent,

"(iv) in the case of property placed in service after December 31, 2025, and before January 1, 2027, 40 percent, and

"(v) in the case of property placed in service after December 31, 2026, and before January 1, 2028, 20 percent.

"(C) RULE FOR PLANTS BEARING FRUITS AND NUTS.—In the case of a specified plant described in paragraph (5), the term 'applicable percentage' means—

"(i) in the case of a plant which is planted or grafted after September 27, 2017, and before January 1, 2023, 100 percent,

"(ii) in the case of a plant which is planted or grafted after December 31,

2022, and before January 1, 2024, 80 percent,

"(iii) in the case of a plant which is planted or grafted after December 31, 2023, and before January 1, 2025, 60 percent,

"(iv) in the case of a plant which is planted or grafted after December 31, 2024, and before January 1, 2026, 40 percent, and

"(v) in the case of a plant which is planted or grafted after December 31, 2025, and before January 1, 2027, 20 percent.".

(3) CONFORMING AMENDMENT.—

(A) Paragraph (5) of section 168(k) is amended by striking subparagraph (F).

(B) Section 168(k) is amended by adding at the end the following new paragraph:

"(8) PHASE DOWN.—In the case of qualified property acquired by the taxpayer before September 28, 2017, and placed in service by the taxpayer after September 27, 2017, paragraph (6) shall be applied by substituting for each percentage therein—

"(A) '50 percent' in the case of—

"(i) property placed in service before January 1, 2018, and

"(ii) property described in subparagraph (B) or (C) of paragraph (2) which is placed in service in 2018,

"(B) '40 percent' in the case of—

"(i) property placed in service in 2018 (other than property described in subparagraph (B) or (C) of paragraph (2)), and

"(ii) property described in subparagraph (B) or (C) of paragraph (2) which is placed in service in 2019,

"(C) '30 percent' in the case of—

"(i) property placed in service in 2019 (other than property described in subparagraph (B) or (C) of paragraph (2)), and

"(ii) property described in subparagraph (B) or (C) of paragraph (2) which is placed in service in 2020, and

"(D) '0 percent' in the case of—

"(i) property placed in service after 2019 (other than property described in subparagraph (B) or (C) of paragraph (2)), and "(ii) property described in subparagraph (B) or (C) of paragraph (2) which is placed in service after 2020.".

(b) EXTENSION.—

(1) IN GENERAL.—Section 168(k) is amended—

(A) in paragraph (2)—

(i) in subparagraph (A)(iii), clauses (i)(III) and (ii) of subparagraph (B), and subparagraph (E)(i), by striking "January 1, 2020" each place it appears and inserting "January 1, 2027", and

(ii) in subparagraph (B)—

(I) in clause (i)(II), by striking "January 1, 2021" and inserting "January 1, 2028", and

(II) in the heading of clause (ii), by striking "PRE-JANUARY 1, 2020" and inserting "PRE-JANUARY 1, 2027", and

(B) in paragraph (5)(A), by striking "January 1, 2020" and inserting "January 1, 2027".

(2) CONFORMING AMENDMENTS.—

(A) Clause (ii) of section 460(c)(6)(B) is amended by striking "January 1, 2020 (January 1, 2021" and inserting "January 1, 2027 (January 1, 2028".

(B) The heading of section 168(k) is amended by striking "ACQUIRED AFTER DECEMBER 31, 2007, AND BEFORE JANUARY 1, 2020".

(c) APPLICATION TO USED PROPERTY.—

(1) IN GENERAL.—Section 168(k)(2)(A)(ii) is amended to read as follows:

"(ii) the original use of which begins with the taxpayer or the acquisition of which by the taxpayer meets the requirements of clause (ii) of subparagraph (E), and".

(2) ACQUISITION REQUIREMENTS.—Section 168(k)(2)(E)(ii) is amended to read as follows:

"(ii) ACQUISITION REQUIREMENTS.—An acquisition of property meets the requirements of this clause if—

"(I) such property was not used by the taxpayer at any time prior to such acquisition, and

"(II) the acquisition of such property meets the requirements of paragraphs (2)(A), (2)(B), (2)(C), and (3) of section 179(d).",

(3) ANTI-ABUSE RULES.—Section 168(k)(2)(E) is further amended by amending clause (iii)(I) to read as follows:

"(I) property is used by a lessor of such property and such use is the lessor's first use of such property,".

(d) EXCEPTION FOR CERTAIN PROPERTY.—Section 168(k), as amended by this section, is amended by adding at the end the following new paragraph:

"(9) EXCEPTION FOR CERTAIN PROPERTY.—The term 'qualified property' shall not include—

"(A) any property which is primarily used in a trade or business described in clause (iv) of section 163(j)(7)(A), or

"(B) any property used in a trade or business that has had floor plan financing indebtedness (as defined in paragraph (9) of section 163(j)), if the floor plan financing interest related to such indebtedness was taken into account under paragraph (1)(C) of such section.".

(e) SPECIAL RULE.—Section 168(k), as amended by this section, is amended by adding at the end the following new paragraph:

"(10) SPECIAL RULE FOR PROPERTY PLACED IN SERVICE DURING CERTAIN PERIODS.—

"(A) IN GENERAL.—In the case of qualified property placed in service by the taxpayer during the first taxable year ending after September 27, 2017, if the taxpayer elects to have this paragraph apply for such taxable year, paragraphs (1)(A) and (5)(A)(i) shall be applied by substituting '50 percent' for 'the applicable percentage'.

"(B) FORM OF ELECTION.—Any election under this paragraph shall be made at such time and in such form and manner as the Secretary may prescribe.".

(f) COORDINATION WITH SECTION 280F.—Clause (iii) of section 168(k)(2)(F) is amended by striking "placed in service by the taxpayer after December 31, 2017" and inserting "acquired by the taxpayer before September 28, 2017, and placed in service by the taxpayer after September 27, 2017".

(g) QUALIFIED FILM AND TELEVISION AND LIVE THEATRICAL PRODUCTIONS.—

(1) IN GENERAL.—Clause (i) of section 168(k)(2)(A), as amended by section 13204, is amended—

(A) in subclause (II), by striking "or",

(B) in subclause (III), by adding "or" after the comma, and

(C) by adding at the end the following:

"(IV) which is a qualified film or television production (as defined in subsection (d) of section 181) for which a deduction would have been allowable under section 181 without regard to subsections (a)(2) and (g) of such section or this subsection, or

"(V) which is a qualified live theatrical production (as defined in subsection (e) of section 181) for which a deduction would have been allowable under section 181 without regard to subsections (a)(2) and (g) of such section or this subsection,".

(2) PRODUCTION PLACED IN SERVICE.—Paragraph (2) of section 168(k) is amended by adding at the end the following:

"(H) PRODUCTION PLACED IN SERVICE.—For purposes of subparagraph (A)—

"(i) a qualified film or television production shall be considered to be placed in service at the time of initial release or broadcast, and

"(ii) a qualified live theatrical production shall be considered to be placed in service at the time of the initial live staged performance.".

(h) EFFECTIVE DATE.—

(1) IN GENERAL.—Except as provided by paragraph (2), the amendments made by this section shall apply to property which—

(A) is acquired after September 27, 2017, and

(B) is placed in service after such date.

For purposes of the preceding sentence, property shall not be treated as acquired after the date on which a written binding contract is entered into for such acquisition.

(2) SPECIFIED PLANTS.—The amendments made by this section shall apply to specified plants planted or grafted after September 27, 2017.

**SEC. 13202. MODIFICATIONS TO DEPRECIATION LIMITATIONS ON LUXURY AUTOMOBILES AND PERSONAL USE PROPERTY.**

(a) LUXURY AUTOMOBILES.—

(1) IN GENERAL.—280F(a)(1)(A) is amended—

(A) in clause (i), by striking "$2,560" and inserting "$10,000",

(B) in clause (ii), by striking "$4,100" and inserting "$16,000",

(C) in clause (iii), by striking "$2,450" and inserting "$9,600", and

(D) in clause (iv), by striking "$1,475" and inserting "$5,760".

(2) CONFORMING AMENDMENTS.—

(A) Clause (ii) of section 280F(a)(1)(B) is amended by striking "$1,475" in the text and heading and inserting "$5,760".

(B) Paragraph (7) of section 280F(d) is amended—

(i) in subparagraph (A), by striking "1988" and inserting "2018", and

(ii) in subparagraph (B)(i)(II), by striking "1987" and inserting "2017".

(b) REMOVAL OF COMPUTER EQUIPMENT FROM LISTED PROPERTY.—

(1) IN GENERAL.—Section 280F(d)(4)(A) is amended—

(A) by inserting "and" at the end of clause (iii),

(B) by striking clause (iv), and

(C) by redesignating clause (v) as clause (iv).

(2) CONFORMING AMENDMENT.—Section 280F(d)(4) is amended by striking subparagraph (B) and by redesignating subparagraph (C) as subparagraph (B).

(c) EFFECTIVE DATE.—The amendments made by this section shall apply to property placed in service after December 31, 2017, in taxable years ending after such date.

**SEC. 13203. MODIFICATIONS OF TREATMENT OF CERTAIN FARM PROPERTY.**

(a) TREATMENT OF CERTAIN FARM PROPERTY AS 5-YEAR PROPERTY.—Clause (vii) of section 168(e)(3)(B) is amended by striking "after December 31, 2008, and which is placed in service before January 1, 2010" and inserting "after December 31, 2017".

(b) REPEAL OF REQUIRED USE OF 150-PERCENT DECLINING BALANCE METHOD.—Section 168(b)(2) is amended by striking subparagraph (B) and by redesignating subparagraphs (C) and (D) as subparagraphs (B) and (C), respectively.

(c) EFFECTIVE DATE.—The amendments made by this section shall apply to property placed in service after December 31, 2017, in taxable years ending after such date.

**SEC. 13204. APPLICABLE RECOVERY PERIOD FOR REAL PROPERTY.**

(a) IMPROVEMENTS TO REAL PROPERTY.—

(1) ELIMINATION OF QUALIFIED LEASEHOLD IMPROVEMENT, QUALIFIED RESTAURANT, AND QUALIFIED RETAIL IMPROVEMENT PROPERTY.—Subsection (e) of section 168 is amended—

(A) in subparagraph (E) of paragraph (3)—

(i) by striking clauses (iv), (v), and (ix),

(ii) in clause (vii), by inserting "and" at the end,

(iii) in clause (viii), by striking ", and" and inserting a period, and

(iv) by redesignating clauses (vi), (vii), and (viii), as so amended, as clauses (iv), (v), and (vi), respectively, and

(B) by striking paragraphs (6), (7), and (8).

(2) APPLICATION OF STRAIGHT LINE METHOD TO QUALIFIED IMPROVEMENT PROPERTY.—Paragraph (3) of section 168(b) is amended—

(A) by striking subparagraphs (G), (H), and (I), and

(B) by inserting after subparagraph (F) the following new subparagraph:

"(G) Qualified improvement property described in subsection (e)(6).".

(3) ALTERNATIVE DEPRECIATION SYSTEM.—

(A) ELECTING REAL PROPERTY TRADE OR BUSINESS.—Subsection (g) of section 168 is amended—

(i) in paragraph (1)—

(I) in subparagraph (D), by striking "and" at the end,

(II) in subparagraph (E), by inserting "and" at the end, and

(III) by inserting after subparagraph (E) the following new subparagraph:

"(F) any property described in paragraph (8),", and

(ii) by adding at the end the following new paragraph:

"(8) ELECTING REAL PROPERTY TRADE OR BUSINESS.—The property described in this paragraph shall consist of any nonresidential real property, residential rental property, and qualified improvement property held by an electing real property trade or business (as defined in 163(j)(7)(B)).".

(B) QUALIFIED IMPROVEMENT PROPERTY.—The table contained in subparagraph (B) of section 168(g)(3) is amended—

(i) by inserting after the item relating to subparagraph (D)(ii) the following new item:

| | |
|---|---|
| "(D)(v) | 20" |

, and

(ii) by striking the item relating to subparagraph (E)(iv) and all that follows through the item relating to subparagraph (E)(ix) and inserting the following:

| | |
|---|---|
| "(E)(iv) | 20 |
| (E)(v) | 30 |
| (E)(vi) | 35". |

(C) APPLICABLE RECOVERY PERIOD FOR RESIDENTIAL RENTAL PROPERTY.—The table contained in subparagraph (C) of section 168(g)(2) is amended by striking clauses (iii)

"(iii) Residential rental property .......... 30 years
(iv) Nonresidential real property .......... 40 years
(v) Any railroad grading or tunnel bore or water utility property .......... 50 years".

(4) CONFORMING AMENDMENTS.—

(A) Clause (i) of section 168(k)(2)(A) is amended—

(i) in subclause (II), by inserting "or" after the comma,

(ii) in subclause (III), by striking "or" at the end, and

(iii) by striking subclause (IV).

(B) Section 168 is amended—

(i) in subsection (e), as amended by paragraph (1)(B), by adding at the end the following:

"(6) QUALIFIED IMPROVEMENT PROPERTY.—

"(A) IN GENERAL.—The term 'qualified improvement property' means any improvement to an interior portion of a building which is nonresidential real property if such improvement is placed in service after the date such building was first placed in service.

"(B) CERTAIN IMPROVEMENTS NOT INCLUDED.—Such term shall not include any improvement for which the expenditure is attributable to—

"(i) the enlargement of the building,

"(ii) any elevator or escalator, or

"(iii) the internal structural framework of the building.", and

(ii) in subsection (k), by striking paragraph (3).

(b) EFFECTIVE DATE.—

(1) IN GENERAL.—Except as provided in paragraph (2), the amendments made by this section shall apply to property placed in service after December 31, 2017.

(2) AMENDMENTS RELATED TO ELECTING REAL PROPERTY TRADE OR BUSINESS.—The amendments made by subsection (a)(3)(A) shall apply to taxable years beginning after December 31, 2017.

**SEC. 13205. USE OF ALTERNATIVE DEPRECIATION SYSTEM FOR ELECTING FARMING BUSINESSES.**

(a) IN GENERAL.—Section 168(g)(1), as amended by section 13204, is amended by striking "and" at the end of subparagraph (E), by inserting "and" at the end of subparagraph (F), and by inserting after subparagraph (F) the following new subparagraph:

"(G) any property with a recovery period of 10 years or more which is held by an electing farming business (as defined in section 163(j)(7)(C)),".

(b) EFFECTIVE DATE.—The amendments made by this section shall apply to taxable years beginning after December 31, 2017.

**SEC. 13206. AMORTIZATION OF RESEARCH AND EXPERIMENTAL EXPENDITURES.**

(a) IN GENERAL.—Section 174 is amended to read as follows:

**"SEC. 174. AMORTIZATION OF RESEARCH AND EXPERIMENTAL EXPENDITURES.**

"(a) IN GENERAL.—In the case of a taxpayer's specified research or experimental expenditures for any taxable year—

"(1) except as provided in paragraph (2), no deduction shall be allowed for such expenditures, and

"(2) the taxpayer shall—

"(A) charge such expenditures to capital account, and

"(B) be allowed an amortization deduction of such expenditures ratably over the 5-year period (15-year period in the case of any specified research or experimental expenditures which are attributable to foreign research (within the meaning of section 41(d)(4)(F))) beginning with the midpoint of the taxable year in which such expenditures are paid or incurred.

"(b) SPECIFIED RESEARCH OR EXPERIMENTAL EXPENDITURES.—For purposes of this section, the term 'specified research or experimental expenditures' means, with respect to any taxable year, research or experimental expenditures which are paid or incurred by the taxpayer during such taxable year in connection with the taxpayer's trade or business.

"(c) SPECIAL RULES.—

"(1) LAND AND OTHER PROPERTY.—This section shall not apply to any expenditure for the acquisition or improvement of land, or for the acquisition or improvement of property to be used in connection with the research or experimentation and of a character which is subject to the allowance under section 167 (relating to allowance for depreciation, etc.) or section 611 (relating to allowance for depletion); but for purposes of this section allowances under section 167, and allowances under section 611, shall be considered as expenditures.

"(2) EXPLORATION EXPENDITURES.—This section shall not apply to any expenditure paid or incurred for the purpose of ascertaining the existence, location, extent, or quality of any deposit of ore or other mineral (including oil and gas).

"(3) SOFTWARE DEVELOPMENT.—For purposes of this section, any amount paid or incurred in connection with the development of any software shall be treated as a research or experimental expenditure.

"(d) TREATMENT UPON DISPOSITION, RETIREMENT, OR ABANDONMENT.—If any property with respect to which specified research or experimental expenditures are paid or incurred is disposed, retired, or abandoned during the period during which such expenditures are allowed as an amortization deduction under this section, no deduction shall be allowed with respect to such expenditures on account of such disposition, retirement, or abandonment and such amortization deduction shall continue with respect to such expenditures.".

(b) CHANGE IN METHOD OF ACCOUNTING.—The amendments made by subsection (a) shall be treated as a change in method of accounting for purposes of section 481 of the Internal Revenue Code of 1986 and—

(1) such change shall be treated as initiated by the taxpayer,

(2) such change shall be treated as made with the consent of the Secretary, and

(3) such change shall be applied only on a cut-off basis for any research or experimental expenditures paid or incurred in taxable years beginning after December 31, 2021, and no adjustments under section 481(a) shall be made.

(c) CLERICAL AMENDMENT.—The table of sections for part VI of subchapter B of chapter 1 is amended by striking the item relating to section 174 and inserting the following new item:

"Sec. 174. Amortization of research and experimental expenditures.".

(d) CONFORMING AMENDMENTS.—

(1) Section 41(d)(1)(A) is amended by striking "expenses under section 174" and inserting "specified research or experimental expenditures under section 174".

(2) Subsection (c) of section 280C is amended—

(A) by striking paragraph (1) and inserting the following:

"(1) IN GENERAL.—If—

"(A) the amount of the credit determined for the taxable year under section 41(a)(1), exceeds

"(B) the amount allowable as a deduction for such taxable year for qualified research ex-the amount chargeable to capital account for the taxable year for such expenses shall be reduced by the amount of such excess.",

(B) by striking paragraph (2),

(C) by redesignating paragraphs (3) (as amended by this Act) and (4) as paragraphs (2) and (3), respectively, and

(D) in paragraph (2), as redesignated by subparagraph (C), by striking "paragraphs (1) and (2)" and inserting "paragraph (1)".

(e) EFFECTIVE DATE.—The amendments made by this section shall apply to amounts paid or incurred in taxable years beginning after December 31, 2021.

**SEC. 13207. EXPENSING OF CERTAIN COSTS OF REPLANTING CITRUS PLANTS LOST BY REASON OF CASUALTY.**

(a) IN GENERAL.—Section 263A(d)(2) is amended by adding at the end the following new subparagraph:

"(C) SPECIAL TEMPORARY RULE FOR CITRUS PLANTS LOST BY REASON OF CASUALTY.—

"(i) IN GENERAL.—In the case of the replanting of citrus plants, subparagraph (A) shall apply to amounts paid or incurred by a person (other than the taxpayer described in subparagraph (A)) if—

"(I) the taxpayer described in subparagraph (A) has an equity interest of not less than 50 percent in the replanted citrus plants at all times during the taxable year in which such amounts were paid or incurred and such other person holds any part of the remaining equity interest, or

"(II) such other person acquired the entirety of such taxpayer's equity interest in the land on which the lost or damaged citrus plants were located at the time of such loss or damage, and the replanting is on such land.

"(ii) TERMINATION.—Clause (i) shall not apply to any cost paid or incurred after the date which is 10 years after the date of the enactment of the Tax Cuts and Jobs Act.".

(b) EFFECTIVE DATE.—The amendment made by this section shall apply to costs paid or incurred after the date of the enactment of this Act.

### Subpart B—Accounting Methods

## SEC. 13221. CERTAIN SPECIAL RULES FOR TAXABLE YEAR OF INCLUSION.

(a) INCLUSION NOT LATER THAN FOR FINANCIAL ACCOUNTING PURPOSES.—Section 451 is amended by redesignating subsections (b) through (i) as subsections (c) through (j), respectively, and by inserting after subsection (a) the following new subsection:

"(b) INCLUSION NOT LATER THAN FOR FINANCIAL ACCOUNTING PURPOSES.—

"(1) INCOME TAKEN INTO ACCOUNT IN FINANCIAL STATEMENT.—

"(A) IN GENERAL.—In the case of a taxpayer the taxable income of which is computed under an accrual method of accounting, the all events test with respect to any item of gross income (or portion thereof) shall not be treated as met any later than when such item (or portion thereof) is taken into account as revenue in—

"(i) an applicable financial statement of the taxpayer, or

"(ii) such other financial statement as the Secretary may specify for purposes of this subsection.

"(B) EXCEPTION.—This paragraph shall

"(i) a taxpayer which does not have a financial statement described in clause (i) or (ii) of subparagraph (A) for a taxable year, or

"(ii) any item of gross income in connection with a mortgage servicing contract.

"(C) ALL EVENTS TEST.—For purposes of this section, the all events test is met with respect to any item of gross income if all the events have occurred which fix the right to receive such income and the amount of such income can be determined with reasonable accuracy.

"(2) COORDINATION WITH SPECIAL METHODS OF ACCOUNTING.—Paragraph (1) shall not apply with respect to any item of gross income for which the taxpayer uses a special method of accounting provided under any other provision of this chapter, other than any provision of part V of subchapter P (except as provided in clause (ii) of paragraph (1)(B)).

"(3) APPLICABLE FINANCIAL STATEMENT.—For purposes of this subsection, the term 'applicable financial statement' means—

"(A) a financial statement which is certified as being prepared in accordance with generally accepted accounting principles and which is—

"(i) a 10–K (or successor form), or annual statement to shareholders, required to be filed by the taxpayer with the United States Securities and Exchange Commission,

"(ii) an audited financial statement of the taxpayer which is used for—

"(I) credit purposes,

"(II) reporting to shareholders, partners, or other proprietors, or to beneficiaries, or

"(III) any other substantial nontax purpose,

but only if there is no statement of the taxpayer described in clause (i), or

"(iii) filed by the taxpayer with any other Federal agency for purposes other than Federal tax purposes, but only if there is no statement of the taxpayer described in clause (i) or (ii),

"(B) a financial statement which is made on the basis of international financial reporting standards and is filed by the taxpayer with an agency of a foreign government which is equivalent to the United States Securities and Exchange Commission and which has reporting standards not less stringent than the standards required by such Commission, but only if there is no statement of the taxpayer described in subparagraph (A), or

"(C) a financial statement filed by the taxpayer with any other regulatory or governmental body specified by the Secretary, but only if there is no statement of the taxpayer described in subparagraph (A) or (B).

"(4) ALLOCATION OF TRANSACTION PRICE.—For purposes of this subsection, in the case of a contract which contains multiple performance obligations, the allocation of the transaction price to each performance obligation shall be equal to the amount allocated to each performance obligation for purposes of including such item in revenue in the applicable financial statement of the taxpayer.

"(5) GROUP OF ENTITIES.—For purposes of paragraph (1), if the financial results of a taxpayer are reported on the applicable financial statement (as defined in paragraph (3)) for a group of entities, such statement shall be treated as the applicable financial statement of the taxpayer.".

(b) TREATMENT OF ADVANCE PAYMENTS.—Section 451, as amended by subsection (a), is amended by redesignating subsections (c) through (j) as subsections (d) through (k), respectively, and by inserting after subsection (b) the following new subsection:

"(c) TREATMENT OF ADVANCE PAYMENTS.—

"(1) IN GENERAL.—A taxpayer which computes taxable income under the accrual method of accounting, and receives any advance payment during the taxable year, shall—

"(A) except as provided in subparagraph (B), include such advance payment in gross income for such taxable year, or

"(B) if the taxpayer elects the application of this subparagraph with respect to the category of advance payments to which such advance payment belongs, the taxpayer shall—

"(i) to the extent that any portion of such advance payment is required under subsection (b) to be included in gross income in the taxable year in which such payment is received, so include such portion, and

"(ii) include the remaining portion of such advance payment in gross income in the taxable year following the taxable year in which such payment is received.

"(2) ELECTION.—

"(A) IN GENERAL.—Except as otherwise provided in this paragraph, the election under paragraph (1)(B) shall be made at such time, in such form and manner, and with respect to such categories of advance payments, as the Secretary may provide.

"(B) PERIOD TO WHICH ELECTION APPLIES.—An election under paragraph (1)(B) shall be effective for the taxable year with respect to which it is first made and for all subsequent taxable years, unless the taxpayer secures the consent of the Secretary to revoke such election. For purposes of this title, the computation of taxable income under an election made under paragraph (1)(B) shall be treated as a method of accounting.

"(3) TAXPAYERS CEASING TO EXIST.—Except as otherwise provided by the Secretary, the election under paragraph (1)(B) shall not apply with respect to advance payments received by the taxpayer during a taxable year if such taxpayer ceases to exist during (or with the close of) such taxable year.

"(4) ADVANCE PAYMENT.—For purposes of this subsection—

"(A) IN GENERAL.—The term 'advance payment' means any payment—

"(i) the full inclusion of which in the gross income of the taxpayer for the taxable year of receipt is a permissible method of accounting under this section (determined without regard to this subsection),

"(ii) any portion of which is included in revenue by the taxpayer in a financial statement described in clause (i) or (ii) of subsection (b)(1)(A) for a subsequent taxable year, and

"(iii) which is for goods, services, or such other items as may be identified by the Secretary for purposes of this clause.

"(B) EXCLUSIONS.—Except as otherwise provided by the Secretary, such term shall not include—

"(i) rent,

"(ii) insurance premiums governed by subchapter L,

"(iii) payments with respect to financial instruments,

"(iv) payments with respect to warranty or guarantee contracts under which a third party is the primary obligor,

"(v) payments subject to section 871(a), 881, 1441, or 1442,

"(vi) payments in property to which section 83 applies, and

"(vii) any other payment identified by the Secretary for purposes of this subparagraph.

"(C) RECEIPT.—For purposes of this subsection, an item of gross income is received by the taxpayer if it is actually or constructively received, or if it is due and payable to the taxpayer.

"(D) ALLOCATION OF TRANSACTION PRICE.—For purposes of this subsection, rules similar to subsection (b)(4) shall apply.".

(c) EFFECTIVE DATE.—The amendments made by this section shall apply to taxable years beginning after December 31, 2017.

(d) COORDINATION WITH SECTION 481.—

(1) IN GENERAL.—In the case of any qualified change in method of accounting for the taxpayer's first taxable year beginning after December 31, 2017—

(A) such change shall be treated as initiated by the taxpayer, and

(B) such change shall be treated as made with the consent of the Secretary of the Treasury.

(2) QUALIFIED CHANGE IN METHOD OF ACCOUNTING.—For purposes of this subsection, the term "qualified change in method of accounting" means any change in method of accounting which—

(A) is required by the amendments made by this section, or

(B) was prohibited under the Internal Revenue Code of 1986 prior to such amendments and is permitted under such Code after such amendments.

(e) SPECIAL RULES FOR ORIGINAL ISSUE DISCOUNT.—Notwithstanding subsection (c), in the case of income from a debt instrument having original issue discount—

(1) the amendments made by this section shall apply to taxable years beginning after December 31, 2018, and

(2) the period for taking into account any adjustments under section 481 by reason of a qualified change in method of accounting (as defined in subsection (d)) shall be 6 years.

## PART IV—BUSINESS-RELATED EXCLUSIONS AND DEDUCTIONS

### SEC. 13301. LIMITATION ON DEDUCTION FOR INTEREST.

(a) IN GENERAL.—Section 163(j) is amended to read as follows:

"(j) LIMITATION ON BUSINESS INTEREST.—

"(1) IN GENERAL.—The amount allowed as a deduction under this chapter for any taxable year for business interest shall not exceed the sum of—

"(A) the business interest income of such taxpayer for such taxable year,

"(B) 30 percent of the adjusted taxable income of such taxpayer for such taxable year, plus

"(C) the floor plan financing interest of such taxpayer for such taxable year.

The amount determined under subparagraph (B) shall not be less than zero.

"(2) CARRYFORWARD OF DISALLOWED BUSINESS INTEREST.—The amount of any business interest not allowed as a deduction for any taxable year by reason of paragraph (1) shall be treated as business interest paid or accrued in the succeeding taxable year.

"(3) EXEMPTION FOR CERTAIN SMALL BUSINESSES.—In the case of any taxpayer (other than a tax shelter prohibited from using the cash receipts and disbursements method of accounting under section 448(a)(3)) which meets the gross receipts test of section 448(c) for any taxable year, paragraph (1) shall not apply to such taxpayer for such taxable year. In the case of any taxpayer which is not a corporation or a partnership, the gross receipts test of section 448(c) shall be applied in the same manner as if such taxpayer were a corporation or partnership.

"(4) APPLICATION TO PARTNERSHIPS, ETC.—

"(A) IN GENERAL.—In the case of any partnership—

"(i) this subsection shall be applied at the partnership level and any deduction for business interest shall be taken into account in determining the non-separately stated taxable income or loss of the partnership, and

"(ii) the adjusted taxable income of each partner of such partnership—

"(I) shall be determined without regard to such partner's distributive share of any items of income, gain, deduction, or loss of such partnership, and

"(II) shall be increased by such partner's distributive share of such partnership's excess taxable income.

For purposes of clause (ii)(II), a partner's distributive share of partnership excess taxable income shall be determined in the same manner as the partner's distributive share of nonseparately stated taxable income or loss of the partnership.

"(B) SPECIAL RULES FOR CARRYFORWARDS.—

"(i) IN GENERAL.—The amount of any business interest not allowed as a deduction to a partnership for any taxable year by reason of paragraph (1) for any taxable year—

"(I) shall not be treated under paragraph (2) as business interest paid or accrued by the partnership in the succeeding taxable year, and

"(II) shall, subject to clause (ii), be treated as excess business interest which is allocated to each partner in the same manner as the non-separately stated taxable income or loss of the partnership.

"(ii) TREATMENT OF EXCESS BUSINESS INTEREST ALLOCATED TO PARTNERS.—If a partner is allocated any excess business interest from a partnership under clause (i) for any taxable year—

"(I) such excess business interest shall be treated as business interest paid or accrued by the partner in the next succeeding taxable year in which the partner is allocated excess taxable income from such partnership, but only to the extent of such excess taxable income, and

"(II) any portion of such excess business interest remaining after the application of subclause (I) shall, subject to the limitations of subclause (I), be treated as business interest paid or accrued in succeeding taxable years.

For purposes of applying this paragraph, excess taxable income allocated to a partner from a partnership for any taxable year shall not be taken into account under paragraph (1)(A) with respect to any business interest other than excess business interest from the partnership until all such excess business interest for such taxable year and all preceding taxable years has been treated as paid or accrued under clause (ii).

"(iii) BASIS ADJUSTMENTS.—

"(I) IN GENERAL.—The adjusted basis of a partner in a partnership interest shall be reduced (but not below zero) by the amount of excess business interest allocated to the partner under clause (i)(II).

"(II) SPECIAL RULE FOR DISPOSITIONS.—If a partner disposes of a partnership interest, the adjusted basis of the partner in the partnership interest shall be increased immediately before the disposition by the amount of the excess (if any) of the amount of the basis reduction under subclause (I) over the portion of any excess business interest allocated to the partner under clause (i)(II) which has previously been treated under clause (ii) as business interest paid or accrued by the partner. The preceding sentence shall also apply to transfers of the partnership interest (including by reason of death) in a transaction in which gain is not recognized in whole or in part. No deduction shall be allowed to the transferor or transferee under this chapter for any excess business interest resulting in a basis increase under this subclause.

"(C) EXCESS TAXABLE INCOME.—The term 'excess taxable income' means, with respect to any partnership, the amount which bears the same ratio to the partnership's adjusted taxable income as—

"(i) the excess (if any) of—

"(I) the amount determined for the partnership under paragraph (1)(B), over

"(II) the amount (if any) by which the business interest of the partnership, reduced by the floor plan financing interest, exceeds the business interest income of the partnership, bears to

"(ii) the amount determined for the partnership under paragraph (1)(B).

"(D) APPLICATION TO S CORPORATIONS.—Rules similar to the rules of subparagraphs (A) and (C) shall apply with respect to any S corporation and its shareholders.

"(5) BUSINESS INTEREST.—For purposes of this subsection, the term 'business interest' means any interest paid or accrued on indebtedness properly allocable to a trade or business. Such term shall not include investment interest (within the meaning of subsection (d)).

"(6) BUSINESS INTEREST INCOME.—For purposes of this subsection, the term 'business interest income' means the amount of interest includible in the gross income of the taxpayer for the taxable year which is properly allocable to a trade or business. Such term shall not include investment income (within the meaning of subsection (d)).

"(7) TRADE OR BUSINESS.—For purposes of this subsection—

"(A) IN GENERAL.—The term 'trade or business' shall not include—

"(i) the trade or business of performing services as an employee,

"(ii) any electing real property trade or business,

"(iii) any electing farming business, or

"(iv) the trade or business of the furnishing or sale of—

"(I) electrical energy, water, or sewage disposal services,

"(II) gas or steam through a local distribution system, or

"(III) transportation of gas or steam by pipeline,

if the rates for such furnishing or sale, as the case may be, have been established or approved by a State or political subdivision thereof, by any agency or instrumentality of the United States, by a public service or public utility commission or other similar body of any State or political subdivision thereof, or by the governing or ratemaking body of an electric cooperative.

"(B) ELECTING REAL PROPERTY TRADE OR BUSINESS.—For purposes of this paragraph, the term 'electing real property trade or business' means any trade or business which is described in section 469(c)(7)(C) and which makes an election under this subparagraph. Any such election shall be made at such time and in such manner as the Secretary shall prescribe, and, once made, shall be irrevocable.

"(C) ELECTING FARMING BUSINESS.—For purposes of this paragraph, the term 'electing farming business' means—

"(i) a farming business (as defined in section 263A(e)(4)) which makes an election under this subparagraph, or

"(ii) any trade or business of a specified agricultural or horticultural cooperative (as defined in section 199A(g)(2)) with respect to which the cooperative makes an election under this subparagraph.

Any such election shall be made at such time and in such manner as the Secretary shall prescribe, and, once made, shall be irrevocable.

"(8) ADJUSTED TAXABLE INCOME.—For purposes of this subsection, the term 'adjusted taxable income' means the taxable income of the taxpayer—

"(A) computed without regard to—

"(i) any item of income, gain, deduction, or loss which is not properly allocable to a trade or business,

"(ii) any business interest or business interest income,

"(iii) the amount of any net operating loss deduction under section 172,

"(iv) the amount of any deduction allowed under section 199A, and

"(v) in the case of taxable years beginning before January 1, 2022, any deduction allowable for depreciation, amortization, or depletion, and

"(B) computed with such other adjustments as provided by the Secretary.

"(9) FLOOR PLAN FINANCING INTEREST DEFINED.—For purposes of this subsection—

"(A) IN GENERAL.—The term 'floor plan financing interest' means interest paid or accrued on floor plan financing indebtedness.

"(B) FLOOR PLAN FINANCING INDEBTEDNESS.—The term 'floor plan financing indebtedness' means indebtedness—

"(i) used to finance the acquisition of motor vehicles held for sale or lease, and

"(ii) secured by the inventory so acquired.

"(C) MOTOR VEHICLE.—The term 'motor vehicle' means a motor vehicle that is any of the following:

"(i) Any self-propelled vehicle designed for transporting persons or property on a public street, highway, or road.

"(ii) A boat.

"(iii) Farm machinery or equipment.

"(10) CROSS REFERENCES.—

"(A) For requirement that an electing real property trade or business use the alternative depreciation system, see section 168(g)(1)(F).

"(B) For requirement that an electing farming business use the alternative depreciation system, see section 168(g)(1)(G).".

(b) TREATMENT OF CARRYFORWARD OF DISALLOWED BUSINESS INTEREST IN CERTAIN CORPORATE ACQUISITIONS.—

(1) IN GENERAL.—Section 381(c) is amended by inserting after paragraph (19) the following new paragraph:

"(20) CARRYFORWARD OF DISALLOWED BUSINESS INTEREST.—The carryover of disallowed business interest described in section 163(j)(2) to taxable years ending after the date of distribution or transfer.".

(2) APPLICATION OF LIMITATION.—Section 382(d) is amended by adding at the end the following new paragraph:

"(3) APPLICATION TO CARRYFORWARD OF DISALLOWED INTEREST.—The term 'pre-change loss' shall include any carryover of disallowed interest described in section 163(j)(2) under rules similar to the rules of paragraph (1).".

(3) CONFORMING AMENDMENT.—Section 382(k)(1) is amended by inserting after the first sentence the following: "Such term shall include any

corporation entitled to use a carryforward of disallowed interest described in section 381(c)(20).''.

(c) EFFECTIVE DATE.—The amendments made by this section shall apply to taxable years beginning after December 31, 2017.

**SEC. 13302. MODIFICATION OF NET OPERATING LOSS DEDUCTION.**

(a) LIMITATION ON DEDUCTION.—

(1) IN GENERAL.—Section 172(a) is amended to read as follows:

''(a) DEDUCTION ALLOWED.—There shall be allowed as a deduction for the taxable year an amount equal to the lesser of—

''(1) the aggregate of the net operating loss carryovers to such year, plus the net operating loss carrybacks to such year, or

''(2) 80 percent of taxable income computed without regard to the deduction allowable under this section.

For purposes of this subtitle, the term 'net operating loss deduction' means the deduction allowed by this subsection.''.

(2) COORDINATION OF LIMITATION WITH CARRYBACKS AND CARRYOVERS.—Section 172(b)(2)

is amended by striking "shall be computed—" and all that follows and inserting "shall—

"(A) be computed with the modifications specified in subsection (d) other than paragraphs (1), (4), and (5) thereof, and by determining the amount of the net operating loss deduction without regard to the net operating loss for the loss year or for any taxable year thereafter,

"(B) not be considered to be less than zero, and

"(C) not exceed the amount determined under subsection (a)(2) for such prior taxable year.".

(3) CONFORMING AMENDMENT.—Section 172(d)(6) is amended by striking "and" at the end of subparagraph (A), by striking the period at the end of subparagraph (B) and inserting "; and", and by adding at the end the following new subparagraph:

"(C) subsection (a)(2) shall be applied by substituting 'real estate investment trust taxable income (as defined in section 857(b)(2) but without regard to the deduction for dividends paid (as defined in section 561))' for 'taxable income'.".

(b) Repeal of Net Operating Loss Carryback; Indefinite Carryforward.—

(1) In general.—Section 172(b)(1)(A) is amended—

(A) by striking "shall be a net operating loss carryback to each of the 2 taxable years" in clause (i) and inserting "except as otherwise provided in this paragraph, shall not be a net operating loss carryback to any taxable year", and

(B) by striking "to each of the 20 taxable years" in clause (ii) and inserting "to each taxable year".

(2) Conforming amendment.—Section 172(b)(1) is amended by striking subparagraphs (B) through (F).

(c) Treatment of Farming Losses.—

(1) Allowance of carrybacks.—Section 172(b)(1), as amended by subsection (b)(2), is amended by adding at the end the following new subparagraph:

"(B) Farming losses.—

"(i) IN GENERAL.—In the case of any portion of a net operating loss for the taxable year which is a farming loss with respect to the taxpayer, such loss shall be a net operating loss carryback to each of the 2 taxable years preceding the taxable year of such loss.

"(ii) FARMING LOSS.—For purposes of this section, the term 'farming loss' means the lesser of—

"(I) the amount which would be the net operating loss for the taxable year if only income and deductions attributable to farming businesses (as defined in section 263A(e)(4)) are taken into account, or

"(II) the amount of the net operating loss for such taxable year.

"(iii) COORDINATION WITH PARAGRAPH (2).—For purposes of applying paragraph (2), a farming loss for any taxable year shall be treated as a separate net operating loss for such taxable year to be taken into account after the remaining portion of the net operating loss for such taxable year.

"(iv) ELECTION.—Any taxpayer entitled to a 2-year carryback under clause (i) from any loss year may elect not to have such clause apply to such loss year. Such election shall be made in such manner as prescribed by the Secretary and shall be made by the due date (including extensions of time) for filing the taxpayer's return for the taxable year of the net operating loss. Such election, once made for any taxable year, shall be irrevocable for such taxable year.".

(2) CONFORMING AMENDMENTS.—

(A) Section 172 is amended by striking subsections (f), (g), and (h), and by redesignating subsection (i) as subsection (f).

(B) Section 537(b)(4) is amended by inserting "(as in effect before the date of enactment of the Tax Cuts and Jobs Act)" after "as defined in section 172(f)".

(d) TREATMENT OF CERTAIN INSURANCE LOSSES.—

(1) TREATMENT OF CARRYFORWARDS AND CARRYBACKS.—Section 172(b)(1), as amended by

subsections (b)(2) and (c)(1), is amended by adding at the end the following new subparagraph:

"(C) INSURANCE COMPANIES.—In the case of an insurance company (as defined in section 816(a)) other than a life insurance company, the net operating loss for any taxable year—

"(i) shall be a net operating loss carryback to each of the 2 taxable years preceding the taxable year of such loss, and

"(ii) shall be a net operating loss carryover to each of the 20 taxable years following the taxable year of the loss.".

(2) EXEMPTION FROM LIMITATION.—Section 172, as amended by subsection (c)(2)(A), is amended by redesignating subsection (f) as subsection (g) and inserting after subsection (e) the following new subsection:

"(f) SPECIAL RULE FOR INSURANCE COMPANIES.—In the case of an insurance company (as defined in section 816(a)) other than a life insurance company—

"(1) the amount of the deduction allowed under subsection (a) shall be the aggregate of the net operating loss carryovers to such year, plus the net operating loss carrybacks to such year, and

"(2) subparagraph (C) of subsection (b)(2) shall not apply.".

(e) EFFECTIVE DATE.—

(1) NET OPERATING LOSS LIMITATION.—The amendments made by subsections (a) and (d)(2) shall apply to losses arising in taxable years beginning after December 31, 2017.

(2) CARRYFORWARDS AND CARRYBACKS.—The amendments made by subsections (b), (c), and (d)(1) shall apply to net operating losses arising in taxable years ending after December 31, 2017.

**SEC. 13303. LIKE-KIND EXCHANGES OF REAL PROPERTY.**

(a) IN GENERAL.—Section 1031(a)(1) is amended by striking "property" each place it appears and inserting "real property".

(b) CONFORMING AMENDMENTS.—

(1)(A) Paragraph (2) of section 1031(a) is amended to read as follows:

"(2) EXCEPTION FOR REAL PROPERTY HELD FOR SALE.—This subsection shall not apply to any exchange of real property held primarily for sale.".

(B) Section 1031 is amended by striking subsection (i).

(2) Section 1031 is amended by striking subsection (e).

(3) Section 1031, as amended by paragraph (2), is amended by inserting after subsection (d) the following new subsection:

"(e) APPLICATION TO CERTAIN PARTNERSHIPS.—For purposes of this section, an interest in a partnership which has in effect a valid election under section 761(a) to be excluded from the application of all of subchapter K shall be treated as an interest in each of the assets of such partnership and not as an interest in a partnership.".

(4) Section 1031(h) is amended to read as follows:

"(h) SPECIAL RULES FOR FOREIGN REAL PROPERTY.—Real property located in the United States and real property located outside the United States are not property of a like kind.".

(5) The heading of section 1031 is amended by striking "**PROPERTY**" and inserting "**REAL PROPERTY**".

(6) The table of sections for part III of subchapter O of chapter 1 is amended by striking the item relating to section 1031 and inserting the following new item:

"Sec. 1031. Exchange of real property held for productive use or investment.".

(c) EFFECTIVE DATE.—

(1) IN GENERAL.—Except as otherwise pro-

this section shall apply to exchanges completed after December 31, 2017.

(2) TRANSITION RULE.—The amendments made by this section shall not apply to any exchange if—

(A) the property disposed of by the taxpayer in the exchange is disposed of on or before December 31 2017, or

(B) the property received by the taxpayer in the exchange is received on or before December 31, 2017.

**SEC. 13304. LIMITATION ON DEDUCTION BY EMPLOYERS OF EXPENSES FOR FRINGE BENEFITS.**

(a) NO DEDUCTION ALLOWED FOR ENTERTAINMENT EXPENSES.—

(1) IN GENERAL.—Section 274(a) is amended—

(A) in paragraph (1)(A), by striking "unless" and all that follows through "trade or business,",

(B) by striking the flush sentence at the end of paragraph (1), and

(C) by striking paragraph (2)(C).

(2) CONFORMING AMENDMENTS.—

(A) Section 274(d) is amended—

(i) by striking paragraph (2) and redesignating paragraphs (3) and (4) as paragraphs (2) and (3), respectively, and

(ii) in the flush text following paragraph (3) (as so redesignated)—

(I) by striking ", entertainment, amusement, recreation, or use of the facility or property," in item (B), and

(II) by striking "(D) the business relationship to the taxpayer of persons entertained, using the facility or property, or receiving the gift" and inserting "(D) the business relationship to the taxpayer of the person receiving the benefit",

(B) Section 274 is amended by striking subsection (l).

(C) Section 274(n) is amended by striking "AND ENTERTAINMENT" in the heading.

(D) Section 274(n)(1) is amended to read as follows:

"(1) IN GENERAL.—The amount allowable as a deduction under this chapter for any expense for food or beverages shall not exceed 50 percent of the amount of such expense which would (but for this paragraph) be allowable as a deduction under this chapter.".

(E) Section 274(n)(2) is amended—

(i) in subparagraph (B), by striking "in the case of an expense for food or beverages,",

(ii) by striking subparagraph (C) and redesignating subparagraphs (D) and (E) as subparagraphs (C) and (D), respectively,

(iii) by striking "of subparagraph (E)" the last sentence and inserting "of subparagraph (D)", and

(iv) by striking "in subparagraph (D)" in the last sentence and inserting "in subparagraph (C)".

(F) Clause (iv) of section 7701(b)(5)(A) is amended to read as follows:

"(iv) a professional athlete who is temporarily in the United States to compete in a sports event—

"(I) which is organized for the primary purpose of benefiting an organization which is described in section 501(c)(3) and exempt from tax under section 501(a),

"(II) all of the net proceeds of which are contributed to such organization, and,

"(III) which utilizes volunteers for substantially all of the work performed in carrying out such event.".

(b) ONLY 50 PERCENT OF EXPENSES FOR MEALS PROVIDED ON OR NEAR BUSINESS PREMISES ALLOWED AS DEDUCTION.—Paragraph (2) of section 274(n), as amended by subsection (a), is amended—

(1) by striking subparagraph (B),

(2) by redesignating subparagraphs (C) and (D) as subparagraphs (B) and (C), respectively,

(3) by striking "of subparagraph (D)" in the last sentence and inserting "of subparagraph (C)", and

(4) by striking "in subparagraph (C)" in the last sentence and inserting "in subparagraph (B)".

(c) TREATMENT OF TRANSPORTATION BENEFITS.—Section 274, as amended by subsection (a), is amended—

(1) in subsection (a)—

(A) in the heading, by striking "OR RECREATION" and inserting "RECREATION, OR QUALIFIED TRANSPORTATION FRINGES", and

(B) by adding at the end the following new paragraph:

"(4) QUALIFIED TRANSPORTATION FRINGES.—No deduction shall be allowed under this chapter for the expense of any qualified transportation fringe (as defined in section 132(f)) provided to an employee of the taxpayer.", and

(2) by inserting after subsection (k) the following new subsection:

"(l) TRANSPORTATION AND COMMUTING BENEFITS.—

"(1) IN GENERAL.—No deduction shall be allowed under this chapter for any expense incurred for providing any transportation, or any payment or reimbursement, to an employee of the taxpayer in connection with travel between the employee's residence and place of employment, except as necessary for ensuring the safety of the employee.

"(2) EXCEPTION.—In the case of any qualified bicycle commuting reimbursement (as described in section 132(f)(5)(F)), this subsection shall not apply for any amounts paid or incurred after December 31, 2017, and before January 1, 2026.".

(d) ELIMINATION OF DEDUCTION FOR MEALS PROVIDED AT CONVENIENCE OF EMPLOYER.—Section 274, as amended by subsection (c), is amended—

(1) by redesignating subsection (o) as subsection (p), and

(2) by inserting after subsection (n) the following new subsection:

"(o) MEALS PROVIDED AT CONVENIENCE OF EMPLOYER.—No deduction shall be allowed under this chapter for—

"(1) any expense for the operation of a facility described in section 132(e)(2), and any expense for food or beverages, including under section 132(e)(1), associated with such facility, or

"(2) any expense for meals described in section 119(a).".

(e) EFFECTIVE DATE.—

(1) IN GENERAL.—Except as provided in paragraph (2), the amendments made by this section shall apply to amounts incurred or paid after December 31, 2017.

(2) EFFECTIVE DATE FOR ELIMINATION OF DEDUCTION FOR MEALS PROVIDED AT CONVENIENCE

OF EMPLOYER.—The amendments made by subsection (d) shall apply to amounts incurred or paid after December 31, 2025.

**SEC. 13305. REPEAL OF DEDUCTION FOR INCOME ATTRIBUTABLE TO DOMESTIC PRODUCTION ACTIVITIES.**

(a) IN GENERAL.—Part VI of subchapter B of chapter 1 is amended by striking section 199 (and by striking the item relating to such section in the table of sections for such part).

(b) CONFORMING AMENDMENTS.—

(1) Sections 74(d)(2)(B), 86(b)(2)(A), 135(c)(4)(A), 137(b)(3)(A), 219(g)(3)(A)(ii), 221(b)(2)(C), 222(b)(2)(C), 246(b)(1), and 469(i)(3)(F)(iii) are each amended by striking "199,".

(2) Section 170(b)(2)(D), as amended by subtitle A, is amended by striking clause (iv), and by redesignating clauses (v) and (vi) as clauses (iv) and (v).

(3) Section 172(d) is amended by striking paragraph (7).

(4) Section 613(a), as amended by section 11011, is amended by striking "and without the deduction under section 199".

(5) Section 613A(d)(1), as amended by section 11011, is amended by striking subparagraph (B) and by redesignating subparagraphs (C), (D), (E), and (F) as subparagraphs (B), (C), (D), and (E), respectively.

(c) EFFECTIVE DATE.—The amendments made by this section shall apply to taxable years beginning after December 31, 2017.

**SEC. 13306. DENIAL OF DEDUCTION FOR CERTAIN FINES, PENALTIES, AND OTHER AMOUNTS.**

(a) DENIAL OF DEDUCTION.—

(1) IN GENERAL.—Subsection (f) of section 162 is amended to read as follows:

"(f) FINES, PENALTIES, AND OTHER AMOUNTS.—

"(1) IN GENERAL.—Except as provided in the following paragraphs of this subsection, no deduction otherwise allowable shall be allowed under this chapter for any amount paid or incurred (whether by suit, agreement, or otherwise) to, or at the direction of, a government or governmental entity in relation to the violation of any law or the investigation or inquiry by such government or entity into the potential violation of any law.

"(2) EXCEPTION FOR AMOUNTS CONSTITUTING RESTITUTION OR PAID TO COME INTO COMPLIANCE WITH LAW.—

"(A) IN GENERAL.—Paragraph (1) shall not apply to any amount that—

"(i) the taxpayer establishes—

"(I) constitutes restitution (including remediation of property) for damage or harm which was or may be caused by the violation of any law or the potential violation of any law, or

"(II) is paid to come into compliance with any law which was violated or otherwise involved in the investigation or inquiry described in paragraph (1),

"(ii) is identified as restitution or as an amount paid to come into compliance with such law, as the case may be, in the court order or settlement agreement, and

"(iii) in the case of any amount of restitution for failure to pay any tax imposed under this title in the same manner as if such amount were such tax, would have been allowed as a deduction under this chapter if it had been timely paid.

The identification under clause (ii) alone shall not be sufficient to make the establishment required under clause (i).

"(B) LIMITATION.—Subparagraph (A) shall not apply to any amount paid or incurred as reimbursement to the government or entity for the costs of any investigation or litigation.

"(3) EXCEPTION FOR AMOUNTS PAID OR INCURRED AS THE RESULT OF CERTAIN COURT ORDERS.—Paragraph (1) shall not apply to any amount paid or incurred by reason of any order of a court in a suit in which no government or governmental entity is a party.

"(4) EXCEPTION FOR TAXES DUE.—Paragraph (1) shall not apply to any amount paid or incurred as taxes due.

"(5) TREATMENT OF CERTAIN NONGOVERNMENTAL REGULATORY ENTITIES.—For purposes of this subsection, the following nongovernmental entities shall be treated as governmental entities:

"(A) Any nongovernmental entity which exercises self-regulatory powers (including imposing sanctions) in connection with a qualified board or exchange (as defined in section 1256(g)(7)).

"(B) To the extent provided in regulations, any nongovernmental entity which exercises self-regulatory powers (including imposing sanctions) as part of performing an essential governmental function.".

(2) EFFECTIVE DATE.—The amendment made by this subsection shall apply to amounts paid or incurred on or after the date of the enactment of this Act, except that such amendments shall not apply to amounts paid or incurred under any binding order or agreement entered into before such date. Such exception shall not apply to an order or agreement requiring court approval unless the approval was obtained before such date.

(b) REPORTING OF DEDUCTIBLE AMOUNTS.—

(1) IN GENERAL.—Subpart B of part III of subchapter A of chapter 61 is amended by inserting after section 6050W the following new section:

**"SEC. 6050X. INFORMATION WITH RESPECT TO CERTAIN FINES, PENALTIES, AND OTHER AMOUNTS.**

"(a) REQUIREMENT OF REPORTING.—

"(1) IN GENERAL.—The appropriate official of any government or any entity described in section

162(f)(5) which is involved in a suit or agreement described in paragraph (2) shall make a return in such form as determined by the Secretary setting forth—

"(A) the amount required to be paid as a result of the suit or agreement to which paragraph (1) of section 162(f) applies,

"(B) any amount required to be paid as a result of the suit or agreement which constitutes restitution or remediation of property, and

"(C) any amount required to be paid as a result of the suit or agreement for the purpose of coming into compliance with any law which was violated or involved in the investigation or inquiry.

"(2) SUIT OR AGREEMENT DESCRIBED.—

"(A) IN GENERAL.—A suit or agreement is described in this paragraph if—

"(i) it is—

"(I) a suit with respect to a violation of any law over which the government or entity has authority and with respect to which there has been a court order, or

"(II) an agreement which is entered into with respect to a violation of any law over which the government or entity has authority, or with respect to an investigation or inquiry by the government or entity into the potential violation of any law over which such government or entity has authority, and

"(ii) the aggregate amount involved in all court orders and agreements with respect to the violation, investigation, or inquiry is $600 or more.

"(B) ADJUSTMENT OF REPORTING THRESHOLD.—The Secretary shall adjust the $600 amount in subparagraph (A)(ii) as necessary in order to ensure the efficient administration of the internal revenue laws.

"(3) TIME OF FILING.—The return required under this subsection shall be filed at the time the agreement is entered into, as determined by the Secretary.

"(b) STATEMENTS TO BE FURNISHED TO INDIVIDUALS INVOLVED IN THE SETTLEMENT.—Every person required to make a return under subsection (a) shall furnish to each person who is a party to the suit or agreement a written statement showing—

"(1) the name of the government or entity, and

"(2) the information supplied to the Secretary under subsection (a)(1).

The written statement required under the preceding sentence shall be furnished to the person at the same time the government or entity provides the Secretary with the information required under subsection (a).

"(c) APPROPRIATE OFFICIAL DEFINED.—For purposes of this section, the term 'appropriate official' means the officer or employee having control of the suit, investigation, or inquiry or the person appropriately designated for purposes of this section.".

(2) CONFORMING AMENDMENT.—The table of sections for subpart B of part III of subchapter A of chapter 61 is amended by inserting after the item relating to section 6050W the following new item:

"Sec. 6050X. Information with respect to certain fines, penalties, and other amounts.".

(3) EFFECTIVE DATE.—The amendments made by this subsection shall apply to amounts paid or incurred on or after the date of the enactment of this Act, except that such amendments shall not apply to amounts paid or incurred under any binding order or agreement entered into before such date. Such ex-

ception shall not apply to an order or agreement requiring court approval unless the approval was obtained before such date.

**SEC. 13307. DENIAL OF DEDUCTION FOR SETTLEMENTS SUBJECT TO NONDISCLOSURE AGREEMENTS PAID IN CONNECTION WITH SEXUAL HARASSMENT OR SEXUAL ABUSE.**

(a) DENIAL OF DEDUCTION.—Section 162 is amended by redesignating subsection (q) as subsection (r) and by inserting after subsection (p) the following new subsection:

"(q) PAYMENTS RELATED TO SEXUAL HARASSMENT AND SEXUAL ABUSE.—No deduction shall be allowed under this chapter for—

"(1) any settlement or payment related to sexual harassment or sexual abuse if such settlement or payment is subject to a nondisclosure agreement, or

"(2) attorney's fees related to such a settlement or payment.".

(b) EFFECTIVE DATE.—The amendments made by this section shall apply to amounts paid or incurred after the date of the enactment of this Act.

## SEC. 13308. REPEAL OF DEDUCTION FOR LOCAL LOBBYING EXPENSES.

(a) IN GENERAL.—Section 162(e) is amended by striking paragraphs (2) and (7) and by redesignating paragraphs (3), (4), (5), (6), and (8) as paragraphs (2), (3), (4), (5), and (6), respectively.

(b) CONFORMING AMENDMENT.—Section 6033(e)(1)(B)(ii) is amended by striking "section 162(e)(5)(B)(ii)" and inserting "section 162(e)(4)(B)(ii)".

(c) EFFECTIVE DATE.—The amendments made by this section shall apply to amounts paid or incurred on or after the date of the enactment of this Act.

## SEC. 13309. RECHARACTERIZATION OF CERTAIN GAINS IN THE CASE OF PARTNERSHIP PROFITS INTERESTS HELD IN CONNECTION WITH PERFORMANCE OF INVESTMENT SERVICES.

(a) IN GENERAL.—Part IV of subchapter O of chapter 1 is amended—

(1) by redesignating section 1061 as section 1062, and

(2) by inserting after section 1060 the following new section:

**"SEC. 1061. PARTNERSHIP INTERESTS HELD IN CONNECTION WITH PERFORMANCE OF SERVICES.**

"(a) IN GENERAL.—If one or more applicable partnership interests are held by a taxpayer at any time during the taxable year, the excess (if any) of—

"(1) the taxpayer's net long-term capital gain with respect to such interests for such taxable year, over

"(2) the taxpayer's net long-term capital gain with respect to such interests for such taxable year computed by applying paragraphs (3) and (4) of sections 1222 by substituting '3 years' for '1 year',

shall be treated as short-term capital gain, notwithstanding section 83 or any election in effect under section 83(b).

"(b) SPECIAL RULE.—To the extent provided by the Secretary, subsection (a) shall not apply to income or gain attributable to any asset not held for portfolio investment on behalf of third party investors.

"(c) APPLICABLE PARTNERSHIP INTEREST.—For purposes of this section—

"(1) IN GENERAL.—Except as provided in this paragraph or paragraph (4), the term 'applicable partnership interest' means any interest in a partnership which, directly or indirectly, is transferred to performance of substantial services by the taxpayer, or any other related person, in any applicable trade or business. The previous sentence shall not apply to an interest held by a person who is employed by another entity that is conducting a trade or business (other than an applicable trade or business) and only provides services to such other entity.

"(2) APPLICABLE TRADE OR BUSINESS.—The term 'applicable trade or business' means any activity conducted on a regular, continuous, and substantial basis which, regardless of whether the activity is conducted in one or more entities, consists, in whole or in part, of—

"(A) raising or returning capital, and

"(B) either—

"(i) investing in (or disposing of) specified assets (or identifying specified assets for such investing or disposition), or

"(ii) developing specified assets.

"(3) SPECIFIED ASSET.—The term 'specified asset' means securities (as defined in section 475(c)(2) without regard to the last sentence thereof), commodities (as defined in section 475(e)(2)), real estate held for rental or investment, cash or cash equivalents, options or derivative contracts with respect to any of the foregoing, and an interest in a partnership to the extent of the partnership's proportionate interest in any of the foregoing.

"(4) EXCEPTIONS.—The term 'applicable partnership interest' shall not include—

"(A) any interest in a partnership directly or indirectly held by a corporation, or

"(B) any capital interest in the partnership which provides the taxpayer with a right to share in partnership capital commensurate with—

"(i) the amount of capital contributed (determined at the time of receipt of such partnership interest), or

"(ii) the value of such interest subject to tax under section 83 upon the receipt or vesting of such interest.

"(5) THIRD PARTY INVESTOR.—The term 'third party investor' means a person who—

"(A) holds an interest in the partnership which does not constitute property held in connection with an applicable trade or business; and

"(B) is not (and has not been) actively engaged, and is (and was) not related to a person so engaged, in (directly or indirectly) providing substantial services described in paragraph (1) for such partnership or any applicable trade or business.

"(d) TRANSFER OF APPLICABLE PARTNERSHIP INTEREST TO RELATED PERSON.—

"(1) IN GENERAL.—If a taxpayer transfers any applicable partnership interest, directly or indirectly, to a person related to the taxpayer, the taxpayer shall include in gross income (as short term capital gain) the excess (if any) of—

"(A) so much of the taxpayer's long-term capital gains with respect to such interest for such taxable year attributable to the sale or exchange of any asset held for not more than 3 years as is allocable to such interest, over

"(B) any amount treated as short term capital gain under subsection (a) with respect to the transfer of such interest.

"(2) RELATED PERSON.—For purposes of this paragraph, a person is related to the taxpayer if—

"(A) the person is a member of the taxpayer's family within the meaning of section 318(a)(1), or

"(B) the person performed a service within the current calendar year or the preceding three calendar years in any applicable trade or business in which or for which the taxpayer performed a service.

"(e) REPORTING.—The Secretary shall require such reporting (at the time and in the manner prescribed by the Secretary) as is necessary to carry out the purposes of this section.

"(f) REGULATIONS.—The Secretary shall issue such regulations or other guidance as is necessary or appropriate to carry out the purposes of this section".

(b) CLERICAL AMENDMENT.—The table of sections for part IV of subchapter O of chapter 1 is amended by striking the item relating to 1061 and inserting the following new items:

"Sec. 1061. Partnership interests held in connection with performance of services.
"Sec. 1062. Cross references.".

(c) EFFECTIVE DATE.—The amendments made by this section shall apply to taxable years beginning after December 31, 2017.

**SEC. 13310. PROHIBITION ON CASH, GIFT CARDS, AND OTHER NON-TANGIBLE PERSONAL PROPERTY AS EMPLOYEE ACHIEVEMENT AWARDS.**

(a) IN GENERAL.—Subparagraph (A) of section

(1) by striking "The term" and inserting the following:

"(i) IN GENERAL.—The term".

(2) by redesignating clauses (i), (ii), and (iii) as subclauses (I), (II), and (III), respectively, and conforming the margins accordingly, and

(3) by adding at the end the following new clause:

"(ii) TANGIBLE PERSONAL PROPERTY.—For purposes of clause (i), the term 'tangible personal property' shall not include—

"(I) cash, cash equivalents, gift cards, gift coupons, or gift certificates (other than arrangements conferring only the right to select and receive tangible personal property from a limited array of such items pre-selected or pre-approved by the employer), or

"(II) vacations, meals, lodging, tickets to theater or sporting events, stocks, bonds, other securities, and other similar items.".

(b) EFFECTIVE DATE.—The amendments made by this section shall apply to amounts paid or incurred after December 31, 2017.

**SEC. 13311. ELIMINATION OF DEDUCTION FOR LIVING EXPENSES INCURRED BY MEMBERS OF CONGRESS.**

(a) IN GENERAL.—Subsection (a) of section 162 is amended in the matter following paragraph (3) by striking "in excess of $3,000".

(b) EFFECTIVE DATE.—The amendment made by this section shall apply to taxable years beginning after the date of the enactment of this Act.

**SEC. 13312. CERTAIN CONTRIBUTIONS BY GOVERNMENTAL ENTITIES NOT TREATED AS CONTRIBUTIONS TO CAPITAL.**

(a) IN GENERAL.—Section 118 is amended—

(1) by striking subsections (b), (c), and (d),

(2) by redesignating subsection (e) as subsection (d), and

(3) by inserting after subsection (a) the following new subsections:

"(b) EXCEPTIONS.—For purposes of subsection (a), the term 'contribution to the capital of the taxpayer' does not include—

"(1) any contribution in aid of construction or any other contribution as a customer or potential customer, and

"(2) any contribution by any governmental entity or civic group (other than a contribution made by a shareholder as such).

"(c) REGULATIONS.—The Secretary shall issue such regulations or other guidance as may be necessary or appropriate to carry out this section, including regulations or other guidance for determining whether any contribution constitutes a contribution in aid of construction.".

(b) EFFECTIVE DATE.—

(1) IN GENERAL.—Except as provided in paragraph (2), the amendments made by this section shall apply to contributions made after the date of enactment of this Act.

(2) EXCEPTION.—The amendments made by this section shall not apply to any contribution, made after the date of enactment of this Act by a governmental entity, which is made pursuant to a master development plan that has been approved prior to such date by a governmental entity.

**SEC. 13313. REPEAL OF ROLLOVER OF PUBLICLY TRADED SECURITIES GAIN INTO SPECIALIZED SMALL BUSINESS INVESTMENT COMPANIES.**

(a) IN GENERAL.—Part III of subchapter O of chapter 1 is amended by striking section 1044 (and by striking the item relating to such section in the table of sections of such part).

(b) CONFORMING AMENDMENTS.—Section 1016(a)(23) is amended—

(1) by striking "1044,", and

(2) by striking "1044(d),".

(c) EFFECTIVE DATE.—The amendments made by this section shall apply to sales after December 31, 2017.

**SEC. 13314. CERTAIN SELF-CREATED PROPERTY NOT TREATED AS A CAPITAL ASSET.**

(a) PATENTS, ETC.—Section 1221(a)(3) is amended by inserting "a patent, invention, model or design (whether or not patented), a secret formula or process," before "a copyright".

(b) CONFORMING AMENDMENT.—Section 1231(b)(1)(C) is amended by inserting "a patent, invention, model or design (whether or not patented), a secret formula or process," before "a copyright".

(c) EFFECTIVE DATE.—The amendments made by this section shall apply to dispositions after December 31,

## PART V—BUSINESS CREDITS

### SEC. 13401. MODIFICATION OF ORPHAN DRUG CREDIT.

(a) CREDIT RATE.—Subsection (a) of section 45C is amended by striking "50 percent" and inserting "25 percent".

(b) ELECTION OF REDUCED CREDIT.—Subsection (b) of section 280C is amended by redesignating paragraph (3) as paragraph (4) and by inserting after paragraph (2) the following new paragraph:

"(3) ELECTION OF REDUCED CREDIT.—

"(A) IN GENERAL.—In the case of any taxable year for which an election is made under this paragraph—

"(i) paragraphs (1) and (2) shall not apply, and

"(ii) the amount of the credit under section 45C(a) shall be the amount determined under subparagraph (B).

"(B) AMOUNT OF REDUCED CREDIT.—The amount of credit determined under this subparagraph for any taxable year shall be the amount equal to the excess of—

"(i) the amount of credit determined under section 45C(a) without regard to this paragraph, over

"(I) the amount described in clause (i), and

"(II) the maximum rate of tax under section 11(b).

"(C) ELECTION.—An election under this paragraph for any taxable year shall be made not later than the time for filing the return of tax for such year (including extensions), shall be made on such return, and shall be made in such manner as the Secretary shall prescribe. Such an election, once made, shall be irrevocable.".

(c) EFFECTIVE DATE.—The amendments made by this section shall apply to taxable years beginning after December 31, 2017.

**SEC. 13402. REHABILITATION CREDIT LIMITED TO CERTIFIED HISTORIC STRUCTURES.**

(a) IN GENERAL.—Subsection (a) of section 47 is amended to read as follows:

"(a) GENERAL RULE.—

"(1) IN GENERAL.—For purposes of section 46, for any taxable year during the 5-year period beginning in the taxable year in which a qualified rehabilitated building is placed in service, the rehabilitation credit for such year is an amount equal to the ratable share for such year.

"(2) RATABLE SHARE.—For purposes of paragraph (1), the ratable share for any taxable year during the period described in such paragraph is the amount equal to 20 percent of the qualified rehabilitation expenditures with respect to the qualified rehabilitated building, as allocated ratably to each year during such period.".

(b) CONFORMING AMENDMENTS.—

(1) Section 47(c) is amended—

(A) in paragraph (1)—

(i) in subparagraph (A), by amending clause (iii) to read as follows:

"(iii) such building is a certified historic structure, and",

(ii) by striking subparagraph (B), and

(iii) by redesignating subparagraphs (C) and (D) as subparagraphs (B) and (C), respectively, and

(B) in paragraph (2)(B), by amending clause (iv) to read as follows:

"(iv) CERTIFIED HISTORIC STRUCTURE.—Any expenditure attributable to the rehabilitation of a qualified rehabilitated building unless the rehabilitation is a certified rehabilitation (within the meaning of subparagraph (C)).".

(2) Paragraph (4) of section 145(d) is amended—

(A) by striking "of section 47(c)(1)(C)" each place it appears and inserting "of section 47(c)(1)(B)", and

(B) by striking "section 47(c)(1)(C)(i)" and inserting "section 47(c)(1)(B)(i)".

(c) EFFECTIVE DATE.—

(1) IN GENERAL.—Except as provided in paragraph (2), the amendments made by this section shall apply to amounts paid or incurred after December 31, 2017.

(2) TRANSITION RULE.—In the case of qualified rehabilitation expenditures with respect to any building—

(A) owned or leased by the taxpayer during the entirety of the period after December 31, 2017, and

(B) with respect to which the 24-month period selected by the taxpayer under clause (i) of section 47(c)(1)(B) of the Internal Revenue Code (as amended by subsection (b)), or the

60-month period applicable under clause (ii) of such section, begins not later than 180 days after the date of the enactment of this Act,

the amendments made by this section shall apply to such expenditures paid or incurred after the end of the taxable year in which the 24-month period, or the 60-month period, referred to in subparagraph (B) ends.

**SEC. 13403. EMPLOYER CREDIT FOR PAID FAMILY AND MEDICAL LEAVE.**

(a) IN GENERAL.—

(1) ALLOWANCE OF CREDIT.—Subpart D of part IV of subchapter A of chapter 1 is amended by adding at the end the following new section:

**"SEC. 45S. EMPLOYER CREDIT FOR PAID FAMILY AND MEDICAL LEAVE.**

"(a) ESTABLISHMENT OF CREDIT.—

"(1) IN GENERAL.—For purposes of section 38, in the case of an eligible employer, the paid family and medical leave credit is an amount equal to the applicable percentage of the amount of wages paid to qualifying employees during any period in which such employees are on family and medical leave.

"(2) APPLICABLE PERCENTAGE.—For purposes of paragraph (1), the term 'applicable percentage' means 12.5 percent increased (but not above 25 percent) by 0.25 percentage points for each percentage point by which the rate of payment (as described under subsection (c)(1)(B)) exceeds 50 percent.

"(b) LIMITATION.—

"(1) IN GENERAL.—The credit allowed under subsection (a) with respect to any employee for any taxable year shall not exceed an amount equal to the product of the normal hourly wage rate of such employee for each hour (or fraction thereof) of actual services performed for the employer and the number of hours (or fraction thereof) for which family and medical leave is taken.

"(2) NON-HOURLY WAGE RATE.—For purposes of paragraph (1), in the case of any employee who is not paid on an hourly wage rate, the wages of such employee shall be prorated to an hourly wage rate under regulations established by the Secretary.

"(3) MAXIMUM AMOUNT OF LEAVE SUBJECT TO CREDIT.—The amount of family and medical leave that may be taken into account with respect to any employee under subsection (a) for any taxable year shall not exceed 12 weeks.

"(c) ELIGIBLE EMPLOYER.—For purposes of this section—

"(1) IN GENERAL.—The term 'eligible employer' means any employer who has in place a written policy that meets the following requirements:

"(A) The policy provides—

"(i) in the case of a qualifying employee who is not a part-time employee (as defined in section 4980E(d)(4)(B)), not less than 2 weeks of annual paid family and medical leave, and

"(ii) in the case of a qualifying employee who is a part-time employee, an amount of annual paid family and medical leave that is not less than an amount which bears the same ratio to the amount of annual paid family and medical leave that is provided to a qualifying employee described in clause (i) as—

"(I) the number of hours the employee is expected to work during any week, bears to

"(II) the number of hours an equivalent qualifying employee described in clause (i) is expected to work during the week.

“(B) The policy requires that the rate of payment under the program is not less than 50 percent of the wages normally paid to such employee for services performed for the employer.

“(2) SPECIAL RULE FOR CERTAIN EMPLOYERS.—

“(A) IN GENERAL.—An added employer shall not be treated as an eligible employer unless such employer provides paid family and medical leave in compliance with a written policy which ensures that the employer—

“(i) will not interfere with, restrain, or deny the exercise of or the attempt to exercise, any right provided under the policy, and

“(ii) will not discharge or in any other manner discriminate against any individual for opposing any practice prohibited by the policy.

“(B) ADDED EMPLOYER; ADDED EMPLOYEE.—For purposes of this paragraph—

“(i) ADDED EMPLOYEE.—The term ‘added employee’ means a qualifying employee who is not covered by title I of the

Family and Medical Leave Act of 1993, as amended.

"(ii) ADDED EMPLOYER.—The term 'added employer' means an eligible employer (determined without regard to this paragraph), whether or not covered by that title I, who offers paid family and medical leave to added employees.

"(3) AGGREGATION RULE.—All persons which are treated as a single employer under subsections (a) and (b) of section 52 shall be treated as a single taxpayer.

"(4) TREATMENT OF BENEFITS MANDATED OR PAID FOR BY STATE OR LOCAL GOVERNMENTS.—For purposes of this section, any leave which is paid by a State or local government or required by State or local law shall not be taken into account in determining the amount of paid family and medical leave provided by the employer.

"(5) NO INFERENCE.—Nothing in this subsection shall be construed as subjecting an employer to any penalty, liability, or other consequence (other than ineligibility for the credit allowed by reason of subsection (a) or recapturing the benefit of such credit) for failure to comply with the requirements of this subsection.

"(d) QUALIFYING EMPLOYEES.—For purposes of this section, the term 'qualifying employee' means any employee (as defined in section 3(e) of the Fair Labor Standards Act of 1938, as amended) who—

"(1) has been employed by the employer for 1 year or more, and

"(2) for the preceding year, had compensation not in excess of an amount equal to 60 percent of the amount applicable for such year under clause (i) of section 414(q)(1)(B).

"(e) FAMILY AND MEDICAL LEAVE.—

"(1) IN GENERAL.—Except as provided in paragraph (2), for purposes of this section, the term 'family and medical leave' means leave for any 1 or more of the purposes described under subparagraph (A), (B), (C), (D), or (E) of paragraph (1), or paragraph (3), of section 102(a) of the Family and Medical Leave Act of 1993, as amended, whether the leave is provided under that Act or by a policy of the employer.

"(2) EXCLUSION.—If an employer provides paid leave as vacation leave, personal leave, or medical or sick leave (other than leave specifically for 1 or more of the purposes referred to in paragraph (1)), that paid leave shall not be considered to be family and medical leave under paragraph (1).

"(3) DEFINITIONS.—In this subsection, the terms 'vacation leave', 'personal leave', and 'medical or sick leave' mean those 3 types of leave, within the meaning of section 102(d)(2) of that Act.

"(f) DETERMINATIONS MADE BY SECRETARY OF TREASURY.—For purposes of this section, any determination as to whether an employer or an employee satisfies the applicable requirements for an eligible employer (as described in subsection (c)) or qualifying employee (as described in subsection (d)), respectively, shall be made by the Secretary based on such information, to be provided by the employer, as the Secretary determines to be necessary or appropriate.

"(g) WAGES.—For purposes of this section, the term 'wages' has the meaning given such term by subsection (b) of section 3306 (determined without regard to any dollar limitation contained in such section). Such term shall not include any amount taken into account for purposes of determining any other credit allowed under this subpart.

"(h) ELECTION TO HAVE CREDIT NOT APPLY.—

"(1) IN GENERAL.—A taxpayer may elect to have this section not apply for any taxable year.

"(2) OTHER RULES.—Rules similar to the rules of paragraphs (2) and (3) of section 51(j) shall apply for purposes of this subsection.

"(i) TERMINATION.—This section shall not apply to wages paid in taxable years beginning after December 31, 2019.".

(b) CREDIT PART OF GENERAL BUSINESS CREDIT.—Section 38(b) is amended by striking "plus" at the end of paragraph (35), by striking the period at the end of paragraph (36) and inserting ", plus", and by adding at the end the following new paragraph:

"(37) in the case of an eligible employer (as defined in section 45S(c)), the paid family and medical leave credit determined under section 45S(a).".

(c) CREDIT ALLOWED AGAINST AMT.—Subparagraph (B) of section 38(c)(4) is amended by redesignating clauses (ix) through (xi) as clauses (x) through (xii), respectively, and by inserting after clause (viii) the following new clause:

"(ix) the credit determined under section 45S,".

(d) CONFORMING AMENDMENTS.—

(1) DENIAL OF DOUBLE BENEFIT.—Section 280C(a) is amended by inserting "45S(a)," after "45P(a),".

(2) ELECTION TO HAVE CREDIT NOT APPLY.—Section 6501(m) is amended by inserting "45S(h)," after "45H(g),".

(3) CLERICAL AMENDMENT.—The table of sections for subpart D of part IV of subchapter A of chapter 1 is amended by adding at the end the following new item:

"Sec. 45S. Employer credit for paid family and medical leave.".

(e) EFFECTIVE DATE.—The amendments made by this section shall apply to wages paid in taxable years beginning after December 31, 2017.

**SEC. 13404. REPEAL OF TAX CREDIT BONDS.**

(a) IN GENERAL.—Part IV of subchapter A of chapter 1 is amended by striking subparts H, I, and J (and by striking the items relating to such subparts in the table of subparts for such part).

(b) PAYMENTS TO ISSUERS.—Subchapter B of chapter 65 is amended by striking section 6431 (and by striking the item relating to such section in the table of sections for such subchapter).

(c) CONFORMING AMENDMENTS.—

(1) Part IV of subchapter U of chapter 1 is

the item relating to such section in the table of sections for such part).

(2) Section 54(l)(3)(B) is amended by inserting "(as in effect before its repeal by the Tax Cuts and Jobs Act)" after "section 1397E(I)".

(3) Section 6211(b)(4)(A) is amended by striking ", and 6431" and inserting "and" before "36B".

(4) Section 6401(b)(1) is amended by striking "G, H, I, and J" and inserting "and G".

(d) EFFECTIVE DATE.—The amendments made by this section shall apply to bonds issued after December 31, 2017.

## PART VI—PROVISIONS RELATED TO SPECIFIC ENTITIES AND INDUSTRIES

### Subpart A—Partnership Provisions

#### SEC. 13501. TREATMENT OF GAIN OR LOSS OF FOREIGN PERSONS FROM SALE OR EXCHANGE OF INTERESTS IN PARTNERSHIPS ENGAGED IN TRADE OR BUSINESS WITHIN THE UNITED STATES.

(a) AMOUNT TREATED AS EFFECTIVELY CONNECTED.—

(1) IN GENERAL.—Section 864(c) is amended by adding at the end the following:

"(8) GAIN OR LOSS OF FOREIGN PERSONS FROM SALE OR EXCHANGE OF CERTAIN PARTNERSHIP INTERESTS.—

"(A) IN GENERAL.—Notwithstanding any other provision of this subtitle, if a nonresident alien individual or foreign corporation owns, directly or indirectly, an interest in a partnership which is engaged in any trade or business within the United States, gain or loss on the sale or exchange of all (or any portion of) such interest shall be treated as effectively connected with the conduct of such trade or business to the extent such gain or loss does not exceed the amount determined under subparagraph (B).

"(B) AMOUNT TREATED AS EFFECTIVELY CONNECTED.—The amount determined under this subparagraph with respect to any partnership interest sold or exchanged—

"(i) in the case of any gain on the sale or exchange of the partnership interest, is—

"(I) the portion of the partner's distributive share of the amount of gain which would have been effectively connected with the conduct of a trade or business within the United States if the partnership had sold all of its assets at their fair market value as of the date of the sale or exchange of such interest, or

"(II) zero if no gain on such deemed sale would have been so effectively connected, and

"(ii) in the case of any loss on the sale or exchange of the partnership interest, is—

"(I) the portion of the partner's distributive share of the amount of loss on the deemed sale described in clause (i)(I) which would have been so effectively connected, or

"(II) zero if no loss on such deemed sale would be have been so effectively connected.

For purposes of this subparagraph, a partner's distributive share of gain or loss on the deemed sale shall be determined in the same manner as such partner's distributive share of the non-separately stated taxable income or loss of such partnership.

"(C) COORDINATION WITH UNITED STATES REAL PROPERTY INTERESTS.—If a partnership described in subparagraph (A) holds any United States real property interest (as defined in section 897(c)) at the time of the sale or exchange of the partnership interest, then the gain or loss treated as effectively connected income under subparagraph (A) shall be reduced by the amount so treated with respect to such United States real property interest under section 897.

"(D) SALE OR EXCHANGE.—For purposes of this paragraph, the term 'sale or exchange' means any sale, exchange, or other disposition.

"(E) SECRETARIAL AUTHORITY.—The Secretary shall prescribe such regulations or other guidance as the Secretary determines appropriate for the application of this paragraph, including with respect to exchanges described in section 332, 351, 354, 355, 356, or 361.".

(2) CONFORMING AMENDMENTS.—Section 864(c)(1) is amended—

(A) by striking "and (7)" in subparagraph (A), and inserting "(7), and (8)", and

(B) by striking "or (7)" in subparagraph (B), and inserting "(7), or (8)".

(b) WITHHOLDING REQUIREMENTS.—Section 1446 is amended by redesignating subsection (f) as subsection (g) and by inserting after subsection (e) the following:

"(f) SPECIAL RULES FOR WITHHOLDING ON DISPOSITIONS OF PARTNERSHIP INTERESTS.—

"(1) IN GENERAL.—Except as provided in this subsection, if any portion of the gain (if any) on any disposition of an interest in a partnership would be treated under section 864(c)(8) as effectively connected with the conduct of a trade or business within the United States, the transferee shall be required to deduct and withhold a tax equal to 10 percent of the amount realized on the disposition.

"(2) EXCEPTION IF NONFOREIGN AFFIDAVIT FURNISHED.—

"(A) IN GENERAL.—No person shall be required to deduct and withhold any amount under paragraph (1) with respect to any disposition if the transferor furnishes to the transferee an affidavit by the transferor stating, under penalty of perjury, the transferor's United States taxpayer identification number and that the transferor is not a foreign person.

"(B) FALSE AFFIDAVIT.—Subparagraph (A) shall not apply to any disposition if—

"(i) the transferee has actual knowledge that the affidavit is false, or the transferee receives a notice (as described in section 1445(d)) from a transferor's agent or transferee's agent that such affidavit or statement is false, or

"(ii) the Secretary by regulations requires the transferee to furnish a copy of such affidavit or statement to the Secretary and the transferee fails to furnish a copy of such affidavit or statement to the Secretary at such time and in such manner as required by such regulations.

"(C) RULES FOR AGENTS.—The rules of section 1445(d) shall apply to a transferor's agent or transferee's agent with respect to any affidavit described in subparagraph (A) in the same manner as such rules apply with respect to the disposition of a United States real property interest under such section.

"(3) AUTHORITY OF SECRETARY TO PRESCRIBE REDUCED AMOUNT.—At the request of the transferor or transferee, the Secretary may prescribe a reduced amount to be withheld under this section if the Secretary determines that to substitute such reduced amount will not jeopardize the collection of the tax imposed under this title with respect to gain treated under section 864(c)(8) as effectively connected with the conduct of a trade or business within the United States.

"(4) PARTNERSHIP TO WITHHOLD AMOUNTS NOT WITHHELD BY THE TRANSFEREE.—If a transferee fails to withhold any amount required to be withheld under paragraph (1), the partnership shall be required to deduct and withhold from distributions to the transferee a tax in an amount equal to the amount the transferee failed to withhold (plus interest under this title on such amount).

"(5) DEFINITIONS.—Any term used in this subsection which is also used under section 1445 shall have the same meaning as when used in such section.

"(6) REGULATIONS.—The Secretary shall prescribe such regulations or other guidance as may be necessary to carry out the purposes of this subsection, including regulations providing for exceptions from the provisions of this subsection.".

(c) EFFECTIVE DATES.—

(1) SUBSECTION (a).—The amendments made by subsection (a) shall apply to sales, exchanges, and dispositions on or after November 27, 2017.

(2) SUBSECTION (b).—The amendment made by subsection (b) shall apply to sales, exchanges, and dispositions after December 31, 2017.

**SEC. 13502. MODIFY DEFINITION OF SUBSTANTIAL BUILT-IN LOSS IN THE CASE OF TRANSFER OF PARTNERSHIP INTEREST.**

(a) IN GENERAL.—Paragraph (1) of section 743(d) is to read as follows:

"(1) IN GENERAL.—For purposes of this section, a partnership has a substantial built-in loss with respect to a transfer of an interest in the partnership if—

"(A) the partnership's adjusted basis in the partnership property exceeds by more than $250,000 the fair market value of such property, or

"(B) the transferee partner would be allocated a loss of more than $250,000 if the partnership assets were sold for cash equal to their fair market value immediately after such transfer.".

(b) EFFECTIVE DATE.—The amendments made by this section shall apply to transfers of partnership interests after December 31, 2017.

**SEC. 13503. CHARITABLE CONTRIBUTIONS AND FOREIGN TAXES TAKEN INTO ACCOUNT IN DETERMINING LIMITATION ON ALLOWANCE OF PARTNER'S SHARE OF LOSS.**

(a) IN GENERAL.—Subsection (d) of section 704 is amended—

(1) by striking "A partner's distributive share" and inserting the following:

"(1) IN GENERAL.—A partner's distributive share",

(2) by striking "Any excess of such loss" and inserting the following:

"(2) CARRYOVER.—Any excess of such loss", and

(3) by adding at the end the following new paragraph:

"(3) SPECIAL RULES.—

"(A) IN GENERAL.—In determining the amount of any loss under paragraph (1), there shall be taken into account the partner's distributive share of amounts described in paragraphs (4) and (6) of section 702(a).

"(B) EXCEPTION.—In the case of a charitable contribution of property whose fair market value exceeds its adjusted basis, subparagraph (A) shall not apply to the extent of the partner's distributive share of such excess.".

(b) EFFECTIVE DATE.—The amendments made by this section shall apply to partnership taxable years beginning after December 31, 2017.

**SEC. 13504. REPEAL OF TECHNICAL TERMINATION OF PARTNERSHIPS.**

(a) IN GENERAL.—Paragraph (1) of section 708(b) is amended—

(1) by striking ", or" at the end of subparagraph (A) and all that follows and inserting a period, and

(2) by striking "only if—" and all that follows through "no part of any business" and inserting the following: "only if no part of any business".

(b) CONFORMING AMENDMENT.—

(1) Section 168(i)(7)(B) is amended by striking the second sentence.

(2) Section 743(e) is amended by striking paragraph (4) and redesignating paragraphs (5), (6), and (7) as paragraphs (4), (5), and (6).

(c) EFFECTIVE DATE.—The amendments made by this section shall apply to partnership taxable years beginning after December 31, 2017.

### Subpart B—Insurance Reforms

**SEC. 13511. NET OPERATING LOSSES OF LIFE INSURANCE COMPANIES.**

(a) IN GENERAL.—Section 805(b) is amended by striking paragraph (4) and by redesignating paragraph (5) as paragraph (4).

(b) CONFORMING AMENDMENTS.—

(1) Part I of subchapter L of chapter 1 is amended by striking section 810 (and by striking the item relating to such section in the table of sections for such part).

(2)(A) Part III of subchapter L of chapter 1 is amended by striking section 844 (and by striking the item relating to such section in the table of sections for such part).

(B) Section 831(b)(3) is amended by striking "except as provided in section 844,"

(3) Section 381 is amended by striking subsection (d).

(4) Section 805(a)(4)(B)(ii) is amended to read as follows:

"(ii) the deduction allowed under section 172,".

(5) Section 805(a) is amended by striking paragraph (5).

(6) Section 805(b)(2)(A)(iv) is amended to read as follows:

"(iv) any net operating loss carryback to the taxable year under section 172, and".

(7) Section 953(b)(1)(B) is amended to read as follows:

"(B) So much of section 805(a)(8) as relates to the deduction allowed under section 172.".

(8) Section 1351(i)(3) is amended by striking "or the operations loss deduction under section 810,".

(c) Effective Date.—The amendments made by this section shall apply to losses arising in taxable years beginning after December 31, 2017.

## SEC. 13512. REPEAL OF SMALL LIFE INSURANCE COMPANY DEDUCTION.

(a) In General.—Part I of subchapter L of chapter 1 is amended by striking section 806 (and by striking the item relating to such section in the table of sections for such part).

(b) CONFORMING AMENDMENTS.—

(1) Section 453B(e) is amended—

(A) by striking "(as defined in section 806(b)(3))" in paragraph (2)(B), and

(B) by adding at the end the following new paragraph:

"(3) NONINSURANCE BUSINESS.—

"(A) IN GENERAL.—For purposes of this subsection, the term 'noninsurance business' means any activity which is not an insurance business.

"(B) CERTAIN ACTIVITIES TREATED AS INSURANCE BUSINESSES.—For purposes of subparagraph (A), any activity which is not an insurance business shall be treated as an insurance business if—

"(i) it is of a type traditionally carried on by life insurance companies for investment purposes, but only if the carrying on of such activity (other than in the case of real estate) does not constitute the active conduct of a trade or business, or "(ii) it involves the performance of administrative services in connection with plans providing life insurance, pension, or accident and health benefits.".

(2) Section 465(c)(7)(D)(v)(II) is amended by striking "section 806(b)(3)" and inserting "section 453B(e)(3)".

(3) Section 801(a)(2) is amended by striking subparagraph (C).

(4) Section 804 is amended by striking "means—" and all that follows and inserting "means the general deductions provided in section 805.".

(5) Section 805(a)(4)(B), as amended by this Act, is amended by striking clause (i) and by redesignating clauses (ii), (iii), and (iv) as clauses (i), (ii), and (iii), respectively.

(6) Section 805(b)(2)(A), as amended by this Act, is amended by striking clause (iii) and by redesignating clauses (iv) and (v) as clauses (iii) and (iv), respectively.

(7) Section 842(c) is amended by striking paragraph (1) and by redesignating paragraphs (2) and (3) as paragraphs (1) and (2), respectively.

(8) Section 953(b)(1), as amended by section 13511, is amended by striking subparagraph (A) and by redesignating subparagraphs (B) and (C) as subparagraphs (A) and (B), respectively.

(c) EFFECTIVE DATE.—The amendments made by this section shall apply to taxable years beginning after December 31, 2017.

**SEC. 13513. ADJUSTMENT FOR CHANGE IN COMPUTING RESERVES.**

(a) IN GENERAL.—Paragraph (1) of section 807(f) is amended to read as follows:

"(1) TREATMENT AS CHANGE IN METHOD OF ACCOUNTING.—If the basis for determining any item referred to in subsection (c) as of the close of any taxable year differs from the basis for such determination as of the close of the preceding taxable year, then so much of the difference between—

"(A) the amount of the item at the close of the taxable year, computed on the new basis, and

"(B) the amount of the item at the close of the taxable year, computed on the old basis,

as is attributable to contracts issued before the taxable year shall be taken into account under section 481 as adjustments attributable to a change in method of accounting initiated by the taxpayer and made with the consent of the Secretary.''.

(b) EFFECTIVE DATE.—The amendments made by this section shall apply to taxable years beginning after December 31, 2017.

**SEC. 13514. REPEAL OF SPECIAL RULE FOR DISTRIBUTIONS TO SHAREHOLDERS FROM PRE-1984 POLICYHOLDERS SURPLUS ACCOUNT.**

(a) IN GENERAL.—Subpart D of part I of subchapter L is amended by striking section 815 (and by striking the item relating to such section in the table of sections for such subpart).

(b) CONFORMING AMENDMENT.—Section 801 is amended by striking subsection (c).

(c) EFFECTIVE DATE.—The amendments made by this section shall apply to taxable years beginning after December 31, 2017.

(d) PHASED INCLUSION OF REMAINING BALANCE OF POLICYHOLDERS SURPLUS ACCOUNTS.—In the case of any stock life insurance company which has a balance (determined as of the close of such company's last taxable year beginning before January 1, 2018) in an existing policyholders surplus account (as defined in section 815 of the Internal Revenue Code of 1986, as in effect before its repeal), the tax imposed by section 801 of such Code for the first 8 taxable years beginning after December 31, 2017, shall be the amount which would be imposed by such section for such year on the sum of—

(1) life insurance company taxable income for such year (within the meaning of such section 801 but not less than zero), plus

(2) 1⁄8 of such balance.

**SEC. 13515. MODIFICATION OF PRORATION RULES FOR PROPERTY AND CASUALTY INSURANCE COMPANIES.**

(a) IN GENERAL.—Section 832(b)(5)(B) is amended—

(1) by striking "15 percent" and inserting "the applicable percentage", and

(2) by inserting at the end the following new sentence: "For purposes of this subparagraph, the applicable percentage is 5.25 percent divided by the highest rate in effect under section 11(b).".

(b) EFFECTIVE DATE.—The amendments made by this section shall apply to taxable years beginning after December 31, 2017.

**SEC. 13516. REPEAL OF SPECIAL ESTIMATED TAX PAYMENTS.**

(a) IN GENERAL.—Part III of subchapter L of chapter 1 is amended by striking section 847 (and by striking the item relating to such section in the table of sections for such part).

(b) EFFECTIVE DATE.—The amendments made by this section shall apply to taxable years beginning after December 31, 2017.

**SEC. 13517. COMPUTATION OF LIFE INSURANCE TAX RESERVES.**

(a) IN GENERAL.—

(1) APPROPRIATE RATE OF INTEREST.—The second sentence of section 807(c) is amended to read as follows: "For purposes of paragraph (3), the appropriate rate of interest is the highest rate or rates permitted to be used to discount the obligations by the National Association of Insurance Commissioners as of the date the reserve is determined.".

(2) METHOD OF COMPUTING RESERVES.—Section 807(d) is amended—

(A) by striking paragraphs (1), (2), (4), and (5),

(B) by redesignating paragraph (6) as paragraph (4),

(C) by inserting before paragraph (3) the following new paragraphs:

"(1) DETERMINATION OF RESERVE.—

"(A) IN GENERAL.—For purposes of this part (other than section 816), the amount of the life insurance reserves for any contract (other than a contract to which subparagraph (B) applies) shall be the greater of—

"(i) the net surrender value of such contract, or

"(ii) 92.81 percent of the reserve determined under paragraph (2).

"(B) VARIABLE CONTRACTS.—For purposes of this part (other than section 816), the amount of the life insurance reserves for a variable contract shall be equal to the sum of—

"(i) the greater of—

"(I) the net surrender value of such contract, or

"(II) the portion of the reserve that is separately accounted for under section 817, plus

"(ii) 92.81 percent of the excess (if any) of the reserve determined under paragraph (2) over the amount in clause (i).

"(C) STATUTORY CAP.—In no event shall the reserves determined under subparagraphs (A) or (B) for any contract as of any time exceed the amount which would be taken into account with respect to such contract as of such time in determining statutory reserves (as defined in paragraph (4)).

"(D) NO DOUBLE COUNTING.—In no event shall any amount or item be taken into account more than once in determining any reserve under this subchapter.

"(2) AMOUNT OF RESERVE.—The amount of the reserve determined under this paragraph with respect to any contract shall be determined by using the tax reserve method applicable to such contract.".

(D) by striking "(other than a qualified long-term care insurance contract, as defined in section 7702B(b)), a 2-year full preliminary term method" in paragraph (3)(A)(iii) and inserting ", the reserve method prescribed by the National Association of Insurance Commissioners which covers such contract as of the date the reserve is determined",

(E) by striking "(as of the date of issuance)" in paragraph (3)(A)(iv)(I) and inserting "(as of the date the reserve is determined)",

(F) by striking "as of the date of the issuance of" in paragraph (3)(A)(iv)(II) and inserting "as of the date the reserve is determined for",

(G) by striking "in effect on the date of the issuance of the contract" in paragraph (3)(B)(i) and inserting "applicable to the contract and in effect as of the date the reserve is determined", and

(H) by striking "in effect on the date of the issuance of the contract" in paragraph (3)(B)(ii) and inserting "applicable to the contract and in effect as of the date the reserve is determined".

(3) SPECIAL RULES.—Section 807(e) is amended—

(A) by striking paragraphs (2) and (5),

(B) by redesignating paragraphs (3), (4), (6), and (7) as paragraphs (2), (3), (4), and (5), respectively,

(C) by amending paragraph (2) (as so redesignated) to read as follows:

"(2) QUALIFIED SUPPLEMENTAL BENEFITS.—

"(A) QUALIFIED SUPPLEMENTAL BENEFITS TREATED SEPARATELY.—For purposes of this part, the amount of the life insurance reserve for any qualified supplemental benefit shall be computed separately as though such benefit were under a separate contract.

"(B) QUALIFIED SUPPLEMENTAL BENEFIT.—For purposes of this paragraph, the term 'qualified supplemental benefit' means any supplemental benefit described in subparagraph (C) if—

"(i) there is a separately identified premium or charge for such benefit, and

"(ii) any net surrender value under the contract attributable to any other benefit is not available to fund such benefit.

"(C) SUPPLEMENTAL BENEFITS.—For purposes of this paragraph, the supplemental benefits described in this subparagraph are any—

"(i) guaranteed insurability,

"(ii) accidental death or disability benefit,

"(iii) convertibility,

"(iv) disability waiver benefit, or

"(v) other benefit prescribed by regulations,

which is supplemental to a contract for which there is a reserve described in subsection (c).", and

(D) by adding at the end the following new paragraph:

"(6) REPORTING RULES.—The Secretary shall require reporting (at such time and in such manner as the Secretary shall prescribe) with respect to the opening balance and closing balance of reserves and with respect to the method of computing reserves for purposes of determining income.".

(4) DEFINITION OF LIFE INSURANCE CONTRACT.—Section 7702 is amended—

(A) by striking clause (i) of subsection (c)(3)(B) and inserting the following:

"(i) reasonable mortality charges which meet the requirements prescribed in regulations to be promulgated by the Secretary or that do not exceed the mortality charges specified in the prevailing commissioners' standard tables as defined in subsection (f)(10)," and

(B) by adding at the end of subsection (f) the following new paragraph:

"(10) Prevailing commissioners' standard tables.—For purposes of subsection (c)(3)(B)(i), the term 'prevailing commissioners' standard tables' means the most recent commissioners' standard tables prescribed by the National Association of Insurance Commissioners which are permitted to be used in computing reserves for that type of contract under the insurance laws of at least 26 States when the contract was issued. If the prevailing commissioners' standard tables as of the beginning of any calendar year (hereinafter in this paragraph referred to as the 'year of change') are different from the prevailing commissioners' standard tables as of the beginning of the preceding calendar year, the issuer may use the prevailing commissioners' standard tables as of the beginning of the preceding calendar year with respect to any contract issued after the change and before the close of the 3-year period beginning on the first day of the year of change.".

(b) Conforming Amendments.—

(1) Section 808 is amended by adding at the end the following new subsection:

"(g) Prevailing State Assumed Interest Rate.—For purposes of this subchapter—

"(1) IN GENERAL.—The term 'prevailing State assumed interest rate' means, with respect to any contract, the highest assumed interest rate permitted to be used in computing life insurance reserves for insurance contracts or annuity contracts (as the case may be) under the insurance laws of at least 26 States. For purposes of the preceding sentence, the effect of nonforfeiture laws of a State on interest rates for reserves shall not be taken into account.

"(2) WHEN RATE DETERMINED.—The prevailing State assumed interest rate with respect to any contract shall be determined as of the beginning of the calendar year in which the contract was issued.".

(2) Paragraph (1) of section 811(d) is amended by striking "the greater of the prevailing State assumed interest rate or applicable Federal interest rate in effect under section 807" and inserting "the interest rate in effect under section 808(g)".

(3) Subparagraph (A) of section 846(f)(6) is amended by striking "except that" and all that follows and inserting "except that the limitation of subsection (a)(3) shall apply, and":

(4) Section 848(e)(1)(B)(iii) is amended by striking "807(e)(4)" and inserting "807(e)(3)".

(5) Subparagraph (B) of section 954(i)(5) is amended by striking "shall be substituted for the prevailing State assumed interest rate," and inserting "shall apply,".

(c) EFFECTIVE DATE.—

(1) IN GENERAL.—The amendments made by this section shall apply to taxable years beginning after December 31, 2017.

(2) TRANSITION RULE.—For the first taxable year beginning after December 31, 2017, the reserve with respect to any contract (as determined under section 807(d) of the Internal Revenue Code of 1986) at the end of the preceding taxable year shall be determined as if the amendments made by this section had applied to such reserve in such preceding taxable year.

(3) TRANSITION RELIEF.—

(A) IN GENERAL.—If—

(i) the reserve determined under section 807(d) of the Internal Revenue Code of 1986 (determined after application of paragraph (2)) with respect to any contract as of the close of the year preceding the first taxable year beginning after December 31, 2017, differs from

(ii) the reserve which would have been determined with respect to such contract as of the close of such taxable year under such section determined without regard to paragraph (2),

then the difference between the amount of the reserve described in clause (i) and the amount of the reserve described in clause (ii) shall be taken into account under the method provided in subparagraph (B).

(B) METHOD.—The method provided in this subparagraph is as follows:

(i) If the amount determined under subparagraph (A)(i) exceeds the amount determined under subparagraph (A)(ii), 1/8 of such excess shall be taken into account, for each of the 8 succeeding taxable years, as a deduction under section 805(a)(2) or 832(c)(4) of such Code, as applicable.

(ii) If the amount determined under subparagraph (A)(ii) exceeds the amount determined under subparagraph (A)(i), 1/8 of such excess shall be included in gross income, for each of the 8 succeeding taxable years, under section 803(a)(2) or 832(b)(1)(C) of such Code, as applicable.

**SEC. 13518. MODIFICATION OF RULES FOR LIFE INSURANCE PRORATION FOR PURPOSES OF DETERMINING THE DIVIDENDS RECEIVED DEDUCTION.**

(a) IN GENERAL.—Section 812 is amended to read as follows:

**"SEC. 812. DEFINITION OF COMPANY'S SHARE AND POLICYHOLDER'S SHARE.**

"(a) COMPANY'S SHARE.—For purposes of section 805(a)(4), the term 'company's share' means, with respect to any taxable year beginning after December 31, 2017, 70 percent.

"(b) POLICYHOLDER'S SHARE.—For purposes of section 807, the term 'policyholder's share' means, with respect to any taxable year beginning after December 31, 2017, 30 percent.".

(b) CONFORMING AMENDMENT.—Section 817A(e)(2) is amended by striking ", 807(d)(2)(B), and 812" and inserting "and 807(d)(2)(B)".

(c) Effective Date.—The amendments made by this section shall apply to taxable years beginning after December 31, 2017.

**SEC. 13519. CAPITALIZATION OF CERTAIN POLICY ACQUISITION EXPENSES.**

(a) In General.—

(1) Section 848(a)(2) is amended by striking "120-month" and inserting "180-month".

(2) Section 848(c)(1) is amended by striking "1.75 percent" and inserting "2.09 percent".

(3) Section 848(c)(2) is amended by striking "2.05 percent" and inserting "2.45 percent".

(4) Section 848(c)(3) is amended by striking "7.7 percent" and inserting "9.2 percent".

(b) Conforming Amendments.—Section 848(b)(1) is amended by striking "120-month" and inserting "180-month".

(c) Effective Date.—

(1) In general.—The amendments made by this section shall apply to net premiums for taxable years beginning after December 31, 2017.

(2) Transition rule.—Specified policy acquisition expenses first required to be capitalized in a taxable year beginning before January 1, 2018, will continue to be allowed as a deduction ratably over

the 120-month period beginning with the first month in the second half of such taxable year.

**SEC. 13520. TAX REPORTING FOR LIFE SETTLEMENT TRANSACTIONS.**

(a) IN GENERAL.—Subpart B of part III of subchapter A of chapter 61, as amended by section 13306, is amended by adding at the end the following new section:

**"SEC. 6050Y. RETURNS RELATING TO CERTAIN LIFE INSURANCE CONTRACT TRANSACTIONS.**

"(a) REQUIREMENT OF REPORTING OF CERTAIN PAYMENTS.—

"(1) IN GENERAL.—Every person who acquires a life insurance contract or any interest in a life insurance contract in a reportable policy sale during any taxable year shall make a return for such taxable year (at such time and in such manner as the Secretary shall prescribe) setting forth—

"(A) the name, address, and TIN of such person,

"(B) the name, address, and TIN of each recipient of payment in the reportable policy sale,

"(C) the date of such sale,

"(D) the name of the issuer of the life insurance contract sold and the policy number of such contract, and

"(E) the amount of each payment.

"(2) STATEMENT TO BE FURNISHED TO PERSONS WITH RESPECT TO WHOM INFORMATION IS REQUIRED.—Every person required to make a return under this subsection shall furnish to each person whose name is required to be set forth in such return a written statement showing—

"(A) the name, address, and phone number of the information contact of the person required to make such return, and

"(B) the information required to be shown on such return with respect to such person, except that in the case of an issuer of a life insurance contract, such statement is not required to include the information specified in paragraph (1)(E).

"(b) REQUIREMENT OF REPORTING OF SELLER'S BASIS IN LIFE INSURANCE CONTRACTS.—

"(1) IN GENERAL.—Upon receipt of the statement required under subsection (a)(2) or upon notice of a transfer of a life insurance contract to a foreign person, each issuer of a life insurance contract shall make a return (at such time and in such manner as the Secretary shall prescribe) setting forth—

"(A) the name, address, and TIN of the seller who transfers any interest in such contract in such sale,

"(B) the investment in the contract (as defined in section 72(e)(6)) with respect to such seller, and

"(C) the policy number of such contract.

"(2) STATEMENT TO BE FURNISHED TO PERSONS WITH RESPECT TO WHOM INFORMATION IS REQUIRED.—Every person required to make a return under this subsection shall furnish to each person whose name is required to be set forth in such return a written statement showing—

"(A) the name, address, and phone number of the information contact of the person required to make such return, and

"(B) the information required to be shown on such return with respect to each seller whose name is required to be set forth in such return.

"(c) REQUIREMENT OF REPORTING WITH RESPECT TO REPORTABLE DEATH BENEFITS.—

"(1) IN GENERAL.—Every person who makes a payment of reportable death benefits during any taxable year shall make a return for such taxable year (at such time and in such manner as the Secretary shall prescribe) setting forth—

"(A) the name, address, and TIN of the person making such payment,

"(B) the name, address, and TIN of each recipient of such payment,

"(C) the date of each such payment,

"(D) the gross amount of each such payment, and

"(E) such person's estimate of the investment in the contract (as defined in section 72(e)(6)) with respect to the buyer.

"(2) STATEMENT TO BE FURNISHED TO PERSONS WITH RESPECT TO WHOM INFORMATION IS REQUIRED.—Every person required to make a return under this subsection shall furnish to each person whose name is required to be set forth in such return a written statement showing—

"(A) the name, address, and phone number of the information contact of the person required to make such return, and

"(B) the information required to be shown on such return with respect to each recipient of payment whose name is required to be set forth in such return.

"(d) DEFINITIONS.—For purposes of this section:

"(1) PAYMENT.—The term 'payment' means, with respect to any reportable policy sale, the amount of cash and the fair market value of any consideration transferred in the sale.

"(2) REPORTABLE POLICY SALE.—The term 'reportable policy sale' has the meaning given such term in section 101(a)(3)(B).

"(3) ISSUER.—The term 'issuer' means any life insurance company that bears the risk with respect to a life insurance contract on the date any return or statement is required to be made under this section.

"(4) REPORTABLE DEATH BENEFITS.—The term 'reportable death benefits' means amounts paid by reason of the death of the insured under a life insurance contract that has been transferred in a reportable policy sale.".

(b) CLERICAL AMENDMENT.—The table of sections for subpart B of part III of subchapter A of chapter 61, as amended by section 13306, is amended by inserting after the item relating to section 6050X the following new item:

"Sec. 6050Y. Returns relating to certain life insurance contract transactions.".

(c) CONFORMING AMENDMENTS.—

(1) Subsection (d) of section 6724 is amended—

(A) by striking "or" at the end of clause (xxiv) of paragraph (1)(B), by striking "and" at the end of clause (xxv) of such paragraph and inserting "or", and by inserting after such clause (xxv) the following new clause:

"(xxvi) section 6050Y (relating to returns relating to certain life insurance contract transactions), and", and

(B) by striking "or" at the end of subparagraph (HH) of paragraph (2), by striking the period at the end of subparagraph (II) of such paragraph and inserting ", or", and by inserting after such subparagraph (II) the following new subparagraph:

"(JJ) subsection (a)(2), (b)(2), or (c)(2) of section 6050Y (relating to returns relating to certain life insurance contract transactions).".

(2) Section 6047 is amended—

(A) by redesignating subsection (g) as sub-

(B) by inserting after subsection (f) the following new subsection:

"(g) INFORMATION RELATING TO LIFE INSURANCE CONTRACT TRANSACTIONS.—This section shall not apply to any information which is required to be reported under section 6050Y.", and

(C) by adding at the end of subsection (h), as so redesignated, the following new paragraph:

"(4) For provisions requiring reporting of information relating to certain life insurance contract transactions, see section 6050Y.".

(d) EFFECTIVE DATE.—The amendments made by this section shall apply to—

(1) reportable policy sales (as defined in section 6050Y(d)(2) of the Internal Revenue Code of 1986 (as added by subsection (a)) after December 31, 2017, and

(2) reportable death benefits (as defined in section 6050Y(d)(4) of such Code (as added by subsection (a)) paid after December 31, 2017.

**SEC. 13521. CLARIFICATION OF TAX BASIS OF LIFE INSURANCE CONTRACTS.**

(a) CLARIFICATION WITH RESPECT TO ADJUSTMENTS.—Paragraph (1) of section 1016(a) is amended by striking subparagraph (A) and all that follows and inserting the following:

"(A) for—

"(i) taxes or other carrying charges described in section 266; or

"(ii) expenditures described in section 173 (relating to circulation expenditures),

for which deductions have been taken by the taxpayer in determining taxable income for the taxable year or prior taxable years; or

"(B) for mortality, expense, or other reasonable charges incurred under an annuity or life insurance contract;".

(b) EFFECTIVE DATE.—The amendment made by this section shall apply to transactions entered into after August 25, 2009.

**SEC. 13522. EXCEPTION TO TRANSFER FOR VALUABLE CONSIDERATION RULES.**

(a) IN GENERAL.—Subsection (a) of section 101 is amended by inserting after paragraph (2) the following new paragraph:

"(3) EXCEPTION TO VALUABLE CONSIDERATION RULES FOR COMMERCIAL TRANSFERS.—

"(A) IN GENERAL.—The second sentence of paragraph (2) shall not apply in the case of a transfer of a life insurance contract, or any interest therein, which is a reportable policy sale.

"(B) REPORTABLE POLICY SALE.—For purposes of this paragraph, the term 'reportable policy sale' means the acquisition of an interest in a life insurance contract, directly or indirectly, if the acquirer has no substantial family, business, or financial relationship with the insured apart from the acquirer's interest in such life insurance contract. For purposes of the preceding sentence, the term 'indirectly' applies to the acquisition of an interest in a partnership, trust, or other entity that holds an interest in the life insurance contract.".

(b) CONFORMING AMENDMENT.—Paragraph (1) of section 101(a) is amended by striking "paragraph (2)" and inserting "paragraphs (2) and (3)".

(c) EFFECTIVE DATE.—The amendments made by this section shall apply to transfers after December 31, 2017.

**SEC. 13523. MODIFICATION OF DISCOUNTING RULES FOR PROPERTY AND CASUALTY INSURANCE COMPANIES.**

(a) MODIFICATION OF RATE OF INTEREST USED TO DISCOUNT UNPAID LOSSES.—Paragraph (2) of section 846(c) is amended to read as follows:

"(2) DETERMINATION OF ANNUAL RATE.—The annual rate determined by the Secretary under this paragraph for any calendar year shall be a rate determined on the basis of the corporate bond yield curve (as defined in section 430(h)(2)(D)(i), determined by substituting '60-month period' for '24-month period' therein).".

(b) MODIFICATION OF COMPUTATIONAL RULES FOR LOSS PAYMENT PATTERNS.—Section 846(d)(3) is amended by striking subparagraphs (B) through (G) and inserting the following new subparagraph:

"(B) TREATMENT OF CERTAIN LOSSES.—

"(i) 3-YEAR LOSS PAYMENT PATTERN.—In the case of any line of business not described in subparagraph (A)(ii), losses paid after the 1st year following the accident year shall be treated as paid equally in the 2nd and 3rd year following the accident year.

"(ii) 10-YEAR LOSS PAYMENT PATTERN.—

"(I) IN GENERAL.—The period taken into account under subparagraph (A)(ii) shall be extended to the extent required under subclause (II).

"(II) COMPUTATION OF EXTENSION.—The amount of losses which would have been treated as paid in the 10th year after the accident year shall be treated as paid in such 10th year and each subsequent year in an amount equal to the amount of the average of the losses treated as paid in the 7th, 8th, and 9th years after the accident year (or, if lesser, the portion of the unpaid losses not theretofore taken into account). To the extent such unpaid losses have not been treated as paid before the 24th year after the accident year, they shall be treated as paid in such 24th year.".

(c) REPEAL OF HISTORICAL PAYMENT PATTERN ELECTION.—Section 846, as amended by this Act, is amended by striking subsection (e) and by redesignating subsections (f) and (g) as subsections (e) and (f), respectively.

(d) EFFECTIVE DATE.—The amendments made by this section shall apply to taxable years beginning after December 31, 2017.

(e) TRANSITIONAL RULE.—For the first taxable year beginning after December 31, 2017—

(1) the unpaid losses and the expenses unpaid (as defined in paragraphs (5)(B) and (6) of section 832(b) of the Internal Revenue Code of 1986) at the end of the preceding taxable year, and

(2) the unpaid losses as defined in sections 807(c)(2) and 805(a)(1) of such Code at the end of the preceding taxable year,

shall be determined as if the amendments made by this section had applied to such unpaid losses and expenses unpaid in the preceding taxable year and by using the interest rate and loss payment patterns applicable to accident years ending with calendar year 2018, and any adjustment shall be taken into account ratably in such first taxable year and the 7 succeeding taxable years. For subsequent taxable years, such amendments shall be applied with respect to such unpaid losses and expenses unpaid by using the interest rate and loss payment patterns applicable to accident years ending with calendar year 2018.

### Subpart C—Banks and Financial Instruments

**SEC. 13531. LIMITATION ON DEDUCTION FOR FDIC PREMIUMS.**

(a) IN GENERAL.—Section 162, as amended by sections 13307, is amended by redesignating subsection (r) as subsection (s) and by inserting after subsection (q) the following new subsection:

"(r) DISALLOWANCE OF FDIC PREMIUMS PAID BY CERTAIN LARGE FINANCIAL INSTITUTIONS.—

"(1) IN GENERAL.—No deduction shall be allowed for the applicable percentage of any FDIC premium paid or incurred by the taxpayer.

"(2) EXCEPTION FOR SMALL INSTITUTIONS.—Paragraph (1) shall not apply to any taxpayer for any taxable year if the total consolidated assets of such taxpayer (determined as of the close of such taxable year) do not exceed $10,000,000,000.

"(3) APPLICABLE PERCENTAGE.—For purposes of this subsection, the term 'applicable percentage' means, with respect to any taxpayer for any taxable year, the ratio (expressed as a percentage but not greater than 100 percent) which—

"(A) the excess of—

"(i) the total consolidated assets of such taxpayer (determined as of the close

"(ii) $10,000,000,000, bears to

"(B) $40,000,000,000.

"(4) FDIC PREMIUMS.—For purposes of this subsection, the term 'FDIC premium' means any assessment imposed under section 7(b) of the Federal Deposit Insurance Act (12 U.S.C. 1817(b)).

"(5) TOTAL CONSOLIDATED ASSETS.—For purposes of this subsection, the term 'total consolidated assets' has the meaning given such term under section 165 of the Dodd-Frank Wall Street Reform and Consumer Protection Act (12 U.S.C. 5365).

"(6) AGGREGATION RULE.—

"(A) IN GENERAL.—Members of an expanded affiliated group shall be treated as a single taxpayer for purposes of applying this subsection.

"(B) EXPANDED AFFILIATED GROUP.—

"(i) IN GENERAL.—For purposes of this paragraph, the term 'expanded affiliated group' means an affiliated group as defined in section 1504(a), determined—

"(I) by substituting 'more than 50 percent' for 'at least 80 percent' each place it appears, and

"(II) without regard to paragraphs (2) and (3) of section 1504(b).

"(ii) CONTROL OF NON-CORPORATE ENTITIES.—A partnership or any other entity (other than a corporation) shall be treated as a member of an expanded affiliated group if such entity is controlled (within the meaning of section 954(d)(3)) by members of such group (including any entity treated as a member of such group by reason of this clause).".

(b) EFFECTIVE DATE.—The amendments made by this section shall apply to taxable years beginning after December 31, 2017.

**SEC. 13532. REPEAL OF ADVANCE REFUNDING BONDS.**

(a) IN GENERAL.—Paragraph (1) of section 149(d) is amended by striking "as part of an issue described in paragraph (2), (3), or (4)." and inserting "to advance refund another bond.".

(b) CONFORMING AMENDMENTS.—

(1) Section 149(d) is amended by striking paragraphs (2), (3), (4), and (6) and by redesignating paragraphs (5) and (7) as paragraphs (2) and (3).

(2) Section 148(f)(4)(C) is amended by striking clause (xiv) and by redesignating clauses (xv) to (xvii) as clauses (xiv) to (xvi).

(c) EFFECTIVE DATE.—The amendments made by this section shall apply to advance refunding bonds issued after December 31, 2017.

### Subpart D—S Corporations

#### SEC. 13541. EXPANSION OF QUALIFYING BENEFICIARIES OF AN ELECTING SMALL BUSINESS TRUST.

(a) NO LOOK-THROUGH FOR ELIGIBILITY PURPOSES.—Section 1361(c)(2)(B)(v) is amended by adding at the end the following new sentence: "This clause shall not apply for purposes of subsection (b)(1)(C).".

(b) EFFECTIVE DATE.—The amendment made by this section shall take effect on January 1, 2018.

#### SEC. 13542. CHARITABLE CONTRIBUTION DEDUCTION FOR ELECTING SMALL BUSINESS TRUSTS.

(a) IN GENERAL.—Section 641(c)(2) is amended by inserting after subparagraph (D) the following new subparagraph:

"(E)(i) Section 642(c) shall not apply.

"(ii) For purposes of section 170(b)(1)(G), adjusted gross income shall be computed in the same manner as in the case of an individual, except that the deductions for costs which are paid or incurred in connection with the administration of the trust and which would not have been incurred if the property were not held in such trust shall be treated as allowable in arriving at adjusted gross income.".

(b) EFFECTIVE DATE.—The amendment made by this section shall apply to taxable years beginning after December 31, 2017.

**SEC. 13543. MODIFICATION OF TREATMENT OF S CORPORATION CONVERSIONS TO C CORPORATIONS.**

(a) ADJUSTMENTS ATTRIBUTABLE TO CONVERSION FROM S CORPORATION TO C CORPORATION.—Section 481 is amended by adding at the end the following new subsection:

"(d) ADJUSTMENTS ATTRIBUTABLE TO CONVERSION FROM S CORPORATION TO C CORPORATION.—

"(1) IN GENERAL.—In the case of an eligible terminated S corporation, any adjustment required by subsection (a)(2) which is attributable to such corporation's revocation described in paragraph (2)(A)(ii) shall be taken into account ratably during the 6-taxable year period beginning with the year of change.

"(2) ELIGIBLE TERMINATED S CORPORATION.—For purposes of this subsection, the term 'eligible terminated S corporation' means any C corporation—

"(A) which—

"(i) was an S corporation on the day before the date of the enactment of the Tax Cuts and Jobs Act, and

"(ii) during the 2-year period beginning on the date of such enactment makes a revocation of its election under section 1362(a), and

"(B) the owners of the stock of which, determined on the date such revocation is made, are the same owners (and in identical proportions) as on the date of such enactment.".

(b) CASH DISTRIBUTIONS FOLLOWING POST-TERMINATION TRANSITION PERIOD FROM S CORPORATION STATUS.—Section 1371 is amended by adding at the end the following new subsection:

"(f) CASH DISTRIBUTIONS FOLLOWING POST-TERMINATION TRANSITION PERIOD.—In the case of a distribution of money by an eligible terminated S corporation (as defined in section 481(d)) after the post-termination transition period, the accumulated adjustments account shall be allocated to such distribution, and the distribution shall be chargeable to accumulated earnings and profits, in the same ratio as the amount of such accumulated adjustments account bears to the amount of such accumulated earnings and profits.".

## PART VII—EMPLOYMENT

### Subpart A—Compensation

**SEC. 13601. MODIFICATION OF LIMITATION ON EXCESSIVE EMPLOYEE REMUNERATION.**

(a) Repeal of Performance-based Compensation and Commission Exceptions for Limitation on Excessive Employee Remuneration.—

(1) In general.—Paragraph (4) of section 162(m) is amended by striking subparagraphs (B) and (C) and by redesignating subparagraphs (D), (E), (F), and (G) as subparagraphs (B), (C), (D), and (E), respectively.

(2) Conforming amendments.—

(A) Paragraphs (5)(E) and (6)(D) of section 162(m) are each amended by striking "subparagraphs (B), (C), and (D)" and inserting "subparagraph (B)".

(B) Paragraphs (5)(G) and (6)(G) of section 162(m) are each amended by striking "(F) and (G)" and inserting "(D) and (E)".

(b) MODIFICATION OF DEFINITION OF COVERED EMPLOYEES.—Paragraph (3) of section 162(m) is amended—

(1) in subparagraph (A), by striking "as of the close of the taxable year, such employee is the chief executive officer of the taxpayer or is" and inserting "such employee is the principal executive officer or principal financial officer of the taxpayer at any time during the taxable year, or was",

(2) in subparagraph (B)—

(A) by striking "4" and inserting "3", and

(B) by striking "(other than the chief executive officer)" and inserting "(other than any individual described in subparagraph (A))", and

(3) by striking "or" at the end of subparagraph (A), by striking the period at the end of subparagraph (B) and inserting ", or", and by adding at the end the following:

"(C) was a covered employee of the taxpayer (or any predecessor) for any preceding taxable year beginning after December 31, 2016.".

(c) EXPANSION OF APPLICABLE EMPLOYER.—

(1) IN GENERAL.—Section 162(m)(2) is amended to read as follows:

"(2) PUBLICLY HELD CORPORATION.—For purposes of this subsection, the term 'publicly held corporation' means any corporation which is an issuer (as defined in section 3 of the Securities Exchange Act of 1934 (15 U.S.C. 78c))—

"(A) the securities of which are required to be registered under section 12 of such Act (15 U.S.C. 78l), or

"(B) that is required to file reports under section 15(d) of such Act (15 U.S.C. 78o(d)).".

(2) CONFORMING AMENDMENT.—Section 162(m)(3), as amended by subsection (b), is amended by adding at the end the following flush sentence:

"Such term shall include any employee who would be described in subparagraph (B) if the reporting described in such subparagraph were required as so described.".

(d) SPECIAL RULE FOR REMUNERATION PAID TO BENEFICIARIES, ETC.—Paragraph (4) of section 162(m), as amended by subsection (a), is amended by adding at the end the following new subparagraph:

"(F) SPECIAL RULE FOR REMUNERATION PAID TO BENEFICIARIES, ETC.—Remuneration shall not fail to be applicable employee remuneration merely because it is includible in the income of, or paid to, a person other than the covered employee, including after the death of the covered employee.''.

(e) EFFECTIVE DATE.—

(1) IN GENERAL.—Except as provided in paragraph (2), the amendments made by this section shall apply to taxable years beginning after December 31, 2017.

(2) EXCEPTION FOR BINDING CONTRACTS.—The amendments made by this section shall not apply to remuneration which is provided pursuant to a written binding contract which was in effect on November 2, 2017, and which was not modified in any material respect on or after such date.

**SEC. 13602. EXCISE TAX ON EXCESS TAX-EXEMPT ORGANIZATION EXECUTIVE COMPENSATION.**

(a) IN GENERAL.—Subchapter D of chapter 42 is amended by adding at the end the following new section:

**''SEC. 4960. TAX ON EXCESS TAX-EXEMPT ORGANIZATION EXECUTIVE COMPENSATION.**

''(a) TAX IMPOSED.—There is hereby imposed a tax equal to the product of the rate of tax under section 11 and the sum of—

''(1) so much of the remuneration paid (other than any excess parachute payment) by an applicable tax-exempt organization for the taxable year with respect to employment of any covered employee in excess of $1,000,000, plus

"(2) any excess parachute payment paid by such an organization to any covered employee.

For purposes of the preceding sentence, remuneration shall be treated as paid when there is no substantial risk of forfeiture (within the meaning of section 457(f)(3)(B)) of the rights to such remuneration.

"(b) LIABILITY FOR TAX.—The employer shall be liable for the tax imposed under subsection (a).

"(c) DEFINITIONS AND SPECIAL RULES.—For purposes of this section—

"(1) APPLICABLE TAX-EXEMPT ORGANIZATION.—The term 'applicable tax-exempt organization' means any organization which for the taxable year—

"(A) is exempt from taxation under section 501(a),

"(B) is a farmers' cooperative organization described in section 521(b)(1),

"(C) has income excluded from taxation under section 115(1), or

"(D) is a political organization described in section 527(e)(1).

"(2) COVERED EMPLOYEE.—For purposes of this section, the term 'covered employee' means any employee (including any former employee) of an applicable tax-exempt organization if the employee—

"(A) is one of the 5 highest compensated employees of the organization for the taxable year, or

"(B) was a covered employee of the organization (or any predecessor) for any preceding taxable year beginning after December 31, 2016.

"(3) REMUNERATION.—For purposes of this section:

"(A) IN GENERAL.—The term 'remuneration' means wages (as defined in section 3401(a)), except that such term shall not include any designated Roth contribution (as defined in section 402A(c)) and shall include amounts required to be included in gross income under section 457(f).

"(B) EXCEPTION FOR REMUNERATION FOR MEDICAL SERVICES.—The term 'remuneration' shall not include the portion of any remuneration paid to a licensed medical professional (including a veterinarian) which is for the performance of medical or veterinary services by such professional.

"(4) REMUNERATION FROM RELATED ORGANIZATIONS.—

"(A) IN GENERAL.—Remuneration of a covered employee by an applicable tax-exempt organization shall include any remuneration paid with respect to employment of such employee by any related person or governmental entity.

"(B) RELATED ORGANIZATIONS.—A person or governmental entity shall be treated as related to an applicable tax-exempt organization if such person or governmental entity—

"(i) controls, or is controlled by, the organization,

"(ii) is controlled by one or more persons which control the organization,

"(iii) is a supported organization (as defined in section 509(f)(3)) during the taxable year with respect to the organization,

"(iv) is a supporting organization described in section 509(a)(3) during the taxable year with respect to the organization, or

"(v) in the case of an organization which is a voluntary employees' beneficiary association described in section 501(c)(9), establishes, maintains, or makes contributions to such voluntary employees' beneficiary association.

"(C) LIABILITY FOR TAX.—In any case in which remuneration from more than one employer is taken into account under this paragraph in determining the tax imposed by subsection (a), each such employer shall be liable for such tax in an amount which bears the same ratio to the total tax determined under subsection (a) with respect to such remuneration as—

"(i) the amount of remuneration paid by such employer with respect to such employee, bears to

"(ii) the amount of remuneration paid by all such employers to such employee.

"(5) EXCESS PARACHUTE PAYMENT.—For purposes of determining the tax imposed by subsection (a)(2)—

"(A) IN GENERAL.—The term 'excess parachute payment' means an amount equal to the excess of any parachute payment over the portion of the base amount allocated to such payment.

"(B) PARACHUTE PAYMENT.—The term 'parachute payment' means any payment in the nature of compensation to (or for the benefit of) a covered employee if—

"(i) such payment is contingent on such employee's separation from employment with the employer, and

"(ii) the aggregate present value of the payments in the nature of compensation to (or for the benefit of) such individual which are contingent on such separation equals or exceeds an amount equal to 3 times the base amount.

"(C) EXCEPTION.—Such term does not include any payment—

"(i) described in section 280G(b)(6) (relating to exemption for payments under qualified plans), "(ii) made under or to an annuity contract described in section 403(b) or a plan described in section 457(b),

"(iii) to a licensed medical professional (including a veterinarian) to the extent that such payment is for the performance of medical or veterinary services by such professional, or

"(iv) to an individual who is not a highly compensated employee as defined in section 414(q).

"(D) BASE AMOUNT.—Rules similar to the rules of 280G(b)(3) shall apply for purposes of determining the base amount.

"(E) PROPERTY TRANSFERS; PRESENT VALUE.—Rules similar to the rules of paragraphs (3) and (4) of section 280G(d) shall apply.

"(6) COORDINATION WITH DEDUCTION LIMITATION.—Remuneration the deduction for which is not allowed by reason of section 162(m) shall not be taken into account for purposes of this section.

"(d) REGULATIONS.—The Secretary shall prescribe such regulations as may be necessary to prevent avoidance of the tax under this section, including regulations to prevent avoidance of such tax through the performance of services other than as an employee or by providing compensation through a pass-through or other entity to avoid such tax.''.

(b) CLERICAL AMENDMENT.—The table of sections for subchapter D of chapter 42 is amended by adding at the end the following new item:

"Sec. 4960. Tax on excess tax-exempt organization executive compensation.''.

(c) EFFECTIVE DATE.—The amendments made by this section shall apply to taxable years beginning after December 31, 2017.

**SEC. 13603. TREATMENT OF QUALIFIED EQUITY GRANTS.**

(a) IN GENERAL.—Section 83 is amended by adding at the end the following new subsection:

"(i) QUALIFIED EQUITY GRANTS.—

"(1) IN GENERAL.—For purposes of this subtitle—

"(A) TIMING OF INCLUSION.—If qualified stock is transferred to a qualified employee who makes an election with respect to such stock under this subsection, subsection (a) shall be applied by including the amount determined under such subsection with respect to such stock in income of the employee in the taxable year determined under subparagraph (B) in lieu

"(B) TAXABLE YEAR DETERMINED.—The taxable year determined under this subparagraph is the taxable year of the employee which includes the earliest of—

"(i) the first date such qualified stock becomes transferable (including, solely for purposes of this clause, becoming transferable to the employer),

"(ii) the date the employee first becomes an excluded employee,

"(iii) the first date on which any stock of the corporation which issued the qualified stock becomes readily tradable on an established securities market (as determined by the Secretary, but not including any market unless such market is recognized as an established securities market by the Secretary for purposes of a provision of this title other than this subsection),

"(iv) the date that is 5 years after the first date the rights of the employee in such stock are transferable or are not subject to a substantial risk of forfeiture, whichever occurs earlier, or "(v) the date on which the employee revokes (at such time and in such manner as the Secretary provides) the election under this subsection with respect to such stock.

"(2) QUALIFIED STOCK.—

"(A) IN GENERAL.—For purposes of this subsection, the term 'qualified stock' means, with respect to any qualified employee, any stock in a corporation which is the employer of such employee, if—

"(i) such stock is received—

"(I) in connection with the exercise of an option, or

"(II) in settlement of a restricted stock unit, and

"(ii) such option or restricted stock unit was granted by the corporation—

"(I) in connection with the performance of services as an employee, and

"(II) during a calendar year in which such corporation was an eligible corporation.

"(B) LIMITATION.—The term 'qualified stock' shall not include any stock if the employee may sell such stock to, or otherwise receive cash in lieu of stock from, the corporation at the time that the rights of the employee in such stock first become transferable or not subject to a substantial risk of forfeiture.

"(C) ELIGIBLE CORPORATION.—For purposes of subparagraph (A)(ii)(II)—

"(i) IN GENERAL.—The term 'eligible corporation' means, with respect to any calendar year, any corporation if—

"(I) no stock of such corporation (or any predecessor of such corporation) is readily tradable on an established securities market (as determined under paragraph (1)(B)(iii)) during any preceding calendar year, and

"(II) such corporation has a written plan under which, in such calendar year, not less than 80 percent of all employees who provide services to such corporation in the United States (or any possession of the

United States) are granted stock options, or are granted restricted stock units, with the same rights and privileges to receive qualified stock.

"(ii) SAME RIGHTS AND PRIVILEGES.—For purposes of clause (i)(II)—

"(I) except as provided in subclauses (II) and (III), the determination of rights and privileges with respect to stock shall be made in a similar manner as under section 423(b)(5),

"(II) employees shall not fail to be treated as having the same rights and privileges to receive qualified stock solely because the number of shares available to all employees is not equal in amount, so long as the number of shares available to each employee is more than a de minimis amount, and

"(III) rights and privileges with respect to the exercise of an option shall not be treated as the same as rights and privileges with respect to the settlement of a restricted stock unit.

"(iii) EMPLOYEE.—For purposes of clause (i)(II), the term 'employee' shall not include any employee described in section 4980E(d)(4) or any excluded employee.

"(iv) SPECIAL RULE FOR CALENDAR YEARS BEFORE 2018.—In the case of any calendar year beginning before January 1, 2018, clause (i)(II) shall be applied without regard to whether the rights and privileges with respect to the qualified stock are the same.

"(3) QUALIFIED EMPLOYEE; EXCLUDED EMPLOYEE.—For purposes of this subsection—

"(A) IN GENERAL.—The term 'qualified employee' means any individual who—

"(i) is not an excluded employee, and

"(ii) agrees in the election made under this subsection to meet such requirements as are determined by the Secretary to be necessary to ensure that the withholding requirements of the corporation under chapter 24 with respect to the qualified stock are met.

"(B) EXCLUDED EMPLOYEE.—The term 'excluded employee' means, with respect to any corporation, any individual—

"(i) who is a 1-percent owner (within the meaning of section 416(i)(1)(B)(ii)) at any time during the calendar year or who was such a 1 percent owner at any time during the 10 preceding calendar years,

"(ii) who is or has been at any prior time—

"(I) the chief executive officer of such corporation or an individual acting in such a capacity, or

"(II) the chief financial officer of such corporation or an individual acting in such a capacity,

"(iii) who bears a relationship described in section 318(a)(1) to any individual described in subclause (I) or (II) of clause (ii), or

"(iv) who is one of the 4 highest compensated officers of such corporation for the taxable year, or was one of the 4 highest compensated officers of such corporation for any of the 10 preceding taxable years, determined with respect to each such taxable year on the basis of the shareholder disclosure rules for compensation under the Securities Exchange Act of 1934 (as if such rules applied to such corporation).

"(4) ELECTION.—

"(A) TIME FOR MAKING ELECTION.—An election with respect to qualified stock shall be made under this subsection no later than 30 days after the first date the rights of the employee in such stock are transferable or are not subject to a substantial risk of forfeiture, whichever occurs earlier, and shall be made in a manner similar to the manner in which an election is made under subsection (b).

"(B) LIMITATIONS.—No election may be made under this section with respect to any qualified stock if—

"(i) the qualified employee has made an election under subsection (b) with respect to such qualified stock,

"(ii) any stock of the corporation which issued the qualified stock is readily tradable on an established securities market (as determined under paragraph (1)(B)(iii)) at any time before the election is made, or

"(iii) such corporation purchased any of its outstanding stock in the calendar year preceding the calendar year which includes the first date the rights of the employee in such stock are transferable or are not subject to a substantial risk of forfeiture, unless—

"(I) not less than 25 percent of the total dollar amount of the stock so purchased is deferral stock, and

"(II) the determination of which individuals from whom deferral stock is purchased is made on a reasonable basis.

"(C) DEFINITIONS AND SPECIAL RULES RELATED TO LIMITATION ON STOCK REDEMPTIONS.—

"(i) DEFERRAL STOCK.—For purposes of this paragraph, the term 'deferral stock' means stock with respect to which an election is in effect under this subsection.

"(ii) DEFERRAL STOCK WITH RESPECT TO ANY INDIVIDUAL NOT TAKEN INTO ACCOUNT IF INDIVIDUAL HOLDS DEFERRAL STOCK WITH LONGER DEFERRAL PERIOD.—Stock purchased by a corporation from any individual shall not be treated as deferral stock for purposes of subparagraph (B)(iii) if such individual (immediately after such purchase) holds any deferral stock with respect to which an election has been in effect under this subsection for a longer period than the election with respect to the stock so purchased.

"(iii) PURCHASE OF ALL OUTSTANDING DEFERRAL STOCK.—The requirements of subclauses (I) and (II) of subparagraph (B)(iii) shall be treated as met if the stock so purchased includes all of the corporation's outstanding deferral stock.

"(iv) REPORTING.—Any corporation which has outstanding deferral stock as of the beginning of any calendar year and which purchases any of its outstanding stock during such calendar year shall include on its return of tax for the taxable year in which, or with which, such calendar year ends the total dollar amount of its outstanding stock so purchased during such calendar year and such other information as the Secretary requires for purposes of administering this paragraph.

"(5) CONTROLLED GROUPS.—For purposes of this subsection, all persons treated as a single employer under section 414(b) shall be treated as 1 corporation.

"(6) NOTICE REQUIREMENT.—Any corporation which transfers qualified stock to a qualified employee shall, at the time that (or a reasonable period before) an amount attributable to such stock would (but for this subsection) first be includible in the gross income of such employee—

"(A) certify to such employee that such stock is qualified stock, and

"(B) notify such employee—

"(i) that the employee may be eligible to elect to defer income on such stock under this subsection, and "(ii) that, if the employee makes such an election—

"(I) the amount of income recognized at the end of the deferral period will be based on the value of the stock at the time at which the rights of the employee in such stock first become transferable or not subject to substantial risk of forfeiture, notwithstanding whether the value of the stock has declined during the deferral period,

"(II) the amount of such income recognized at the end of the deferral period will be subject to withholding under section 3401(i) at the rate determined under section 3402(t), and

"(III) the responsibilities of the employee (as determined by the Secretary under paragraph (3)(A)(ii)) with respect to such withholding.

"(7) RESTRICTED STOCK UNITS.—This section (other than this subsection), including any election under subsection (b), shall not apply to restricted stock units.".

(b) WITHHOLDING.—

(1) TIME OF WITHHOLDING.—Section 3401 is amended by adding at the end the following new subsection:

"(i) QUALIFIED STOCK FOR WHICH AN ELECTION IS IN EFFECT UNDER SECTION 83(I).—For purposes of subsection (a), qualified stock (as defined in section 83(i)) with respect to which an election is made under section 83(i) shall be treated as wages—

"(1) received on the earliest date described in section 83(i)(1)(B), and

"(2) in an amount equal to the amount included in income under section 83 for the taxable year which includes such date.".

(2) AMOUNT OF WITHHOLDING.—Section 3402 is amended by adding at the end the following new subsection:

"(t) RATE OF WITHHOLDING FOR CERTAIN STOCK.—In the case of any qualified stock (as defined in section 83(i)(2)) with respect to which an election is made under section 83(i)—

"(1) the rate of tax under subsection (a) shall not be less than the maximum rate of tax in effect under section 1, and

"(2) such stock shall be treated for purposes of section 3501(b) in the same manner as a non-cash fringe benefit.".

(c) COORDINATION WITH OTHER DEFERRED COMPENSATION RULES.—

(1) ELECTION TO APPLY DEFERRAL TO STATUTORY OPTIONS.—

(A) INCENTIVE STOCK OPTIONS.—Section 422(b) is amended by adding at the end the following: "Such term shall not include any option if an election is made under section 83(i) with respect to the stock received in connection with the exercise of such option.".

(B) EMPLOYEE STOCK PURCHASE PLANS.—Section 423 is amended—

(i) in subsection (b)(5), by striking "and" before "the plan" and by inserting ", and the rules of section 83(i) shall apply in determining which employees have a right to make an election under such section" before the semicolon at the end, and

(ii) by adding at the end the following new subsection:

"(d) COORDINATION WITH QUALIFIED EQUITY GRANTS.—An option for which an election is made under section 83(i) with respect to the stock received in connection with its exercise shall not be considered as granted pursuant an employee stock purchase plan.".

(2) EXCLUSION FROM DEFINITION OF NONQUALIFIED DEFERRED COMPENSATION PLAN.—Subsection (d) of section 409A is amended by adding at the end the following new paragraph:

"(7) TREATMENT OF QUALIFIED STOCK.—An arrangement under which an employee may receive qualified stock (as defined in section 83(i)(2)) shall not be treated as a nonqualified deferred compensation plan with respect to such employee solely because of such employee's election, or ability to make an election, to defer recognition of income under section 83(i).".

(d) INFORMATION REPORTING.—Section 6051(a) is amended by striking "and" at the end of paragraph (14)(B), by striking the period at the end of paragraph (15) and inserting a comma, and by inserting after paragraph (15) the following new paragraphs:

"(16) the amount includible in gross income under subparagraph (A) of section 83(i)(1) with respect to an event described in subparagraph (B) of such section which occurs in such calendar year, and

"(17) the aggregate amount of income which is being deferred pursuant to elections under section 83(i), determined as of the close of the calendar year.".

(e) PENALTY FOR FAILURE OF EMPLOYER TO PROVIDE NOTICE OF TAX CONSEQUENCES.—Section 6652 is amended by adding at the end the following new subsection:

"(p) FAILURE TO PROVIDE NOTICE UNDER SECTION 83(I).—In the case of each failure to provide a notice as required by section 83(i)(6), at the time prescribed therefor, unless it is shown that such failure is due to reasonable cause and not to willful neglect, there shall be paid, on notice and demand of the Secretary and in the same manner as tax, by the person failing to provide such notice, an amount equal to $100 for each such failure, but the total amount imposed on such person for all such failures during any calendar year shall not exceed $50,000.".

(f) EFFECTIVE DATES.—

(1) IN GENERAL.—Except as provided in paragraph (2), the amendments made by this section shall apply to stock attributable to options exercised, or restricted stock units settled, after December 31, 2017.

(2) REQUIREMENT TO PROVIDE NOTICE.—The amendments made by subsection (e) shall apply to failures after December 31, 2017.

(g) TRANSITION RULE.—Until such time as the Secretary (or the Secretary's delegate) issues regulations or other guidance for purposes of implementing the requirements of paragraph (2)(C)(i)(II) of section 83(i) of the Internal Revenue Code of 1986 (as added by this section), or the requirements of paragraph (6) of such section, a corporation shall be treated as being in compliance with such requirements (respectively) if such corporation complies with a reasonable good faith interpretation of such requirements.

**SEC. 13604. INCREASE IN EXCISE TAX RATE FOR STOCK COMPENSATION OF INSIDERS IN EXPATRIATED CORPORATIONS.**

(a) IN GENERAL.—Section 4985(a)(1) is amended by striking "section 1(h)(1)(C)" and inserting "section 1(h)(1)(D)".

(b) EFFECTIVE DATE.—The amendment made by this section shall apply to corporations first becoming expatriated corporations (as defined in section 4985 of the Internal Revenue Code of 1986) after the date of enactment of this Act.

### Subpart B—Retirement Plans

**SEC. 13611. REPEAL OF SPECIAL RULE PERMITTING RECHARACTERIZATION OF ROTH CONVERSIONS.**

(a) IN GENERAL.—Section 408A(d)(6)(B) is amended by adding at the end the following new clause:

"(iii) CONVERSIONS.—Subparagraph (A) shall not apply in the case of a qualified rollover contribution to which subsection (d)(3) applies (including by reason of subparagraph (C) thereof).".

(b) EFFECTIVE DATE.—The amendments made by this section shall apply to taxable years beginning after December 31, 2017.

**SEC. 13612. MODIFICATION OF RULES APPLICABLE TO LENGTH OF SERVICE AWARD PLANS.**

(a) MAXIMUM DEFERRAL AMOUNT.—Clause (ii) of section 457(e)(11)(B) is amended by striking "$3,000" and inserting "$6,000".

(b) COST OF LIVING ADJUSTMENT.—Subparagraph (B) of section 457(e)(11) is amended by adding at the end the following:

"(iii) COST OF LIVING ADJUSTMENT.—In the case of taxable years beginning after December 31, 2017, the Sec-under clause (ii) at the same time and in the same manner as under section 415(d), except that the base period shall be the calendar quarter beginning July 1, 2016, and any increase under this paragraph that is not a multiple of $500 shall be rounded to the next lowest multiple of $500.".

(c) APPLICATION OF LIMITATION ON ACCRUALS.—Subparagraph (B) of section 457(e)(11), as amended by subsection (b), is amended by adding at the end the following:

"(iv) SPECIAL RULE FOR APPLICATION OF LIMITATION ON ACCRUALS FOR CERTAIN PLANS.—In the case of a plan described in subparagraph (A)(ii) which is a defined benefit plan (as defined in section 414(j)), the limitation under clause (ii) shall apply to the actuarial present value of the aggregate amount of length of service awards accruing with respect to any year of service. Such actuarial present value with respect to any year shall be calculated using reasonable actuarial assumptions and methods, assuming payment will be made under the most valuable form of payment under the plan with payment commencing at the later of the earliest age at which unreduced benefits are payable under the plan or the participant's age at the time of the calculation.".

(d) EFFECTIVE DATE.—The amendments made by this section shall apply to taxable years beginning after December 31, 2017.

**SEC. 13613. EXTENDED ROLLOVER PERIOD FOR PLAN LOAN OFFSET AMOUNTS.**

(a) IN GENERAL.—Paragraph (3) of section 402(c) is amended by adding at the end the following new subparagraph:

"(C) ROLLOVER OF CERTAIN PLAN LOAN OFFSET AMOUNTS.—

"(i) IN GENERAL.—In the case of a qualified plan loan offset amount, paragraph (1) shall not apply to any transfer of such amount made after the due date (including extensions) for filing the return of tax for the taxable year in which such amount is treated as distributed from a qualified employer plan.

"(ii) QUALIFIED PLAN LOAN OFFSET AMOUNT.—For purposes of this subparagraph, the term 'qualified plan loan offset amount' means a plan loan offset amount which is treated as distributed from a qualified employer plan to a participant or beneficiary solely by reason of—

"(I) the termination of the qualified employer plan, or

"(II) the failure to meet the repayment terms of the loan from such plan because of the severance from employment of the participant.

"(iii) PLAN LOAN OFFSET AMOUNT.—For purposes of clause (ii), the term 'plan loan offset amount' means the amount by which the participant's accrued benefit under the plan is reduced in order to repay a loan from the plan.

"(iv) LIMITATION.—This subparagraph shall not apply to any plan loan offset amount unless such plan loan offset amount relates to a loan to which section 72(p)(1) does not apply by reason of section 72(p)(2).

"(v) QUALIFIED EMPLOYER PLAN.—For purposes of this subsection, the term 'qualified employer plan' has the meaning given such term by section 72(p)(4).".

(b) CONFORMING AMENDMENTS.—Section 402(c)(3) is amended—

(1) by striking "TRANSFER MUST BE MADE WITHIN 60 DAYS OF RECEIPT" in the heading and inserting "TIME LIMIT ON TRANSFERS", and

(2) by striking "subparagraph (B)" in subparagraph (A) and inserting "subparagraphs (B) and (C)".

(c) EFFECTIVE DATE.—The amendments made by this section shall apply to plan loan offset amounts which are treated as distributed in taxable years beginning after December 31, 2017.

## PART VIII—EXEMPT ORGANIZATIONS

### SEC. 13701. EXCISE TAX BASED ON INVESTMENT INCOME OF PRIVATE COLLEGES AND UNIVERSITIES.

(a) IN GENERAL.—Chapter 42 is amended by adding at the end the following new subchapter:

## "Subchapter H—Excise Tax Based on Investment Income of Private Colleges and Universities

"Sec. 4968. Excise tax based on investment income of private colleges and uni-

**"SEC. 4968. EXCISE TAX BASED ON INVESTMENT INCOME OF PRIVATE COLLEGES AND UNIVERSITIES.**

"(a) TAX IMPOSED.—There is hereby imposed on each applicable educational institution for the taxable year a tax equal to 1.4 percent of the net investment income of such institution for the taxable year.

"(b) APPLICABLE EDUCATIONAL INSTITUTION.—For purposes of this subchapter—

"(1) IN GENERAL.—The term 'applicable educational institution' means an eligible educational institution (as defined in section 25A(f)(2))—

"(A) which had at least 500 tuition-paying students during the preceding taxable year,

"(B) more than 50 percent of the tuition-paying students of which are located in the United States,

"(C) which is not described in the first sentence of section 511(a)(2)(B) (relating to State colleges and universities), and

"(D) the aggregate fair market value of the assets of which at the end of the preceding taxable year (other than those assets which are used directly in carrying out the institution's exempt purpose) is at least $500,000 per student of the institution.

"(2) STUDENTS.—For purposes of paragraph (1), the number of students of an institution (including for purposes of determining the number of students at a particular location) shall be based on the daily average number of full-time students attending such institution (with part-time students taken into account on a full-time student equivalent basis).

"(c) NET INVESTMENT INCOME.—For purposes of this section, net investment income shall be determined under rules similar to the rules of section 4940(c).

"(d) ASSETS AND NET INVESTMENT INCOME OF RELATED ORGANIZATIONS.—

"(1) IN GENERAL.—For purposes of subsections (b)(1)(C) and (c), assets and net investment income of any related organization with respect to an educational institution shall be treated as assets and net investment income, respectively, of the educational institution, except that—

"(A) no such amount shall be taken into account with respect to more than 1 educational institution, and

"(B) unless such organization is controlled by such institution or is described in section 509(a)(3) with respect to such institution for the taxable year, assets and net investment income which are not intended or available for the use or benefit of the educational institution shall not be taken into account.

"(2) RELATED ORGANIZATION.—For purposes of this subsection, the term 'related organization' means, with respect to an educational institution, any organization which—

"(A) controls, or is controlled by, such institution,

"(B) is controlled by 1 or more persons which also control such institution, or

"(C) is a supported organization (as defined in section 509(f)(3)), or an organization described in section 509(a)(3), during the taxable year with respect to such institution.".

(b) CLERICAL AMENDMENT.—The table of subchapters for chapter 42 is amended by adding at the end the following new item:

"SUBCHAPTER H—EXCISE TAX BASED ON INVESTMENT INCOME OF PRIVATE COLLEGES AND UNIVERSITIES".

(c) EFFECTIVE DATE.—The amendments made by this section shall apply to taxable years beginning after December 31, 2017.

**SEC. 13702. UNRELATED BUSINESS TAXABLE INCOME SEPARATELY COMPUTED FOR EACH TRADE OR BUSINESS ACTIVITY.**

(a) IN GENERAL.—Subsection (a) of section 512 is amended by adding at the end the following new paragraph:

"(6) SPECIAL RULE FOR ORGANIZATION WITH MORE THAN 1 UNRELATED TRADE OR BUSINESS.—In the case of any organization with more than 1 unrelated trade or business—

"(A) unrelated business taxable income, including for purposes of determining any net operating loss deduction, shall be computed separately with respect to each such trade or business and without regard to subsection (b)(12),

"(B) the unrelated business taxable income of such organization shall be the sum of the unrelated business taxable income so computed with respect to each such trade or business, less a specific deduction under subsection (b)(12), and

"(C) for purposes of subparagraph (B), unrelated business taxable income with respect to any such trade or business shall not be less than zero.".

(1) IN GENERAL.—Except to the extent provided in paragraph (2), the amendment made by this section shall apply to taxable years beginning after December 31, 2017.

(2) CARRYOVERS OF NET OPERATING LOSSES.—If any net operating loss arising in a taxable year beginning before January 1, 2018, is carried over to a taxable year beginning on or after such date—

(A) subparagraph (A) of section 512(a)(6) of the Internal Revenue Code of 1986, as added by this Act, shall not apply to such net operating loss, and

(B) the unrelated business taxable income of the organization, after the application of subparagraph (B) of such section, shall be reduced by the amount of such net operating loss.

**SEC. 13703. UNRELATED BUSINESS TAXABLE INCOME INCREASED BY AMOUNT OF CERTAIN FRINGE BENEFIT EXPENSES FOR WHICH DEDUCTION IS DISALLOWED.**

(a) IN GENERAL.—Section 512(a), as amended by this Act, is further amended by adding at the end the following new paragraph:

"(7) INCREASE IN UNRELATED BUSINESS TAXABLE INCOME BY DISALLOWED FRINGE.—Unrelated business taxable income of an organization shall be increased by any amount for which a deduction is not allowable under this chapter by reason of section 274 and which is paid or incurred by such organization for any qualified transportation fringe (as defined in section 132(f)), any parking facility used in connection with qualified parking (as defined in section 132(f)(5)(C)), or any on-premises athletic facility (as defined in section 132(j)(4)(B)). The preceding sentence shall not apply to the extent the amount paid or incurred is directly connected with an unrelated trade or business which is regularly carried on by the organization. The Secretary shall issue such regulations or other guidance as may be necessary or appropriate to carry out the purposes of this paragraph, including regulations or other guidance providing for the appropriate allocation of depreciation and other costs with respect to facilities used for parking or for on-premises athletic facilities.".

(b) EFFECTIVE DATE.—The amendment made by this section shall apply to amounts paid or incurred after December 31, 2017.

**SEC. 13704. REPEAL OF DEDUCTION FOR AMOUNTS PAID IN EXCHANGE FOR COLLEGE ATHLETIC EVENT SEATING RIGHTS.**

(a) In General.—Section 170(l) is amended—

(1) by striking paragraph (1) and inserting the following:

"(1) In general.—No deduction shall be allowed under this section for any amount described in paragraph (2).", and

(2) in paragraph (2)(B), by striking "such amount would be allowable as a deduction under this section but for the fact that".

(b) Effective Date.—The amendments made by this section shall apply to contributions made in taxable years beginning after December 31, 2017.

**SEC. 13705. REPEAL OF SUBSTANTIATION EXCEPTION IN CASE OF CONTRIBUTIONS REPORTED BY DONEE.**

(a) In General.—Section 170(f)(8) is amended by striking subparagraph (D) and by redesignating subparagraph (E) as subparagraph (D).

(b) Effective Date.—The amendments made by this section shall apply to contributions made in taxable years beginning after December 31, 2016.

## PART IX—OTHER PROVISIONS

### Subpart A—Craft Beverage Modernization and Tax Reform

#### SEC. 13801. PRODUCTION PERIOD FOR BEER, WINE, AND DISTILLED SPIRITS.

(a) IN GENERAL.—Section 263A(f) is amended—

(1) by redesignating paragraph (4) as paragraph (5), and

(2) by inserting after paragraph (3) the following new paragraph:

"(4) EXEMPTION FOR AGING PROCESS OF BEER, WINE, AND DISTILLED SPIRITS.—

"(A) IN GENERAL.—For purposes of this subsection, the production period shall not include the aging period for—

"(i) beer (as defined in section 5052(a)),

"(ii) wine (as described in section 5041(a)), or

"(iii) distilled spirits (as defined in section 5002(a)(8)), except such spirits that are unfit for use for beverage purposes.

"(B) TERMINATION.—This paragraph shall not apply to interest costs paid or accrued

(b) CONFORMING AMENDMENT.—Paragraph (5)(B)(ii) of section 263A(f), as redesignated by this section, is amended by inserting "except as provided in paragraph (4)," before "ending on the date".

(c) EFFECTIVE DATE.—The amendments made by this section shall apply to interest costs paid or accrued in calendar years beginning after December 31, 2017.

**SEC. 13802. REDUCED RATE OF EXCISE TAX ON BEER.**

(a) IN GENERAL.—Paragraph (1) of section 5051(a) is amended to read as follows:

"(1) IN GENERAL.—

"(A) IMPOSITION OF TAX.—A tax is hereby imposed on all beer brewed or produced, and removed for consumption or sale, within the United States, or imported into the United States. Except as provided in paragraph (2), the rate of such tax shall be the amount determined under this paragraph.

"(B) RATE.—Except as provided in subparagraph (C), the rate of tax shall be $18 for per barrel.

"(C) SPECIAL RULE.—In the case of beer removed after December 31, 2017, and before January 1, 2020, the rate of tax shall be—

"(i) $16 on the first 6,000,000 barrels of beer—

"(I) brewed by the brewer and removed during the calendar year for consumption or sale, or

"(II) imported by the importer into the United States during the calendar year, and

"(ii) $18 on any barrels of beer to which clause (i) does not apply.

"(D) BARREL.—For purposes of this section, a barrel shall contain not more than 31 gallons of beer, and any tax imposed under this section shall be applied at a like rate for any other quantity or for fractional parts of a barrel.".

(b) REDUCED RATE FOR CERTAIN DOMESTIC PRODUCTION.—Subparagraph (A) of section 5051(a)(2) is amended—

(1) in the heading, by striking "$7 A BARREL", and

(2) by inserting "($3.50 in the case of beer removed after December 31, 2017, and before January 1, 2020)" after "$7".

(c) APPLICATION OF REDUCED TAX RATE FOR FOREIGN MANUFACTURERS AND IMPORTERS.—Subsection (a) of section 5051 is amended—

(1) in subparagraph (C)(i)(II) of paragraph (1), as amended by subsection (a), by inserting "but only if the importer is an electing importer under paragraph (4) and the barrels have been assigned to the importer pursuant to such paragraph" after "during the calendar year", and

(2) by adding at the end the following new paragraph:

"(4) REDUCED TAX RATE FOR FOREIGN MANUFACTURERS AND IMPORTERS.—

"(A) IN GENERAL.—In the case of any barrels of beer which have been brewed or produced outside of the United States and imported into the United States, the rate of tax applicable under clause (i) of paragraph (1)(C) (referred to in this paragraph as the 'reduced tax rate') may be assigned by the brewer (provided that the brewer makes an election described in subparagraph (B)(ii)) to any electing importer of such barrels pursuant to the requirements established by the Secretary under subparagraph (B).

"(B) ASSIGNMENT.—The Secretary shall, through such rules, regulations, and procedures as are determined appropriate, establish procedures for assignment of the reduced tax rate provided under this paragraph, which shall include—

"(i) a limitation to ensure that the number of barrels of beer for which the reduced tax rate has been assigned by a brewer—

"(I) to any importer does not exceed the number of barrels of beer brewed or produced by such brewer during the calendar year which were imported into the United States by such importer, and

"(II) to all importers does not exceed the 6,000,000 barrels to which the reduced tax rate applies,

"(ii) procedures that allow the election of a brewer to assign and an importer to receive the reduced tax rate provided under this paragraph,

"(iii) requirements that the brewer provide any information as the Secretary determines necessary and appropriate for purposes of carrying out this paragraph, and

"(iv) procedures that allow for revocation of eligibility of the brewer and the importer for the reduced tax rate provided under this paragraph in the case of any erroneous or fraudulent information provided under clause (iii) which the Secretary deems to be material to qualifying for such reduced rate.

"(C) CONTROLLED GROUP.—For purposes of this section, any importer making an election described in subparagraph (B)(ii) shall be deemed to be a member of the controlled group of the brewer, as described under paragraph (5).".

(d) CONTROLLED GROUP AND SINGLE TAXPAYER RULES.—Subsection (a) of section 5051, as amended by this section, is amended—

(1) in paragraph (2)—

(A) by striking subparagraph (B), and

(B) by redesignating subparagraph (C) as subparagraph (B), and

(2) by adding at the end the following new paragraph:

"(5) CONTROLLED GROUP AND SINGLE TAXPAYER RULES.—

"(A) IN GENERAL.—Except as provided in subparagraph (B), in the case of a controlled group, the 6,000,000 barrel quantity specified in paragraph (1)(C)(i) and the 2,000,000 barrel quantity specified in paragraph (2)(A) shall be applied to the controlled group, and the 6,000,000 barrel quantity specified in paragraph (1)(C)(i) and the 60,000 barrel quantity specified in paragraph (2)(A) shall be apportioned among the brewers who are members of such group in such manner as the Secretary or their delegate shall by regulations prescribe. For purposes of the preceding sentence, the term 'controlled group' has the meaning assigned to it by subsection (a) of section 1563, except that for such purposes the phrase 'more than 50 percent' shall be substituted for the phrase 'at least 80 percent' in each place it appears in such subsection. Under regulations prescribed by the Secretary, principles similar to the principles of the preceding two sentences shall be applied to a group of brewers under common control where one or more of the brewers is not a corporation.

"(B) FOREIGN MANUFACTURERS AND IMPORTERS.—For purposes of paragraph (4), in the case of a controlled group, the 6,000,000 barrel quantity specified in paragraph (1)(C)(i) shall be applied to the controlled group and apportioned among the members of such group in such manner as the Secretary shall by regulations prescribe. For purposes of the preceding sentence, the term 'controlled group' has the meaning given such term under subparagraph (A). Under regulations prescribed by the Secretary, principles similar to the principles of the preceding two sentences shall be applied to a group of brewers under common control where one or more of the brewers is not a corporation.

"(C) SINGLE TAXPAYER.—Pursuant to rules issued by the Secretary, two or more entities (whether or not under common control) that produce beer marketed under a similar brand, license, franchise, or other arrangement shall be treated as a single taxpayer for purposes of the application of this subsection.".

(e) Effective Date.—The amendments made by this section shall apply to beer removed after December 31, 2017.

**SEC. 13803. TRANSFER OF BEER BETWEEN BONDED FACILITIES.**

(a) In General.—Section 5414 is amended—

(1) by striking "Beer may be removed" and inserting "(a) In General—Beer may be removed", and

(2) by adding at the end the following:

"(b) Transfer of Beer Between Bonded Facilities.—

"(1) In general.—Beer may be removed from one bonded brewery to another bonded brewery, without payment of tax, and may be mingled with beer at the receiving brewery, subject to such conditions, including payment of the tax, and in such containers, as the Secretary by regulations shall prescribe, which shall include—

"(A) any removal from one brewery to another brewery belonging to the same brewer,

"(B) any removal from a brewery owned by one corporation to a brewery owned by another corporation when—

"(i) one such corporation owns the controlling interest in the other such corporation, or

"(ii) the controlling interest in each such corporation is owned by the same person or persons, and

"(C) any removal from one brewery to another brewery when—

"(i) the proprietors of transferring and receiving premises are independent of each other and neither has a proprietary interest, directly or indirectly, in the business of the other, and

"(ii) the transferor has divested itself of all interest in the beer so transferred and the transferee has accepted responsibility for payment of the tax.

"(2) TRANSFER OF LIABILITY FOR TAX.—For purposes of paragraph (1)(C), such relief from liability shall be effective from the time of removal from the transferor's bonded premises, or from the time of divestment of interest, whichever is later.

"(3) TERMINATION.—This subsection shall not apply to any calendar quarter beginning after December 31, 2019.".

(b) REMOVAL FROM BREWERY BY PIPELINE.—Section 5412 is amended by inserting "pursuant to section 5414 or" before "by pipeline".

(c) EFFECTIVE DATE.—The amendments made by this section shall apply to any calendar quarters beginning after December 31, 2017.

**SEC. 13804. REDUCED RATE OF EXCISE TAX ON CERTAIN WINE.**

(a) IN GENERAL.—Section 5041(c) is amended by adding at the end the following new paragraph:

"(8) SPECIAL RULE FOR 2018 AND 2019.—

"(A) IN GENERAL.—In the case of wine removed after December 31, 2017, and before January 1, 2020, paragraphs (1) and (2) shall not apply and there shall be allowed as a credit against any tax imposed by this title (other than chapters 2, 21, and 22) an amount equal to the sum of—

"(i) $1 per wine gallon on the first 30,000 wine gallons of wine, plus

"(ii) 90 cents per wine gallon on the first 100,000 wine gallons of wine to which clause (i) does not apply, plus "(iii) 53.5 cents per wine gallon on the first 620,000 wine gallons of wine to which clauses (i) and (ii) do not apply,

which are produced by the producer and removed during the calendar year for consumption or sale, or which are imported by the importer into the United States during the calendar year.

"(B) ADJUSTMENT OF CREDIT FOR HARD CIDER.—In the case of wine described in subsection (b)(6), subparagraph (A) of this paragraph shall be applied—

"(i) in clause (i) of such subparagraph, by substituting '6.2 cents' for '$1',

"(ii) in clause (ii) of such subparagraph, by substituting '5.6 cents' for '90 cents', and

"(iii) in clause (iii) of such subparagraph, by substituting '3.3 cents' for '53.5 cents'.",

(b) CONTROLLED GROUP AND SINGLE TAXPAYER RULES.—Paragraph (4) of section 5041(c) is amended by striking "section 5051(a)(2)(B)" and inserting "section 5051(a)(5)".

(c) Allowance of Credit for Foreign Manufacturers and Importers.—Subsection (c) of section 5041, as amended by subsection (a), is amended—

(1) in subparagraph (A) of paragraph (8), by inserting "but only if the importer is an electing importer under paragraph (9) and the wine gallons of wine have been assigned to the importer pursuant to such paragraph" after "into the United States during the calendar year", and

(2) by adding at the end the following new paragraph:

"(9) Allowance of credit for foreign manufacturers and importers.—

"(A) In general.—In the case of any wine gallons of wine which have been produced outside of the United States and imported into the United States, the credit allowable under paragraph (8) (referred to in this paragraph as the 'tax credit') may be assigned by the person who produced such wine (referred to in this paragraph as the 'foreign producer'), provided that such person makes an election described in subparagraph (B)(ii), to any electing importer of such wine gallons pursuant to the requirements established by the Secretary under subparagraph (B).

"(B) ASSIGNMENT.—The Secretary shall, through such rules, regulations, and procedures as are determined appropriate, establish procedures for assignment of the tax credit provided under this paragraph, which shall include—

"(i) a limitation to ensure that the number of wine gallons of wine for which the tax credit has been assigned by a foreign producer—

"(I) to any importer does not exceed the number of wine gallons of wine produced by such foreign producer during the calendar year which were imported into the United States by such importer, and

"(II) to all importers does not exceed the 750,000 wine gallons of wine to which the tax credit applies,

"(ii) procedures that allow the election of a foreign producer to assign and an importer to receive the tax credit provided under this paragraph, "(iii) requirements that the foreign producer provide any information as the Secretary determines necessary and appropriate for purposes of carrying out this paragraph, and

"(iv) procedures that allow for revocation of eligibility of the foreign producer and the importer for the tax credit provided under this paragraph in the case of any erroneous or fraudulent information provided under clause (iii) which the Secretary deems to be material to qualifying for such credit.

"(C) CONTROLLED GROUP.—For purposes of this section, any importer making an election described in subparagraph (B)(ii) shall be deemed to be a member of the controlled group of the foreign producer, as described under paragraph (4).".

(d) EFFECTIVE DATE.—The amendments made by this section shall apply to wine removed after December 31, 2017.

**SEC. 13805. ADJUSTMENT OF ALCOHOL CONTENT LEVEL FOR APPLICATION OF EXCISE TAX RATES.**

(a) IN GENERAL.—Paragraphs (1) and (2) of section 5041(b) are each amended by inserting "(16 percent in the case of wine removed after December 31, 2017, and before January 1, 2020" after "14 percent".

(b) EFFECTIVE DATE.—The amendments made by this section shall apply to wine removed after December 31, 2017.

**SEC. 13806. DEFINITION OF MEAD AND LOW ALCOHOL BY VOLUME WINE.**

(a) IN GENERAL.—Section 5041 is amended—

(1) in subsection (a), by striking "Still wines" and inserting "Subject to subsection (h), still wines", and

(2) by adding at the end the following new subsection:

"(h) MEAD AND LOW ALCOHOL BY VOLUME WINE.—

"(1) IN GENERAL.—For purposes of subsections (a) and (b)(1), mead and low alcohol by volume wine shall be deemed to be still wines containing not more than 16 percent of alcohol by volume.

"(2) DEFINITIONS.—

"(A) MEAD.—For purposes of this section, the term 'mead' means a wine—

"(i) containing not more than 0.64 gram of carbon dioxide per hundred milliliters of wine, except that the Secretary shall by regulations prescribe such tolerances to this limitation as may be reasonably necessary in good commercial practice,

"(ii) which is derived solely from honey and water,

"(iii) which contains no fruit product or fruit flavoring, and

"(iv) which contains less than 8.5 percent alcohol by volume.

"(B) LOW ALCOHOL BY VOLUME WINE.—For purposes of this section, the term 'low alcohol by volume wine' means a wine—

"(i) containing not more than 0.64 gram of carbon dioxide per hundred milliliters of wine, except that the Secretary shall by regulations prescribe such tolerances to this limitation as may be reasonably necessary in good commercial practice, "(ii) which is derived—

"(I) primarily from grapes, or

"(II) from grape juice concentrate and water,

"(iii) which contains no fruit product or fruit flavoring other than grape, and

"(iv) which contains less than 8.5 percent alcohol by volume.

"(3) TERMINATION.—This subsection shall not apply to wine removed after December 31, 2019.".

(b) EFFECTIVE DATE.—The amendments made by this section shall apply to wine removed after December 31, 2017.

**SEC. 13807. REDUCED RATE OF EXCISE TAX ON CERTAIN DISTILLED SPIRITS.**

(a) IN GENERAL.—Section 5001 is amended by redesignating subsection (c) as subsection (d) and by inserting after subsection (b) the following new subsection:

"(c) REDUCED RATE FOR 2018 AND 2019.—

"(1) IN GENERAL.—In the case of a distilled spirits operation, the otherwise applicable tax rate under subsection (a)(1) shall be—

"(A) $2.70 per proof gallon on the first 100,000 proof gallons of distilled spirits, and

"(B) $13.34 per proof gallon on the first 22,130,000 of proof gallons of distilled spirits to which subparagraph (A) does not apply,

which have been distilled or processed by such operation and removed during the calendar year for consumption or sale, or which have been imported by the importer into the United States during the calendar year.

"(2) CONTROLLED GROUPS.—

"(A) IN GENERAL.—In the case of a controlled group, the proof gallon quantities specified under subparagraphs (A) and (B) of paragraph (1) shall be applied to such group and apportioned among the members of such group in such manner as the Secretary or their delegate shall by regulations prescribe.

"(B) DEFINITION.—For purposes of subparagraph (A), the term 'controlled group' shall have the meaning given such term by subsection (a) of section 1563, except that 'more than 50 percent' shall be substituted for 'at least 80 percent' each place it appears in such subsection.

"(C) RULES FOR NON-CORPORATIONS.— Under regulations prescribed by the Secretary, principles similar to the principles of subparagraphs (A) and (B) shall be applied to a group under common control where one or more of the persons is not a corporation.

"(D) SINGLE TAXPAYER.—Pursuant to rules issued by the Secretary, two or more entities (whether or not under common control) that produce distilled spirits marketed under a similar brand, license, franchise, or other arrangement shall be treated as a single taxpayer for purposes of the application of this subsection.

"(3) TERMINATION.—This subsection shall not apply to distilled spirits removed after December 31, 2019.".

(b) CONFORMING AMENDMENT.—Section 7652(f)(2) is amended by striking "section 5001(a)(1)" and inserting "subsection (a)(1) of section 5001, determined as if subsection (c)(1) of such section did not apply".

(c) APPLICATION OF REDUCED TAX RATE FOR FOREIGN MANUFACTURERS AND IMPORTERS.—Subsection (c) of section 5001, as added by subsection (a), is amended—

(1) in paragraph (1), by inserting "but only if the importer is an electing importer under paragraph (3) and the proof gallons of distilled spirits

have been assigned to the importer pursuant to such paragraph'' after ''into the United States during the calendar year'', and

(2) by redesignating paragraph (3) as paragraph (4) and by inserting after paragraph (2) the following new paragraph:

''(3) REDUCED TAX RATE FOR FOREIGN MANUFACTURERS AND IMPORTERS.—

''(A) IN GENERAL.—In the case of any proof gallons of distilled spirits which have been produced outside of the United States and imported into the United States, the rate of tax applicable under paragraph (1) (referred to in this paragraph as the 'reduced tax rate') may be assigned by the distilled spirits operation (provided that such operation makes an election described in subparagraph (B)(ii)) to any electing importer of such proof gallons pursuant to the requirements established by the Secretary under subparagraph (B).

''(B) ASSIGNMENT.—The Secretary shall, through such rules, regulations, and procedures as are determined appropriate, establish procedures for assignment of the reduced tax rate provided under this paragraph, which shall include—

"(i) a limitation to ensure that the number of proof gallons of distilled spirits for which the reduced tax rate has been assigned by a distilled spirits operation—

"(I) to any importer does not exceed the number of proof gallons produced by such operation during the calendar year which were imported into the United States by such importer, and

"(II) to all importers does not exceed the 22,230,000 proof gallons of distilled spirits to which the reduced tax rate applies,

"(ii) procedures that allow the election of a distilled spirits operation to assign and an importer to receive the reduced tax rate provided under this paragraph,

"(iii) requirements that the distilled spirits operation provide any information as the Secretary determines necessary and appropriate for purposes of carrying out this paragraph, and "(iv) procedures that allow for revocation of eligibility of the distilled spirits operation and the importer for the reduced tax rate provided under this paragraph in the case of any erroneous or fraudulent information provided under clause (iii) which the Secretary deems to be material to qualifying for such reduced rate.

"(C) CONTROLLED GROUP.—

"(i) IN GENERAL.—For purposes of this section, any importer making an election described in subparagraph (B)(ii) shall be deemed to be a member of the controlled group of the distilled spirits operation, as described under paragraph (2).

"(ii) APPORTIONMENT.—For purposes of this paragraph, in the case of a controlled group, rules similar to section 5051(a)(5)(B) shall apply.".

(d) EFFECTIVE DATE.—The amendments made by this section shall apply to distilled spirits removed after December 31, 2017.

**SEC. 13808. BULK DISTILLED SPIRITS.**

(a) IN GENERAL.—Section 5212 is amended by adding at the end the following sentence: "In the case of distilled spirits transferred in bond after December 31, 2017, and before January 1, 2020, this section shall be applied without regard to whether distilled spirits are bulk distilled spirits.''.

(b) EFFECTIVE DATE.—The amendments made by this section shall apply distilled spirits transferred in bond after December 31, 2017.

**Subpart B—Miscellaneous Provisions**

**SEC. 13821. MODIFICATION OF TAX TREATMENT OF ALASKA NATIVE CORPORATIONS AND SETTLEMENT TRUSTS.**

(a) EXCLUSION FOR ANCSA PAYMENTS ASSIGNED TO ALASKA NATIVE SETTLEMENT TRUSTS.—

(1) IN GENERAL.—Part III of subchapter B of chapter 1 is amended by inserting before section 140 the following new section:

**"SEC. 139G. ASSIGNMENTS TO ALASKA NATIVE SETTLEMENT TRUSTS.**

''(a) IN GENERAL.—In the case of a Native Corporation, gross income shall not include the value of any payments that would otherwise be made, or treated as being made, to such Native Corporation pursuant to, or as required by, any provision of the Alaska Native Claims Settlement Act (43 U.S.C. 1601 et seq.), including any payment that would otherwise be made to a Village Corporation pursuant to section 7(j) of the Alaska Native Claims Settlement Act (43 U.S.C. 1606(j)), provided that any such payments—

"(1) are assigned in writing to a Settlement Trust, and

"(2) were not received by such Native Corporation prior to the assignment described in paragraph (1).

"(b) INCLUSION IN GROSS INCOME.—In the case of a Settlement Trust which has been assigned payments described in subsection (a), gross income shall include such payments when received by such Settlement Trust pursuant to the assignment and shall have the same character as if such payments were received by the Native Corporation.

"(c) AMOUNT AND SCOPE OF ASSIGNMENT.—The amount and scope of any assignment under subsection (a) shall be described with reasonable particularity and may either be in a percentage of one or more such payments or in a fixed dollar amount.

"(d) DURATION OF ASSIGNMENT; REVOCABILITY.—Any assignment under subsection (a) shall specify—

"(1) a duration either in perpetuity or for a period of time, and

"(2) whether such assignment is revocable.

"(e) PROHIBITION ON DEDUCTION.—Notwithstanding section 247, no deduction shall be allowed to a Native Corporation for purposes of any amounts described in subsection (a).

"(f) DEFINITIONS.—For purposes of this section, the terms 'Native Corporation' and 'Settlement Trust' have the same meaning given such terms under section 646(h).".

(2) CONFORMING AMENDMENT.—The table of sections for part III of subchapter B of chapter 1 is amended by inserting before the item relating to section 140 the following new item:

"Sec. 139G. Assignments to Alaska Native Settlement Trusts.".

(3) EFFECTIVE DATE.—The amendments made by this subsection shall apply to taxable years beginning after December 31, 2016.

(b) DEDUCTION OF CONTRIBUTIONS TO ALASKA NATIVE SETTLEMENT TRUSTS.—

(1) IN GENERAL.—Part VIII of subchapter B of chapter 1 is amended by inserting before section 248 the following new section:

**"SEC. 247. CONTRIBUTIONS TO ALASKA NATIVE SETTLEMENT TRUSTS.**

"(a) IN GENERAL.—In the case of a Native Corporation, there shall be allowed a deduction for any contribu-

Trust (regardless of whether an election under section 646 is in effect for such Settlement Trust) for which the Native Corporation has made an annual election under subsection (e).

"(b) AMOUNT OF DEDUCTION.—The amount of the deduction under subsection (a) shall be equal to—

"(1) in the case of a cash contribution (regardless of the method of payment, including currency, coins, money order, or check), the amount of such contribution, or

"(2) in the case of a contribution not described in paragraph (1), the lesser of—

"(A) the Native Corporation's adjusted basis in the property contributed, or

"(B) the fair market value of the property contributed.

"(c) LIMITATION AND CARRYOVER.—

"(1) IN GENERAL.—Subject to paragraph (2), the deduction allowed under subsection (a) for any taxable year shall not exceed the taxable income (as determined without regard to such deduction) of the Native Corporation for the taxable year in which the contribution was made.

"(2) CARRYOVER.—If the aggregate amount of contributions described in subsection (a) for any taxable year exceeds the limitation under paragraph (1), such excess shall be treated as a contribution described in subsection (a) in each of the 15 succeeding years in order of time.

"(d) DEFINITIONS.—For purposes of this section, the terms 'Native Corporation' and 'Settlement Trust' have the same meaning given such terms under section 646(h).

"(e) MANNER OF MAKING ELECTION.—

"(1) IN GENERAL.—For each taxable year, a Native Corporation may elect to have this section apply for such taxable year on the income tax return or an amendment or supplement to the return of the Native Corporation, with such election to have effect solely for such taxable year.

"(2) REVOCATION.—Any election made by a Native Corporation pursuant to this subsection may be revoked pursuant to a timely filed amendment or supplement to the income tax return of such Native Corporation.

"(f) ADDITIONAL RULES.—

"(1) EARNINGS AND PROFITS.—Notwithstanding section 646(d)(2), in the case of a Native Corporation which claims a deduction under this section for any taxable year, the earnings and profits of such Native Corporation for such taxable year shall be reduced by the amount of such deduction.

"(2) GAIN OR LOSS.—No gain or loss shall be recognized by the Native Corporation with respect to a contribution of property for which a deduction is allowed under this section.

"(3) INCOME.—Subject to subsection (g), a Settlement Trust shall include in income the amount of any deduction allowed under this section in the taxable year in which the Settlement Trust actually receives such contribution.

"(4) PERIOD.—The holding period under section 1223 of the Settlement Trust shall include the period the property was held by the Native Corporation.

"(5) BASIS.—The basis that a Settlement Trust has for which a deduction is allowed under this section shall be equal to the lesser of—

"(A) the adjusted basis of the Native Corporation in such property immediately before such contribution, or

"(B) the fair market value of the property immediately before such contribution.

"(6) PROHIBITION.—No deduction shall be allowed under this section with respect to any contributions made to a Settlement Trust which are in violation of subsection (a)(2) or (c)(2) of section 39 of the Alaska Native Claims Settlement Act (43 U.S.C. 1629e).

"(g) ELECTION BY SETTLEMENT TRUST TO DEFER INCOME RECOGNITION.—

"(1) IN GENERAL.—In the case of a contribution which consists of property other than cash, a Settlement Trust may elect to defer recognition of any income related to such property until the sale or exchange of such property, in whole or in part, by the Settlement Trust.

"(2) TREATMENT.—In the case of property described in paragraph (1), any income or gain realized on the sale or exchange of such property shall be treated as—

"(A) for such amount of the income or gain as is equal to or less than the amount of income which would be included in income at the time of contribution under subsection (f)(3) but for the taxpayer's election under this subsection, ordinary income, and

"(B) for any amounts of the income or gain which are in excess of the amount of income which would be included in income at the time of contribution under subsection (f)(3) but for the taxpayer's election under this subsection, having the same character as if this subsection did not apply.

"(3) ELECTION.—

"(A) IN GENERAL.—For each taxable year, a Settlement Trust may elect to apply this subsection for any property described in paragraph (1) which was contributed during such year. Any property to which the election applies shall be identified and described with reasonable particularity on the income tax return or an amendment or supplement to the return of the Settlement Trust, with such election to have effect solely for such taxable year.

"(B) REVOCATION.—Any election made by a Settlement Trust pursuant to this subsection may be revoked pursuant to a timely filed amendment or supplement to the income tax return of such Settlement Trust.

"(C) CERTAIN DISPOSITIONS.—

"(i) IN GENERAL.—In the case of any property for which an election is in effect under this subsection and which is disposed of within the first taxable year subsequent to the taxable year in which such property was contributed to the Settlement Trust—

"(I) this section shall be applied as if the election under this subsection had not been made,

"(II) any income or gain which would have been included in the year of contribution under subsection (f)(3) but for the taxpayer's election under this subsection shall be included in income for the taxable year of such contribution, and

"(III) the Settlement Trust shall pay any increase in tax resulting from such inclusion, including any applicable interest, and increased by 10 percent of the amount of such increase with interest.

"(ii) ASSESSMENT.—Notwithstanding section 6501(a), any amount described in subclause (III) of clause (i) may be assessed, or a proceeding in court with respect to such amount may be initiated without assessment, within 4 years after the date on which the return making the election under this subsection for such property was filed.".

(2) CONFORMING AMENDMENT.—The table of sections for part VIII of subchapter B of chapter 1 is amended by inserting before the item relating to section 248 the following new item:

"Sec. 247. Contributions to Alaska Native Settlement Trusts.".

(3) EFFECTIVE DATE.—

(A) IN GENERAL.—The amendments made by this subsection shall apply to taxable years for which the period of limitation on refund or credit under section 6511 of the Internal Revenue Code of 1986 has not expired.

(B) ONE-YEAR WAIVER OF STATUTE OF LIMITATIONS.—If the period of limitation on a credit or refund resulting from the amendments made by paragraph (1) expires before the end of the 1-year period beginning on the date of the enactment of this Act, refund or credit of such overpayment (to the extent attributable to such amendments) may, nevertheless, be made or allowed if claim therefor is filed before the close of such 1-year period.

(c) INFORMATION REPORTING FOR DEDUCTIBLE CONTRIBUTIONS TO ALASKA NATIVE SETTLEMENT TRUSTS.—

(1) IN GENERAL.—Section 6039H is amended—

(A) in the heading, by striking "**SPONSORING**", and

(B) by adding at the end the following new subsection:

"(e) DEDUCTIBLE CONTRIBUTIONS BY NATIVE CORPORATIONS TO ALASKA NATIVE SETTLEMENT TRUSTS.—

"(1) IN GENERAL.—Any Native Corporation (as defined in subsection (m) of section 3 of the Alaska Native Claims Settlement Act (43 U.S.C. 1602(m))) which has made a contribution to a Settlement Trust (as defined in subsection (t) of such section) to which an election under subsection (e) of section 247 applies shall provide such Settlement Trust with a statement regarding such election not later than January 31 of the calendar year subsequent to the calendar year in which the contribution was made.

"(2) CONTENT OF STATEMENT.—The statement described in paragraph (1) shall include—

"(A) the total amount of contributions to which the election under subsection (e) of section 247 applies,

"(B) for each contribution, whether such contribution was in cash,

"(C) for each contribution which consists of property other than cash, the date that such property was acquired by the Native Corporation and the adjusted basis and fair market value of such property on the date such property was contributed to the Settlement Trust,

"(D) the date on which each contribution was made to the Settlement Trust, and

"(E) such information as the Secretary determines to be necessary or appropriate for the identification of each contribution and the accurate inclusion of income relating to such contributions by the Settlement Trust.".

(2) CONFORMING AMENDMENT.—The item relating to section 6039H in the table of sections for subpart A of part III of subchapter A of chapter 61 is amended to read as follows:

"Sec. 6039H. Information With Respect to Alaska Native Settlement Trusts and Native Corporations.".

(3) EFFECTIVE DATE.—The amendments made by this subsection shall apply to taxable years beginning after December 31, 2016.

**SEC. 13822. AMOUNTS PAID FOR AIRCRAFT MANAGEMENT SERVICES.**

(a) IN GENERAL.—Subsection (e) of section 4261 is amended by adding at the end the following new paragraph:

"(5) AMOUNTS PAID FOR AIRCRAFT MANAGEMENT SERVICES.—

"(A) IN GENERAL.—No tax shall be imposed by this section or section 4271 on any amounts paid by an aircraft owner for aircraft management services related to—

"(i) maintenance and support of the aircraft owner's aircraft, or

"(ii) flights on the aircraft owner's aircraft.

"(B) AIRCRAFT MANAGEMENT SERVICES.—For purposes of subparagraph (A), the term 'aircraft management services' includes—

"(i) assisting an aircraft owner with administrative and support services, such as scheduling, flight planning, and weather forecasting, "(ii) obtaining insurance,

"(iii) maintenance, storage and fueling of aircraft,

"(iv) hiring, training, and provision of pilots and crew,

"(v) establishing and complying with safety standards, and

"(vi) such other services as are necessary to support flights operated by an aircraft owner.

"(C) LESSEE TREATED AS AIRCRAFT OWNER.—

"(i) IN GENERAL.—For purposes of this paragraph, the term 'aircraft owner' includes a person who leases the aircraft other than under a disqualified lease.

"(ii) DISQUALIFIED LEASE.—For purposes of clause (i), the term 'disqualified lease' means a lease from a person providing aircraft management services with respect to such aircraft (or a related person (within the meaning of section 465(b)(3)(C)) to the person providing such services), if such lease is for a term of 31 days or less.

"(D) PRO RATA ALLOCATION.—In the case of amounts paid to any person which (but for this subsection) are subject to the tax imposed by subsection (a), a portion of which consists of amounts described in subparagraph (A), this paragraph shall apply on a pro rata basis only to the portion which consists of amounts described in such subparagraph.".

(b) EFFECTIVE DATE.—The amendment made by this section shall apply to amounts paid after the date of the enactment of this Act.

**SEC. 13823. OPPORTUNITY ZONES.**

(a) IN GENERAL.—Chapter 1 is amended by adding at the end the following:

## "Subchapter Z—Opportunity Zones



**"SEC. 1400Z–1. DESIGNATION.**

"(a) QUALIFIED OPPORTUNITY ZONE DEFINED.—For the purposes of this subchapter, the term 'qualified opportunity zone' means a population census tract that is a low-income community that is designated as a qualified opportunity zone.

"(b) DESIGNATION.—

"(1) IN GENERAL.—For purposes of subsection

community is designated as a qualified opportunity zone if—

"(A) not later than the end of the determination period, the chief executive officer of the State in which the tract is located—

"(i) nominates the tract for designation as a qualified opportunity zone, and

"(ii) notifies the Secretary in writing of such nomination, and

"(B) the Secretary certifies such nomination and designates such tract as a qualified opportunity zone before the end of the consideration period.

"(2) EXTENSION OF PERIODS.—A chief executive officer of a State may request that the Secretary extend either the determination or consideration period, or both (determined without regard to this subparagraph), for an additional 30 days.

"(c) OTHER DEFINITIONS.—For purposes of this subsection—

"(1) LOW-INCOME COMMUNITIES.—The term 'low-income community' has the same meaning as when used in section 45D(e).

"(2) DEFINITION OF PERIODS.—

"(A) CONSIDERATION PERIOD.—The term 'consideration period' means the 30-day period beginning on the date on which the Secretary receives notice under subsection (b)(1)(A)(ii), as extended under subsection (b)(2).

"(B) DETERMINATION PERIOD.—The term 'determination period' means the 90-day period beginning on the date of the enactment of the Tax Cuts and Jobs Act, as extended under subsection (b)(2).

"(3) STATE.—For purposes of this section, the term 'State' includes any possession of the United States.

"(d) NUMBER OF DESIGNATIONS.—

"(1) IN GENERAL.—Except as provided by paragraph (2), the number of population census tracts in a State that may be designated as qualified opportunity zones under this section may not exceed 25 percent of the number of low-income communities in the State.

"(2) EXCEPTION.—If the number of low-income communities in a State is less than 100, then a total of 25 of such tracts may be designated as qualified opportunity zones.

"(e) DESIGNATION OF TRACTS CONTIGUOUS WITH LOW-INCOME COMMUNITIES.—

"(1) IN GENERAL.—A population census tract that is not a low-income community may be designated as a qualified opportunity zone under this section if—

"(A) the tract is contiguous with the low-income community that is designated as a qualified opportunity zone, and

"(B) the median family income of the tract does not exceed 125 percent of the median family income of the low-income community with which the tract is contiguous.

"(2) LIMITATION.—Not more than 5 percent of the population census tracts designated in a State as a qualified opportunity zone may be designated under paragraph (1).

"(f) PERIOD FOR WHICH DESIGNATION IS IN EFFECT.—A designation as a qualified opportunity zone shall remain in effect for the period beginning on the date of the designation and ending at the close of the 10th calendar year beginning on or after such date of designation.

**"SEC. 1400Z–2. SPECIAL RULES FOR CAPITAL GAINS INVESTED IN OPPORTUNITY ZONES.**

"(a) IN GENERAL.—

"(1) TREATMENT OF GAINS.—In the case of gain from the sale to, or exchange with, an unrelated person of any property held by the taxpayer, at the election of the taxpayer—

"(A) gross income for the taxable year shall not include so much of such gain as does not exceed the aggregate amount invested by the taxpayer in a qualified opportunity fund during the 180-day period beginning on the date of such sale or exchange,

"(B) the amount of gain excluded by subparagraph (A) shall be included in gross income as provided by subsection (b), and

"(C) subsection (c) shall apply.

"(2) ELECTION.—No election may be made under paragraph (1)—

"(A) with respect to a sale or exchange if an election previously made with respect to such sale or exchange is in effect, or

"(B) with respect to any sale or exchange after December 31, 2026.

"(b) DEFERRAL OF GAIN INVESTED IN OPPORTUNITY ZONE PROPERTY.—

"(1) YEAR OF INCLUSION.—Gain to which subsection (a)(1)(B) applies shall be included in income in the taxable year which includes the earlier of—

"(A) the date on which such investment is sold or exchanged, or

"(B) December 31, 2026.

"(2) AMOUNT INCLUDIBLE.—

"(A) IN GENERAL.—The amount of gain included in gross income under subsection (a)(1)(A) shall be the excess of—

"(i) the lesser of the amount of gain excluded under paragraph (1) or the fair market value of the investment as determined as of the date described in paragraph (1), over

"(ii) the taxpayer's basis in the investment.

"(B) DETERMINATION OF BASIS.—

"(i) IN GENERAL.—Except as otherwise provided in this clause or subsection (c), the taxpayer's basis in the investment shall be zero.

"(ii) INCREASE FOR GAIN RECOGNIZED UNDER SUBSECTION (a)(1)(B).—The basis in the investment shall be increased by the amount of gain recognized by reason of subsection (a)(1)(B) with respect to such property.

"(iii) INVESTMENTS HELD FOR 5 YEARS.—In the case of any investment held for at least 5 years, the basis of such investment shall be increased by an amount equal to 10 percent of the amount of gain deferred by reason of subsection (a)(1)(A).

"(iv) INVESTMENTS HELD FOR 7 YEARS.—In the case of any investment held by the taxpayer for at least 7 years, in addition to any adjustment made under clause (iii), the basis of such property shall be increased by an amount equal to 5 percent of the amount of gain deferred by reason of subsection (a)(1)(A).

"(c) SPECIAL RULE FOR INVESTMENTS HELD FOR AT LEAST 10 YEARS.—In the case of any investment held by the taxpayer for at least 10 years and with respect to which the taxpayer makes an election under this clause, the basis of such property shall be equal to the fair market value of such investment on the date that the investment is sold or exchanged.

"(d) QUALIFIED OPPORTUNITY FUND.—For purposes of this section—

"(1) IN GENERAL.—The term 'qualified opportunity fund' means any investment vehicle which is organized as a corporation or a partnership for the purpose of investing in qualified opportunity zone property (other than another qualified opportunity fund) that holds at least 90 percent of its assets in qualified opportunity zone property, determined by the average of the percentage of qualified opportunity zone property held in the fund as measured—

"(A) on the last day of the first 6-month period of the taxable year of the fund, and

"(B) on the last day of the taxable year of the fund.

"(2) QUALIFIED OPPORTUNITY ZONE PROPERTY.—

"(A) IN GENERAL.—The term 'qualified opportunity zone property' means property which is—

"(i) qualified opportunity zone stock,

"(ii) qualified opportunity zone partnership interest, or

"(iii) qualified opportunity zone business property.

"(B) QUALIFIED OPPORTUNITY ZONE STOCK.—

"(i) IN GENERAL.—Except as provided in clause (ii), the term 'qualified opportunity zone stock' means any stock in a domestic corporation if—

"(I) such stock is acquired by the qualified opportunity fund after December 31, 2017, at its original issue (directly or through an underwriter) from the corporation solely in exchange for cash,

"(II) as of the time such stock was issued, such corporation was a qualified opportunity zone business (or, in the case of a new corporation, such corporation was being organized for purposes of being a qualified opportunity zone business), and

"(III) during substantially all of the qualified opportunity fund's holding period for such stock, such corporation qualified as a qualified opportunity zone business.

"(ii) REDEMPTIONS.—A rule similar to the rule of section 1202(c)(3) shall apply for purposes of this paragraph.

"(C) QUALIFIED OPPORTUNITY ZONE PARTNERSHIP INTEREST.—The term 'qualified opportunity zone partnership interest' means any capital or profits interest in a domestic partnership if—

"(i) such interest is acquired by the qualified opportunity fund after December 31, 2017, from the partnership solely in exchange for cash,

"(ii) as of the time such interest was acquired, such partnership was a qualified opportunity zone business (or, in the case of a new partnership, such partnership was being organized for purposes of being a qualified opportunity zone business), and

"(iii) during substantially all of the qualified opportunity fund's holding period for such interest, such partnership qualified as a qualified opportunity zone business.

"(D) QUALIFIED OPPORTUNITY ZONE BUSINESS PROPERTY.—

"(i) IN GENERAL.—The term 'qualified opportunity zone business property' means tangible property used in a trade or business of the qualified opportunity fund if—

"(I) such property was acquired by the qualified opportunity fund by purchase (as defined in section 179(d)(2)) after December 31, 2017,

"(II) the original use of such property in the qualified opportunity zone commences with the qualified opportunity fund or the qualified opportunity fund substantially improves the property, and

"(III) during substantially all of the qualified opportunity fund's holding period for such property, substantially all of the use of such property was in a qualified opportunity zone.

"(ii) SUBSTANTIAL IMPROVEMENT.—For purposes of subparagraph (A)(ii), property shall be treated as substantially improved by the qualified opportunity fund only if, during any 30-month period beginning after the date of acquisition of such property, additions to basis with respect to such property in the hands of the qualified opportunity fund exceed an amount equal to the adjusted basis of such property at the beginning of such 30-month period in the hands of the qualified opportunity fund.

"(iii) RELATED PARTY.—For purposes of subparagraph (A)(i), the related person rule of section 179(d)(2) shall be applied pursuant to paragraph (8) of this subsection in lieu of the application of such rule in section 179(d)(2)(A).

"(3) QUALIFIED OPPORTUNITY ZONE BUSINESS.—

"(A) IN GENERAL.—The term 'qualified opportunity zone business' means a trade or business—

"(i) in which substantially all of the tangible property owned or leased by the taxpayer is qualified opportunity zone business property (determined by substituting 'qualified opportunity zone business' for 'qualified opportunity fund' each place it appears in paragraph (2)(D)),

"(ii) which satisfies the requirements of paragraphs (2), (4), and (8) of section 1397C(b), and

"(iii) which is not described in section 144(c)(6)(B).

"(B) SPECIAL RULE.—For purposes of subparagraph (A), tangible property that ceases to be a qualified opportunity zone business property shall continue to be treated as a qualified opportunity zone business property for the lesser of—

"(i) 5 years after the date on which such tangible property ceases to be so qualified, or

"(ii) the date on which such tangible property is no longer held by the qualified opportunity zone business.

"(e) APPLICABLE RULES.—

"(1) TREATMENT OF INVESTMENTS WITH MIXED FUNDS.—In the case of any investment in a qualified opportunity fund only a portion of which consists of investments of gain to which an election under subsection (a) is in effect—

"(A) such investment shall be treated as 2 separate investments, consisting of—

"(i) one investment that only includes amounts to which the election under subsection (a) applies, and

"(ii) a separate investment consisting of other amounts, and

"(B) subsections (a), (b), and (c) shall only apply to the investment described in subparagraph (A)(i).

"(2) RELATED PERSONS.—For purposes of this section, persons are related to each other if such persons are described in section 267(b) or 707(b)(1), determined by substituting '20 percent' for '50 percent' each place it occurs in such sections.

"(3) DECEDENTS.—In the case of a decedent, amounts recognized under this section shall, if not properly includible in the gross income of the decedent, be includible in gross income as provided by section 691.

"(4) REGULATIONS.—The Secretary shall prescribe such regulations as may be necessary or appropriate to carry out the purposes of this section, including—

"(A) rules for the certification of qualified opportunity funds for the purposes of this section,

"(B) rules to ensure a qualified opportunity fund has a reasonable period of time to reinvest the return of capital from investments in qualified opportunity zone stock and qualified opportunity zone partnership interests, and to reinvest proceeds received from the sale or disposition of qualified opportunity zone property, and

"(C) rules to prevent abuse.

"(f) FAILURE OF QUALIFIED OPPORTUNITY FUND TO MAINTAIN INVESTMENT STANDARD.—

"(1) IN GENERAL.—If a qualified opportunity fund fails to meet the 90-percent requirement of subsection (c)(1), the qualified opportunity fund shall pay a penalty for each month it fails to meet the requirement in an amount equal to the product of—

"(A) the excess of—

"(i) the amount equal to 90 percent of its aggregate assets, over "(ii) the aggregate amount of qualified opportunity zone property held by the fund, multiplied by

"(B) the underpayment rate established under section 6621(a)(2) for such month.

"(2) SPECIAL RULE FOR PARTNERSHIPS.—In the case that the qualified opportunity fund is a partnership, the penalty imposed by paragraph (1) shall be taken into account proportionately as part of the distributive share of each partner of the partnership.

"(3) REASONABLE CAUSE EXCEPTION.—No penalty shall be imposed under this subsection with respect to any failure if it is shown that such failure is due to reasonable cause.".

(b) BASIS ADJUSTMENTS.—Section 1016(a) is amended by striking "and" at the end of paragraph (36), by striking the period at the end of paragraph (37) and inserting ", and", and by inserting after paragraph (37) the following:

"(38) to the extent provided in subsections (b)(2) and (c) of section 1400Z–2.".

(c) CLERICAL AMENDMENT.—The table of subchapters for chapter 1 is amended by adding at the end the following new item:

(d) EFFECTIVE DATE.—The amendments made by this section shall take effect on the date of the enactment of this Act.

# Subtitle D—International Tax Provisions

## PART I—OUTBOUND TRANSACTIONS

### Subpart A—Establishment of Participation Exemption System for Taxation of Foreign Income

#### SEC. 14101. DEDUCTION FOR FOREIGN-SOURCE PORTION OF DIVIDENDS RECEIVED BY DOMESTIC CORPORATIONS FROM SPECIFIED 10-PERCENT OWNED FOREIGN CORPORATIONS.

(a) IN GENERAL.—Part VIII of subchapter B of chapter 1 is amended by inserting after section 245 the following new section:

**"SEC. 245A. DEDUCTION FOR FOREIGN SOURCE-PORTION OF DIVIDENDS RECEIVED BY DOMESTIC CORPORATIONS FROM SPECIFIED 10-PERCENT OWNED FOREIGN CORPORATIONS.**

"(a) IN GENERAL.—In the case of any dividend received from a specified 10-percent owned foreign corporation by a domestic corporation which is a United States shareholder with respect to such foreign corporation, there shall be allowed as a deduction an amount equal to the foreign-source portion of such dividend.

"(b) SPECIFIED 10-PERCENT OWNED FOREIGN CORPORATION.—For purposes of this section—

"(1) IN GENERAL.—The term 'specified 10-percent owned foreign corporation' means any foreign corporation with respect to which any domestic corporation is a United States shareholder with respect to such corporation.

"(2) EXCLUSION OF PASSIVE FOREIGN INVESTMENT COMPANIES.—Such term shall not include any corporation which is a passive foreign investment company (as defined in section 1297) with respect to the shareholder and which is not a controlled foreign corporation.

"(c) FOREIGN-SOURCE PORTION.—For purposes of this section—

"(1) IN GENERAL.—The foreign-source portion of any dividend from a specified 10-percent owned foreign corporation is an amount which bears the same ratio to such dividend as—

"(A) the undistributed foreign earnings of the specified 10-percent owned foreign corporation, bears to

"(B) the total undistributed earnings of such foreign corporation.

"(2) UNDISTRIBUTED EARNINGS.—The term 'undistributed earnings' means the amount of the earnings and profits of the specified 10-percent owned foreign corporation (computed in accordance with sections 964(a) and 986)—

"(A) as of the close of the taxable year of the specified 10-percent owned foreign corporation in which the dividend is distributed, and

"(B) without diminution by reason of dividends distributed during such taxable year.

"(3) UNDISTRIBUTED FOREIGN EARNINGS.—The term 'undistributed foreign earnings' means the portion of the undistributed earnings which is attributable to neither—

"(A) income described in subparagraph (A) of section 245(a)(5), nor

"(B) dividends described in subparagraph (B) of such section (determined without regard to section 245(a)(12)).

"(d) DISALLOWANCE OF FOREIGN TAX CREDIT, ETC.—

"(1) IN GENERAL.—No credit shall be allowed under section 901 for any taxes paid or accrued (or treated as paid or accrued) with respect to any dividend for which a deduction is allowed under this section.

"(2) DENIAL OF DEDUCTION.—No deduction shall be allowed under this chapter for any tax for which credit is not allowable under section 901 by reason of paragraph (1) (determined by treating the taxpayer as having elected the benefits of subpart A of part III of subchapter N).

"(e) SPECIAL RULES FOR HYBRID DIVIDENDS.—

"(1) IN GENERAL.—Subsection (a) shall not apply to any dividend received by a United States shareholder from a controlled foreign corporation if the dividend is a hybrid dividend.

"(2) HYBRID DIVIDENDS OF TIERED CORPORATIONS.—If a controlled foreign corporation with respect to which a domestic corporation is a United States shareholder receives a hybrid dividend from any other controlled foreign corporation with respect to which such domestic corporation is also a United States shareholder, then, notwithstanding any other provision of this title—

"(A) the hybrid dividend shall be treated for purposes of section 951(a)(1)(A) as subpart F income of the receiving controlled foreign corporation for the taxable year of the controlled foreign corporation in which the dividend was received, and

"(B) the United States shareholder shall include in gross income an amount equal to the shareholder's pro rata share (determined in the same manner as under section 951(a)(2)) of the subpart F income described in subparagraph (A).

"(3) DENIAL OF FOREIGN TAX CREDIT, ETC.—The rules of subsection (d) shall apply to any hybrid dividend received by, or any amount included under paragraph (2) in the gross income of, a United States shareholder.

"(4) HYBRID DIVIDEND.—The term 'hybrid dividend' means an amount received from a controlled foreign corporation—

"(A) for which a deduction would be allowed under subsection (a) but for this subsection, and

"(B) for which the controlled foreign corporation received a deduction (or other tax benefit) with respect to any income, war profits, or excess profits taxes imposed by any foreign country or possession of the United States.

"(f) SPECIAL RULE FOR PURGING DISTRIBUTIONS OF PASSIVE FOREIGN INVESTMENT COMPANIES.—Any amount which is treated as a dividend under section 1291(d)(2)(B) shall not be treated as a dividend for purposes of this section.

"(g) REGULATIONS.—The Secretary shall prescribe such regulations or other guidance as may be necessary or appropriate to carry out the provisions of this section, including regulations for the treatment of United States shareholders owning stock of a specified 10 percent owned foreign corporation through a partnership.".

(b) APPLICATION OF HOLDING PERIOD REQUIREMENT.—Subsection (c) of section 246 is amended—

(1) by striking "or 245" in paragraph (1) and inserting "245, or 245A", and

(2) by adding at the end the following new paragraph:

"(5) SPECIAL RULES FOR FOREIGN SOURCE PORTION OF DIVIDENDS RECEIVED FROM SPECIFIED 10-PERCENT OWNED FOREIGN CORPORATIONS.—

"(A) 1-YEAR HOLDING PERIOD REQUIREMENT.—For purposes of section 245A—

"(i) paragraph (1)(A) shall be applied—

"(I) by substituting '365 days' for '45 days' each place it appears, and

"(II) by substituting '731-day period' for '91-day period', and

"(ii) paragraph (2) shall not apply.

"(B) STATUS MUST BE MAINTAINED DURING HOLDING PERIOD.—For purposes of applying paragraph (1) with respect to section 245A, the taxpayer shall be treated as holding the stock referred to in paragraph (1) for any period only if—

"(i) the specified 10-percent owned foreign corporation referred to in section 245A(a) is a specified 10-percent owned foreign corporation at all times during such period, and

"(ii) the taxpayer is a United States shareholder with respect to such specified 10-percent owned foreign corporation at all times during such period.".

(c) APPLICATION OF RULES GENERALLY APPLICABLE TO DEDUCTIONS FOR DIVIDENDS RECEIVED.—

(1) TREATMENT OF DIVIDENDS FROM CERTAIN CORPORATIONS.—Paragraph (1) of section 246(a) is

amended by striking "and 245" and inserting "245, and 245A".

(2) COORDINATION WITH SECTION 1059.—Subparagraph (B) of section 1059(b)(2) is amended by striking "or 245" and inserting "245, or 245A".

(d) COORDINATION WITH FOREIGN TAX CREDIT LIMITATION.—Subsection (b) of section 904 is amended by adding at the end the following new paragraph:

"(5) TREATMENT OF DIVIDENDS FOR WHICH DEDUCTION IS ALLOWED UNDER SECTION 245A.—For purposes of subsection (a), in the case of a domestic corporation which is a United States shareholder with respect to a specified 10-percent owned foreign corporation, such shareholder's taxable income from sources without the United States (and entire taxable income) shall be determined without regard to—

"(A) the foreign-source portion of any dividend received from such foreign corporation, and

"(B) any deductions properly allocable or apportioned to—

"(i) income (other than amounts includible under section 951(a)(1) or 951A(a)) with respect to stock of such specified 10-percent owned foreign corporation, or

"(ii) such stock to the extent income with respect to such stock is other than amounts includible under section 951(a)(1) or 951A(a).

Any term which is used in section 245A and in this paragraph shall have the same meaning for purposes of this paragraph as when used in such section.".

(e) CONFORMING AMENDMENTS.—

(1) Subsection (b) of section 951 is amended by striking "subpart" and inserting "title".

(2) Subsection (a) of section 957 is amended by striking "subpart" in the matter preceding paragraph (1) and inserting "title".

(3) The table of sections for part VIII of subchapter B of chapter 1 is amended by inserting after the item relating to section 245 the following new item:

"Sec. 245A. Deduction for foreign source-portion of dividends received by domestic corporations from certain 10-percent owned foreign corporations.".

(f) EFFECTIVE DATE.—The amendments made by this section shall apply to distributions made after (and, in the case of the amendments made by subsection (d), deductions with respect to taxable years ending after) De-

**SEC. 14102. SPECIAL RULES RELATING TO SALES OR TRANSFERS INVOLVING SPECIFIED 10-PERCENT OWNED FOREIGN CORPORATIONS.**

(a) SALES BY UNITED STATES PERSONS OF STOCK.—

(1) IN GENERAL.—Section 1248 is amended by redesignating subsection (j) as subsection (k) and by inserting after subsection (i) the following new subsection:

"(j) COORDINATION WITH DIVIDENDS RECEIVED DEDUCTION.—In the case of the sale or exchange by a domestic corporation of stock in a foreign corporation held for 1 year or more, any amount received by the domestic corporation which is treated as a dividend by reason of this section shall be treated as a dividend for purposes of applying section 245A.".

(2) EFFECTIVE DATE.—The amendments made by this subsection shall apply to sales or exchanges after December 31, 2017.

(b) BASIS IN SPECIFIED 10-PERCENT OWNED FOREIGN CORPORATION REDUCED BY NONTAXED PORTION OF DIVIDEND FOR PURPOSES OF DETERMINING LOSS.—

(1) IN GENERAL.—Section 961 is amended by adding at the end the following new subsection:

"(d) BASIS IN SPECIFIED 10-PERCENT OWNED FOR-

OF DIVIDEND FOR PURPOSES OF DETERMINING LOSS.—If a domestic corporation received a dividend from a specified 10-percent owned foreign corporation (as defined in section 245A) in any taxable year, solely for purposes of determining loss on any disposition of stock of such foreign corporation in such taxable year or any subsequent taxable year, the basis of such domestic corporation in such stock shall be reduced (but not below zero) by the amount of any deduction allowable to such domestic corporation under section 245A with respect to such stock except to the extent such basis was reduced under section 1059 by reason of a dividend for which such a deduction was allowable.''.

(2) EFFECTIVE DATE.—The amendments made by this subsection shall apply to distributions made after December 31, 2017.

(c) SALE BY A CFC OF A LOWER TIER CFC.—

(1) IN GENERAL.—Section 964(e) is amended by adding at the end the following new paragraph:

``(4) COORDINATION WITH DIVIDENDS RECEIVED DEDUCTION.—

``(A) IN GENERAL.—If, for any taxable year of a controlled foreign corporation beginning after December 31, 2017, any amount is treated as a dividend under paragraph (1) by reason of a sale or exchange by the controlled foreign corporation of stock in another foreign corporation held for 1 year or more, then, notwithstanding any other provision of this title—

"(i) the foreign-source portion of such dividend shall be treated for purposes of section 951(a)(1)(A) as subpart F income of the selling controlled foreign corporation for such taxable year,

"(ii) a United States shareholder with respect to the selling controlled foreign corporation shall include in gross income for the taxable year of the shareholder with or within which such taxable year of the controlled foreign corporation ends an amount equal to the shareholder's pro rata share (determined in the same manner as under section 951(a)(2)) of the amount treated as subpart F income under clause (i), and

"(iii) the deduction under section 245A(a) shall be allowable to the United States shareholder with respect to the subpart F income included in gross income under clause (ii) in the same manner as if such subpart F income were a dividend received by the shareholder from the selling controlled foreign corporation.

"(B) APPLICATION OF BASIS OR SIMILAR ADJUSTMENT.—For purposes of this title, in the case of a sale or exchange by a controlled foreign corporation of stock in another foreign corporation in a taxable year of the selling controlled foreign corporation beginning after December 31, 2017, rules similar to the rules of section 961(d) shall apply.

"(C) FOREIGN-SOURCE PORTION.—For purposes of this paragraph, the foreign-source portion of any amount treated as a dividend under paragraph (1) shall be determined in the same manner as under section 245A(c).".

(2) EFFECTIVE DATE.—The amendments made by this subsection shall apply to sales or exchanges after December 31, 2017.

(d) TREATMENT OF FOREIGN BRANCH LOSSES TRANSFERRED TO SPECIFIED 10-PERCENT OWNED FOREIGN CORPORATIONS.—

(1) IN GENERAL.—Part II of subchapter B of chapter 1 is amended by adding at the end the following new section:

**"SEC. 91. CERTAIN FOREIGN BRANCH LOSSES TRANSFERRED TO SPECIFIED 10-PERCENT OWNED FOREIGN CORPORATIONS.**

"(a) IN GENERAL.—If a domestic corporation transfers substantially all of the assets of a foreign branch (within the meaning of section 367(a)(3)(C), as in effect before the date of the enactment of the Tax Cuts and Jobs Act) to a specified 10-percent owned foreign corporation (as defined in section 245A) with respect to which it is a United States shareholder after such transfer, such domestic corporation shall include in gross income for the taxable year which includes such transfer an amount equal to the transferred loss amount with respect to such transfer.

"(b) TRANSFERRED LOSS AMOUNT.—For purposes of this section, the term 'transferred loss amount' means, with respect to any transfer of substantially all of the assets of a foreign branch, the excess (if any) of—

"(1) the sum of losses—

"(A) which were incurred by the foreign branch after December 31, 2017, and before the transfer, and

"(B) with respect to which a deduction was allowed to the taxpayer, over

"(2) the sum of—

"(A) any taxable income of such branch for a taxable year after the taxable year in which the loss was incurred and through the close of the taxable year of the transfer, and

"(B) any amount which is recognized under section 904(f)(3) on account of the transfer.

"(c) REDUCTION FOR RECOGNIZED GAINS.—The transferred loss amount shall be reduced (but not below zero) by the amount of gain recognized by the taxpayer on account of the transfer (other than amounts taken into account under subsection (b)(2)(B)).

"(d) SOURCE OF INCOME.—Amounts included in gross income under this section shall be treated as derived from sources within the United States.

"(e) BASIS ADJUSTMENTS.—Consistent with such regulations or other guidance as the Secretary shall prescribe, proper adjustments shall be made in the adjusted basis of the taxpayer's stock in the specified 10-percent owned foreign corporation to which the transfer is made, and in the transferee's adjusted basis in the property transferred, to reflect amounts included in gross income under this section.".

(2) CLERICAL AMENDMENT.—The table of sections for part II of subchapter B of chapter 1 is

amended by adding at the end the following new item:

"Sec. 91. Certain foreign branch losses transferred to specified 10-percent owned foreign corporations.".

(3) EFFECTIVE DATE.—The amendments made by this subsection shall apply to transfers after December 31, 2017.

(4) TRANSITION RULE.—The amount of gain taken into account under section 91(c) of the Internal Revenue Code of 1986, as added by this subsection, shall be reduced by the amount of gain which would be recognized under section 367(a)(3)(C) (determined without regard to the amendments made by subsection (e)) with respect to losses incurred before January 1, 2018.

(e) REPEAL OF ACTIVE TRADE OR BUSINESS EXCEPTION UNDER SECTION 367.—

(1) IN GENERAL.—Section 367(a) is amended by striking paragraph (3) and redesignating paragraphs (4), (5), and (6) as paragraphs (3), (4), and (5), respectively.

(2) CONFORMING AMENDMENTS.—Section 367(a)(4), as redesignated by paragraph (1), is amended—

(A) by striking "Paragraphs (2) and (3)" and inserting "Paragraph (2)", and

(B) by striking "PARAGRAPHS (2) AND (3)" in the heading and inserting "PARAGRAPH (2)".

(3) EFFECTIVE DATE.—The amendments made by this subsection shall apply to transfers after December 31, 2017.

**SEC. 14103. TREATMENT OF DEFERRED FOREIGN INCOME UPON TRANSITION TO PARTICIPATION EXEMPTION SYSTEM OF TAXATION.**

(a) IN GENERAL.—Section 965 is amended to read as follows:

**"SEC. 965. TREATMENT OF DEFERRED FOREIGN INCOME UPON TRANSITION TO PARTICIPATION EXEMPTION SYSTEM OF TAXATION.**

"(a) TREATMENT OF DEFERRED FOREIGN INCOME AS SUBPART F INCOME.—In the case of the last taxable year of a deferred foreign income corporation which begins before January 1, 2018, the subpart F income of such foreign corporation (as otherwise determined for such taxable year under section 952) shall be increased by the greater of—

"(1) the accumulated post-1986 deferred foreign income of such corporation determined as of November 2, 2017, or

"(2) the accumulated post-1986 deferred foreign income of such corporation determined as of December 31, 2017.

"(b) REDUCTION IN AMOUNTS INCLUDED IN GROSS INCOME OF UNITED STATES SHAREHOLDERS OF SPECIFIED FOREIGN CORPORATIONS WITH DEFICITS IN EARNINGS AND PROFITS.—

"(1) IN GENERAL.—In the case of a taxpayer which is a United States shareholder with respect to at least one deferred foreign income corporation and at least one E&P deficit foreign corporation, the amount which would (but for this subsection) be taken into account under section 951(a)(1) by reason of subsection (a) as such United States shareholder's pro rata share of the subpart F income of each deferred foreign income corporation shall be reduced by the amount of such United States shareholder's aggregate foreign E&P deficit which is allocated under paragraph (2) to such deferred foreign income corporation.

"(2) ALLOCATION OF AGGREGATE FOREIGN E&P DEFICIT.—The aggregate foreign E&P deficit of any United States shareholder shall be allocated among the deferred foreign income corporations of such

United States shareholder in an amount which bears the same proportion to such aggregate as—

"(A) such United States shareholder's pro rata share of the accumulated post-1986 deferred foreign income of each such deferred foreign income corporation, bears to

"(B) the aggregate of such United States shareholder's pro rata share of the accumulated post-1986 deferred foreign income of all deferred foreign income corporations of such United States shareholder.

"(3) DEFINITIONS RELATED TO E&P DEFICITS.—For purposes of this subsection—

"(A) AGGREGATE FOREIGN E&P DEFICIT.—

"(i) IN GENERAL.—The term 'aggregate foreign E&P deficit' means, with respect to any United States shareholder, the lesser of—

"(I) the aggregate of such shareholder's pro rata shares of the specified E&P deficits of the E&P deficit foreign corporations of such shareholder, or

"(II) the amount determined under paragraph (2)(B).

"(ii) ALLOCATION OF DEFICIT.—If the amount described in clause (i)(II) is less than the amount described in clause (i)(I), then the shareholder shall designate, in such form and manner as the Secretary determines—

"(I) the amount of the specified E&P deficit which is to be taken into account for each E&P deficit corporation with respect to the taxpayer, and

"(II) in the case of an E&P deficit corporation which has a qualified deficit (as defined in section 952), the portion (if any) of the deficit taken into account under subclause (I) which is attributable to a qualified deficit, including the qualified activities to which such portion is attributable.

"(B) E&P DEFICIT FOREIGN CORPORATION.—The term 'E&P deficit foreign corporation' means, with respect to any taxpayer, any specified foreign corporation with respect to which such taxpayer is a United States shareholder, if, as of November 2, 2017—

"(i) such specified foreign corporation has a deficit in post-1986 earnings and profits,

"(ii) such corporation was a specified foreign corporation, and

"(iii) such taxpayer was a United States shareholder of such corporation.

"(C) SPECIFIED E&P DEFICIT.—The term 'specified E&P deficit' means, with respect to any E&P deficit foreign corporation, the amount of the deficit referred to in subparagraph (B).

"(4) TREATMENT OF EARNINGS AND PROFITS IN FUTURE YEARS.—

"(A) REDUCED EARNINGS AND PROFITS TREATED AS PREVIOUSLY TAXED INCOME WHEN DISTRIBUTED.—For purposes of applying section 959 in any taxable year beginning with the taxable year described in subsection (a), with respect to any United States shareholder of a deferred foreign income corporation, an amount equal to such shareholder's reduction under paragraph (1) which is allocated to such deferred foreign income corporation under this subsection shall be treated as an amount which was included in the gross income of such United States shareholder under section 951(a).

"(B) E&P DEFICITS.—For purposes of this title, with respect to any taxable year beginning with the taxable year described in subsection (a), a United States shareholder's pro rata share of the earnings and profits of any E&P deficit foreign corporation under this subsection shall be increased by the amount of the specified E&P deficit of such corporation taken into account by such shareholder under paragraph (1), and, for purposes of section 952, such increase shall be attributable to the same activity to which the deficit so taken into account was attributable.

"(5) NETTING AMONG UNITED STATES SHAREHOLDERS IN SAME AFFILIATED GROUP.—

"(A) IN GENERAL.—In the case of any affiliated group which includes at least one E&P net surplus shareholder and one E&P net deficit shareholder, the amount which would (but for this paragraph) be taken into account under section 951(a)(1) by reason of subsection (a) by each such E&P net surplus shareholder shall be reduced (but not below zero) by such shareholder's applicable share of the affiliated group's aggregate unused E&P deficit.

"(B) E&P NET SURPLUS SHAREHOLDER.—For purposes of this paragraph, the term 'E&P net surplus shareholder' means any United States shareholder which would (determined without regard to this paragraph) take into account an amount greater than zero under section 951(a)(1) by reason of subsection (a).

"(C) E&P NET DEFICIT SHAREHOLDER.—For purposes of this paragraph, the term 'E&P net deficit shareholder' means any United States shareholder if—

"(i) the aggregate foreign E&P deficit with respect to such shareholder (as defined in paragraph (3)(A) without regard to clause (i)(II) thereof), exceeds

"(ii) the amount which would (but for this subsection) be taken into account by such shareholder under section 951(a)(1) by reason of subsection (a).

"(D) AGGREGATE UNUSED E&P DEFICIT.—For purposes of this paragraph—

"(i) IN GENERAL.—The term 'aggregate unused E&P deficit' means, with respect to any affiliated group, the lesser of—

"(I) the sum of the excesses described in subparagraph (C), determined with respect to each E&P net deficit shareholder in such group, or

"(II) the amount determined under subparagraph (E)(ii).

"(ii) REDUCTION WITH RESPECT TO E&P NET DEFICIT SHAREHOLDERS WHICH ARE NOT WHOLLY OWNED BY THE AFFILIATED GROUP.—If the group ownership percentage of any E&P net deficit shareholder is less than 100 percent, the amount of the excess described in subparagraph (C) which is taken into account under clause (i)(I) with respect to such E&P net deficit shareholder shall be such group ownership percentage of such amount.

"(E) APPLICABLE SHARE.—For purposes of this paragraph, the term 'applicable share' means, with respect to any E&P net surplus shareholder in any affiliated group, the amount which bears the same proportion to such group's aggregate unused E&P deficit as—

"(i) the product of—

"(I) such shareholder's group ownership percentage, multiplied by

"(II) the amount which would (but for this paragraph) be taken into account under section 951(a)(1) by reason of subsection (a) by such shareholder, bears to

"(ii) the aggregate amount determined under clause (i) with respect to all E&P net surplus shareholders in such group.

"(F) GROUP OWNERSHIP PERCENTAGE.—For purposes of this paragraph, the term 'group ownership percentage' means, with respect to any United States shareholder in any affiliated group, the percentage of the value of the stock of such United States shareholder which is held by other includible corporations in such affiliated group. Notwithstanding the preceding sentence, the group ownership percentage of the common parent of the affiliated group is 100 percent. Any term used in this subparagraph which is also used in section 1504 shall have the same meaning as when used in such section.

"(c) APPLICATION OF PARTICIPATION EXEMPTION TO INCLUDED INCOME.—

"(1) IN GENERAL.—In the case of a United States shareholder of a deferred foreign income corporation, there shall be allowed as a deduction for the taxable year in which an amount is included in the gross income of such United States shareholder under section 951(a)(1) by reason of this section an amount equal to the sum of—

"(A) the United States shareholder's 8 percent rate equivalent percentage of the excess (if any) of—

"(i) the amount so included as gross income, over

"(ii) the amount of such United States shareholder's aggregate foreign cash position, plus

"(B) the United States shareholder's 15.5 percent rate equivalent percentage of so much of the amount described in subparagraph (A)(ii)

as does not exceed the amount described in subparagraph (A)(i).

"(2) 8 AND 15.5 PERCENT RATE EQUIVALENT PERCENTAGES.—For purposes of this subsection—

"(A) 8 PERCENT RATE EQUIVALENT PERCENTAGE.—The term '8 percent rate equivalent percentage' means, with respect to any United States shareholder for any taxable year, the percentage which would result in the amount to which such percentage applies being subject to a 8 percent rate of tax determined by only taking into account a deduction equal to such percentage of such amount and the highest rate of tax specified in section 11 for such taxable year. In the case of any taxable year of a United States shareholder to which section 15 applies, the highest rate of tax under section 11 before the effective date of the change in rates and the highest rate of tax under section 11 after the effective date of such change shall each be taken into account under the preceding sentence in the same proportions as the portion of such taxable year which is before and after such effective date, respectively.

"(B) 15.5 PERCENT RATE EQUIVALENT PERCENTAGE.—The term '15.5 percent rate equivalent percentage' means, with respect to any United States shareholder for any taxable year, the percentage determined under subparagraph (A) applied by substituting '15.5 percent rate of tax' for '8 percent rate of tax'.

"(3) AGGREGATE FOREIGN CASH POSITION.—For purposes of this subsection—

"(A) IN GENERAL.—The term 'aggregate foreign cash position' means, with respect to any United States shareholder, the greater of—

"(i) the aggregate of such United States shareholder's pro rata share of the cash position of each specified foreign corporation of such United States shareholder determined as of the close of the last taxable year of such specified foreign corporation which begins before January 1, 2018, or

"(ii) one half of the sum of—

"(I) the aggregate described in clause (i) determined as of the close of the last taxable year of each such specified foreign corporation which ends before November 2, 2017, plus

"(II) the aggregate described in clause (i) determined as of the close of the taxable year of each such specified foreign corporation which precedes the taxable year referred to in subclause (I).

"(B) CASH POSITION.—For purposes of this paragraph, the cash position of any specified foreign corporation is the sum of—

"(i) cash held by such foreign corporation,

"(ii) the net accounts receivable of such foreign corporation, plus

"(iii) the fair market value of the following assets held by such corporation:

"(I) Personal property which is of a type that is actively traded and for which there is an established financial market.

"(II) Commercial paper, certificates of deposit, the securities of the Federal government and of any State or foreign government.

"(III) Any foreign currency.

"(IV) Any obligation with a term of less than one year.

"(V) Any asset which the Secretary identifies as being economically equivalent to any asset described in this subparagraph.

"(C) NET ACCOUNTS RECEIVABLE.—For purposes of this paragraph, the term 'net accounts receivable' means, with respect to any specified foreign corporation, the excess (if any) of—

"(i) such corporation's accounts receivable, over

"(ii) such corporation's accounts payable (determined consistent with the rules of section 461).

"(D) PREVENTION OF DOUBLE COUNTING.—Cash positions of a specified foreign corporation described in clause (ii), (iii)(I), or (iii)(IV) of subparagraph (B) shall not be taken into account by a United States shareholder under subparagraph (A) to the extent that such United States shareholder demonstrates to the satisfaction of the Secretary that such amount is so taken into account by such United States shareholder with respect to another specified foreign corporation.

"(E) CASH POSITIONS OF CERTAIN NON-CORPORATE ENTITIES TAKEN INTO ACCOUNT.—An entity (other than a corporation) shall be treated as a specified foreign corporation of a United States shareholder for purposes of determining such United States shareholder's aggregate foreign cash position if any interest in such entity is held by a specified foreign corporation of such United States shareholder (determined after application of this subparagraph) and such entity would be a specified foreign corporation of such United States shareholder if such entity were a foreign corporation.

"(F) ANTI-ABUSE.—If the Secretary determines that a principal purpose of any transaction was to reduce the aggregate foreign cash position taken into account under this subsection, such transaction shall be disregarded for purposes of this subsection.

"(d) DEFERRED FOREIGN INCOME CORPORATION; ACCUMULATED POST-1986 DEFERRED FOREIGN INCOME.—For purposes of this section—

"(1) DEFERRED FOREIGN INCOME CORPORATION.—The term 'deferred foreign income corporation' means, with respect to any United States shareholder, any specified foreign corporation of such United States shareholder which has accumulated post-1986 deferred foreign income (as of the date referred to in paragraph (1) or (2) of subsection (a)) greater than zero.

"(2) ACCUMULATED POST-1986 DEFERRED FOREIGN INCOME.—The term 'accumulated post-1986 deferred foreign income' means the post-1986 earnings and profits except to the extent such earnings—

"(A) are attributable to income of the specified foreign corporation which is effectively connected with the conduct of a trade or business within the United States and subject to tax under this chapter, or

"(B) in the case of a controlled foreign corporation, if distributed, would be excluded from the gross income of a United States shareholder under section 959.

To the extent provided in regulations or other guidance prescribed by the Secretary, in the case of any controlled foreign corporation which has shareholders which are not United States shareholders, accumulated post-1986 deferred foreign income shall be appropriately reduced by amounts which would be described in subparagraph (B) if such shareholders were United States shareholders.

"(3) POST-1986 EARNINGS AND PROFITS.—The term 'post-1986 earnings and profits' means the earnings and profits of the foreign corporation (computed in accordance with sections 964(a) and 986, and by only taking into account periods when the foreign corporation was a specified foreign corporation) accumulated in taxable years beginning after December 31, 1986, and determined—

"(A) as of the date referred to in paragraph (1) or (2) of subsection (a), whichever is applicable with respect to such foreign corporation, and

"(B) without diminution by reason of dividends distributed during the taxable year described in subsection (a) other than dividends distributed to another specified foreign corporation.

"(e) SPECIFIED FOREIGN CORPORATION.—

"(1) IN GENERAL.—For purposes of this section, the term 'specified foreign corporation' means—

"(A) any controlled foreign corporation, and

"(B) any foreign corporation with respect to which one or more domestic corporations is a United States shareholder.

"(2) APPLICATION TO CERTAIN FOREIGN CORPORATIONS.—For purposes of sections 951 and 961, a foreign corporation described in paragraph (1)(B) shall be treated as a controlled foreign corporation solely for purposes of taking into account the subpart F income of such corporation under subsection (a) (and for purposes of applying subsection (f)).

"(3) EXCLUSION OF PASSIVE FOREIGN INVESTMENT COMPANIES.—Such term shall not include any corporation which is a passive foreign investment company (as defined in section 1297) with respect to the shareholder and which is not a controlled foreign corporation.

"(f) DETERMINATIONS OF PRO RATA SHARE.—

"(1) IN GENERAL.—For purposes of this section, the determination of any United States shareholder's pro rata share of any amount with respect to any specified foreign corporation shall be determined under rules similar to the rules of section 951(a)(2) by treating such amount in the same manner as subpart F income (and by treating such specified foreign corporation as a controlled foreign corporation).

"(2) SPECIAL RULES.—The portion which is included in the income of a United States shareholder under section 951(a)(1) by reason of subsection (a) which is equal to the deduction allowed under subsection (c) by reason of such inclusion—

"(A) shall be treated as income exempt from tax for purposes of sections 705(a)(1)(B) and 1367(a)(1)(A), and

"(B) shall not be treated as income exempt from tax for purposes of determining whether an adjustment shall be made to an accumulated adjustment account under section 1368(e)(1)(A).

"(g) DISALLOWANCE OF FOREIGN TAX CREDIT, ETC.—

"(1) IN GENERAL.—No credit shall be allowed under section 901 for the applicable percentage of any taxes paid or accrued (or treated as paid or accrued) with respect to any amount for which a deduction is allowed under this section.

"(2) APPLICABLE PERCENTAGE.—For purposes of this subsection, the term 'applicable percentage' means the amount (expressed as a percentage) equal to the sum of—

"(A) 0.771 multiplied by the ratio of—

"(i) the excess to which subsection (c)(1)(A) applies, divided by

"(ii) the sum of such excess plus the amount to which subsection (c)(1)(B) applies, plus

"(B) 0.557 multiplied by the ratio of—

"(i) the amount to which subsection (c)(1)(B) applies, divided by

"(ii) the sum described in subparagraph (A)(ii).

"(3) DENIAL OF DEDUCTION.—No deduction shall be allowed under this chapter for any tax for which credit is not allowable under section 901 by reason of paragraph (1) (determined by treating the taxpayer as having elected the benefits of subpart A of part III of subchapter N).

"(4) COORDINATION WITH SECTION 78.—With respect to the taxes treated as paid or accrued by a domestic corporation with respect to amounts which are includible in gross income of such domestic corporation by reason of this section, section 78 shall apply only to so much of such taxes as bears the same proportion to the amount of such taxes as—

"(A) the excess of—

"(i) the amounts which are includible in gross income of such domestic corporation by reason of this section, over

"(ii) the deduction allowable under subsection (c) with respect to such amounts, bears to

"(B) such amounts.

"(h) ELECTION TO PAY LIABILITY IN INSTALLMENTS.—

"(1) IN GENERAL.—In the case of a United States shareholder of a deferred foreign income corporation, such United States shareholder may elect to pay the net tax liability under this section in 8 installments of the following amounts:

"(A) 8 percent of the net tax liability in the case of each of the first 5 of such installments,

"(B) 15 percent of the net tax liability in the case of the 6th such installment,

"(C) 20 percent of the net tax liability in the case of the 7th such installment, and

"(D) 25 percent of the net tax liability in the case of the 8th such installment.

"(2) DATE FOR PAYMENT OF INSTALLMENTS.—If an election is made under paragraph (1), the first installment shall be paid on the due date (determined without regard to any extension of time for filing the return) for the return of tax for the taxable year described in subsection (a) and each succeeding installment shall be paid on the due date (as so determined) for the return of tax for the taxable year following the taxable year with respect to which the preceding installment was made.

"(3) ACCELERATION OF PAYMENT.—If there is an addition to tax for failure to timely pay any installment required under this subsection, a liquidation or sale of substantially all the assets of the taxpayer (including in a title 11 or similar case), a cessation of business by the taxpayer, or any similar circumstance, then the unpaid portion of all remaining installments shall be due on the date of such event (or in the case of a title 11 or similar case, the day before the petition is filed). The preceding sentence shall not apply to the sale of substantially all the assets of a taxpayer to a buyer if such buyer enters into an agreement with the Secretary under which such buyer is liable for the remaining installments due under this subsection in the same manner as if such buyer were the taxpayer.

"(4) PRORATION OF DEFICIENCY TO INSTALLMENTS.—If an election is made under paragraph (1) to pay the net tax liability under this section in installments and a deficiency has been assessed with respect to such net tax liability, the deficiency shall be prorated to the installments payable under paragraph (1). The part of the deficiency so prorated to any installment the date for payment of which has not arrived shall be collected at the same time as, and as a part of, such installment. The part of the deficiency so prorated to any installment the date for payment of which has arrived shall be paid upon notice and demand from the Secretary. This subsection shall not apply if the deficiency is due to negligence, to intentional disregard of rules and regulations, or to fraud with intent to evade tax.

"(5) ELECTION.—Any election under paragraph (1) shall be made not later than the due date for the return of tax for the taxable year described in subsection (a) and shall be made in such manner as the Secretary shall provide.

"(6) NET TAX LIABILITY UNDER THIS SECTION.—For purposes of this subsection—

"(A) IN GENERAL.—The net tax liability under this section with respect to any United States shareholder is the excess (if any) of—

"(i) such taxpayer's net income tax for the taxable year in which an amount is included in the gross income of such United States shareholder under section 951(a)(1) by reason of this section, over

"(ii) such taxpayer's net income tax for such taxable year determined—

"(I) without regard to this section, and

"(II) without regard to any income or deduction properly attributable to a dividend received by such United States shareholder from any deferred foreign income corporation.

"(B) NET INCOME TAX.—The term 'net income tax' means the regular tax liability reduced by the credits allowed under subparts A, B, and D of part IV of subchapter A.

"(i) SPECIAL RULES FOR S CORPORATION SHAREHOLDERS.—

"(1) IN GENERAL.—In the case of any S corporation which is a United States shareholder of a deferred foreign income corporation, each shareholder of such S corporation may elect to defer payment of such shareholder's net tax liability under this section with respect to such S corporation until the shareholder's taxable year which includes the triggering event with respect to such liability. Any net tax liability payment of which is deferred under the preceding sentence shall be assessed on the return of tax as an addition to tax in the shareholder's taxable year which includes such triggering event.

"(2) TRIGGERING EVENT.—

"(A) IN GENERAL.—In the case of any shareholder's net tax liability under this section with respect to any S corporation, the triggering event with respect to such liability is whichever of the following occurs first:

"(i) Such corporation ceases to be an S corporation (determined as of the first day of the first taxable year that such corporation is not an S corporation).

"(ii) A liquidation or sale of substantially all the assets of such S corporation (including in a title 11 or similar case), a cessation of business by such S corporation, such S corporation ceases to exist, or any similar circumstance.

"(iii) A transfer of any share of stock in such S corporation by the taxpayer (including by reason of death, or otherwise).

"(B) PARTIAL TRANSFERS OF STOCK.—In the case of a transfer of less than all of the taxpayer's shares of stock in the S corporation, such transfer shall only be a triggering event with respect to so much of the taxpayer's net tax liability under this section with respect to such S corporation as is properly allocable to such stock.

"(C) TRANSFER OF LIABILITY.—A transfer described in clause (iii) of subparagraph (A) shall not be treated as a triggering event if the transferee enters into an agreement with the Secretary under which such transferee is liable for net tax liability with respect to such stock in the same manner as if such transferee were the taxpayer.

"(3) NET TAX LIABILITY.—A shareholder's net tax liability under this section with respect to any S corporation is the net tax liability under this section which would be determined under subsection (h)(6) if the only subpart F income taken into account by such shareholder by reason of this section were allocations from such S corporation.

"(4) ELECTION TO PAY DEFERRED LIABILITY IN INSTALLMENTS.—In the case of a taxpayer which elects to defer payment under paragraph (1)—

"(A) subsection (h) shall be applied separately with respect to the liability to which such election applies,

"(B) an election under subsection (h) with respect to such liability shall be treated as timely made if made not later than the due date for the return of tax for the taxable year in which the triggering event with respect to such liability occurs,

"(C) the first installment under subsection (h) with respect to such liability shall be paid not later than such due date (but determined without regard to any extension of time for filing the return), and

"(D) if the triggering event with respect to any net tax liability is described in paragraph (2)(A)(ii), an election under subsection (h) with respect to such liability may be made only with the consent of the Secretary.

"(5) JOINT AND SEVERAL LIABILITY OF S CORPORATION.—If any shareholder of an S corporation elects to defer payment under paragraph (1), such S corporation shall be jointly and severally liable for such payment and any penalty, addition to tax, or additional amount attributable thereto.

"(6) EXTENSION OF LIMITATION ON COLLECTION.—Any limitation on the time period for the collection of a liability deferred under this subsection shall not be treated as beginning before the date of the triggering event with respect to such liability.

"(7) ANNUAL REPORTING OF NET TAX LIABILITY.—

"(A) IN GENERAL.—Any shareholder of an S corporation which makes an election under paragraph (1) shall report the amount of such shareholder's deferred net tax liability on such shareholder's return of tax for the taxable year for which such election is made and on the return of tax for each taxable year thereafter until such amount has been fully assessed on such returns.

"(B) DEFERRED NET TAX LIABILITY.—For purposes of this paragraph, the term 'deferred net tax liability' means, with respect to any taxable year, the amount of net tax liability payment of which has been deferred under paragraph (1) and which has not been assessed on a return of tax for any prior taxable year.

"(C) FAILURE TO REPORT.—In the case of any failure to report any amount required to be reported under subparagraph (A) with respect to any taxable year before the due date for the return of tax for such taxable year, there shall be assessed on such return as an addition to tax 5 percent of such amount.

"(8) ELECTION.—Any election under paragraph (1)—

"(A) shall be made by the shareholder of the S corporation not later than the due date for such shareholder's return of tax for the taxable year which includes the close of the taxable year of such S corporation in which the amount described in subsection (a) is taken into account, and

"(B) shall be made in such manner as the Secretary shall provide.

"(j) REPORTING BY S CORPORATION.—Each S corporation which is a United States shareholder of a specified foreign corporation shall report in its return of tax under section 6037(a) the amount includible in its gross income for such taxable year by reason of this section and the amount of the deduction allowable by subsection (c). Any copy provided to a shareholder under section 6037(b) shall include a statement of such shareholder's pro rata share of such amounts.

"(k) EXTENSION OF LIMITATION ON ASSESSMENT.—Notwithstanding section 6501, the limitation on the time period for the assessment of the net tax liability under this section (as defined in subsection (h)(6)) shall not expire before the date that is 6 years after the return for the taxable year described in such subsection was filed.

"(l) RECAPTURE FOR EXPATRIATED ENTITIES.—

"(1) IN GENERAL.—If a deduction is allowed under subsection (c) to a United States shareholder and such shareholder first becomes an expatriated entity at any time during the 10-year period beginning on the date of the enactment of the Tax Cuts and Jobs Act (with respect to a surrogate foreign corporation which first becomes a surrogate foreign corporation during such period), then—

"(A) the tax imposed by this chapter shall be increased for the first taxable year in which such taxpayer becomes an expatriated entity by an amount equal to 35 percent of the amount of the deduction allowed under subsection (c), and

"(B) no credits shall be allowed against the increase in tax under subparagraph (A).

"(2) EXPATRIATED ENTITY.—For purposes of this subsection, the term 'expatriated entity' has the same meaning given such term under section 7874(a)(2), except that such term shall not include an entity if the surrogate foreign corporation with respect to the entity is treated as a domestic corporation under section 7874(b).

"(3) SURROGATE FOREIGN CORPORATION.—For purposes of this subsection, the term 'surrogate foreign corporation' has the meaning given such term in section 7874(a)(2)(B).

"(m) SPECIAL RULES FOR UNITED STATES SHAREHOLDERS WHICH ARE REAL ESTATE INVESTMENT TRUSTS.—

"(1) IN GENERAL.—If a real estate investment trust is a United States shareholder in 1 or more deferred foreign income corporations—

"(A) any amount required to be taken into account under section 951(a)(1) by reason of this section shall not be taken into account as gross income of the real estate investment trust for purposes of applying paragraphs (2) and (3) of section 856(c) to any taxable year for which such amount is taken into account under section 951(a)(1), and

"(B) if the real estate investment trust elects the application of this subparagraph, notwithstanding subsection (a), any amount required to be taken into account under section 951(a)(1) by reason of this section shall, in lieu of the taxable year in which it would otherwise be included in gross income (for purposes of the computation of real estate investment trust taxable income under section 857(b)), be included in gross income as follows:

"(i) 8 percent of such amount in the case of each of the taxable years in the 5-taxable year period beginning with the taxable year in which such amount would otherwise be included.

"(ii) 15 percent of such amount in the case of the 1st taxable year following such period.

"(iii) 20 percent of such amount in the case of the 2nd taxable year following such period.

"(iv) 25 percent of such amount in the case of the 3rd taxable year following such period.

"(2) RULES FOR TRUSTS ELECTING DEFERRED INCLUSION.—

"(A) ELECTION.—Any election under paragraph (1)(B) shall be made not later than the due date for the first taxable year in the 5-taxable year period described in clause (i) of paragraph (1)(B) and shall be made in such manner as the Secretary shall provide.

"(B) SPECIAL RULES.—If an election under paragraph (1)(B) is in effect with respect to any real estate investment trust, the following rules shall apply:

"(i) APPLICATION OF PARTICIPATION EXEMPTION.—For purposes of subsection (c)(1)—

"(I) the aggregate amount to which subparagraph (A) or (B) of subsection (c)(1) applies shall be determined without regard to the election,

"(II) each such aggregate amount shall be allocated to each taxable year described in paragraph (1)(B) in the same proportion as the amount included in the gross income of such United States shareholder under section 951(a)(1) by reason of this section is allocated to each such taxable year.

"(III) NO INSTALLMENT PAYMENTS.—The real estate investment trust may not make an election under subsection (g) for any taxable year described in paragraph (1)(B).

"(ii) ACCELERATION OF INCLUSION.—If there is a liquidation or sale of substantially all the assets of the real estate investment trust (including in a title 11 or similar case), a cessation of business by such trust, or any similar circumstance, then any amount not yet included in gross income under paragraph (1)(B) shall be included in gross income as of the day before the date of the event and the unpaid portion of any tax liability with respect to such inclusion shall be due on the date of such event (or in the case of a title 11 or similar case, the day before the petition is filed).

"(n) ELECTION NOT TO APPLY NET OPERATING LOSS DEDUCTION.—

"(1) IN GENERAL.—If a United States shareholder of a deferred foreign income corporation elects the application of this subsection for the taxable year described in subsection (a), then the amount described in paragraph (2) shall not be taken into account—

"(A) in determining the amount of the net operating loss deduction under section 172 of such shareholder for such taxable year, or

"(B) in determining the amount of taxable income for such taxable year which may be reduced by net operating loss carryovers or carrybacks to such taxable year under section 172.

"(2) AMOUNT DESCRIBED.—The amount described in this paragraph is the sum of—

"(A) the amount required to be taken into account under section 951(a)(1) by reason of this section (determined after the application of subsection (c)), plus

"(B) in the case of a domestic corporation which chooses to have the benefits of subpart A of part III of subchapter N for the taxable year, the taxes deemed to be paid by such corporation under subsections (a) and (b) of section 960 for such taxable year with respect to the amount described in subparagraph (A) which are treated as a dividends under section 78.

"(3) ELECTION.—Any election under this subsection shall be made not later than the due date (including extensions) for filing the return of tax for the taxable year and shall be made in such manner as the Secretary shall prescribe.

"(o) REGULATIONS.—The Secretary shall prescribe such regulations or other guidance as may be necessary or appropriate to carry out the provisions of this section, including—

"(1) regulations or other guidance to provide appropriate basis adjustments, and

"(2) regulations or other guidance to prevent the avoidance of the purposes of this section, including through a reduction in earnings and profits, through changes in entity classification or accounting methods, or otherwise.".

(b) CLERICAL AMENDMENT.—The table of sections for subpart F of part III of subchapter N of chapter 1 is amended by striking the item relating to section 965 and inserting the following:

"Sec. 965. Treatment of deferred foreign income upon transition to participation exemption system of taxation.".

### Subpart B—Rules Related to Passive and Mobile Income

## CHAPTER 1—TAXATION OF FOREIGN-DERIVED INTANGIBLE INCOME AND GLOBAL INTANGIBLE LOW-TAXED INCOME

### SEC. 14201. CURRENT YEAR INCLUSION OF GLOBAL INTANGIBLE LOW-TAXED INCOME BY UNITED STATES SHAREHOLDERS.

(a) IN GENERAL.—Subpart F of part III of subchapter N of chapter 1 is amended by inserting after section 951 the following new section:

**"SEC. 951A. GLOBAL INTANGIBLE LOW-TAXED INCOME INCLUDED IN GROSS INCOME OF UNITED STATES SHAREHOLDERS.**

"(a) In General.—Each person who is a United States shareholder of any controlled foreign corporation for any taxable year of such United States shareholder shall include in gross income such shareholder's global intangible low-taxed income for such taxable year.

"(b) Global Intangible Low-taxed Income.—For purposes of this section—

"(1) In general.—The term 'global intangible low-taxed income' means, with respect to any United States shareholder for any taxable year of such United States shareholder, the excess (if any) of—

"(A) such shareholder's net CFC tested income for such taxable year, over

"(B) such shareholder's net deemed tangible income return for such taxable year.

"(2) Net deemed tangible income return.—The term 'net deemed tangible income return' means, with respect to any United States shareholder for any taxable year, the excess of—

"(A) 10 percent of the aggregate of such shareholder's pro rata share of the qualified business asset investment of each controlled for-shareholder is a United States shareholder for such taxable year (determined for each taxable year of each such controlled foreign corporation which ends in or with such taxable year of such United States shareholder), over

"(B) the amount of interest expense taken into account under subsection (c)(2)(A)(ii) in determining the shareholder's net CFC tested income for the taxable year to the extent the interest income attributable to such expense is not taken into account in determining such shareholder's net CFC tested income.

"(c) NET CFC TESTED INCOME.—For purposes of this section—

"(1) IN GENERAL.—The term 'net CFC tested income' means, with respect to any United States shareholder for any taxable year of such United States shareholder, the excess (if any) of—

"(A) the aggregate of such shareholder's pro rata share of the tested income of each controlled foreign corporation with respect to which such shareholder is a United States shareholder for such taxable year of such United States shareholder (determined for each taxable year of such controlled foreign corporation which ends in or with such taxable year of such United States shareholder), over

"(B) the aggregate of such shareholder's pro rata share of the tested loss of each controlled foreign corporation with respect to which such shareholder is a United States shareholder for such taxable year of such United States shareholder (determined for each taxable year of such controlled foreign corporation which ends in or with such taxable year of such United States shareholder).

"(2) TESTED INCOME; TESTED LOSS.—For purposes of this section—

"(A) TESTED INCOME.—The term 'tested income' means, with respect to any controlled foreign corporation for any taxable year of such controlled foreign corporation, the excess (if any) of—

"(i) the gross income of such corporation determined without regard to—

"(I) any item of income described in section 952(b),

"(II) any gross income taken into account in determining the subpart F income of such corporation,

"(III) any gross income excluded from the foreign base company income (as defined in section 954) and the insurance income (as defined in section 953) of such corporation by reason of section 954(b)(4),

"(IV) any dividend received from a related person (as defined in section 954(d)(3)), and

"(V) any foreign oil and gas extraction income (as defined in section 907(c)(1)) of such corporation, over

"(ii) the deductions (including taxes) properly allocable to such gross income under rules similar to the rules of section 954(b)(5) (or to which such deductions would be allocable if there were such gross income).

"(B) TESTED LOSS.—

"(i) IN GENERAL.—The term 'tested loss' means, with respect to any controlled foreign corporation for any taxable year of such controlled foreign corporation, the excess (if any) of the amount described in subparagraph (A)(ii) over the amount described in subparagraph (A)(i).

"(ii) COORDINATION WITH SUBPART F TO DENY DOUBLE BENEFIT OF LOSSES.—Section 952(c)(1)(A) shall be applied by increasing the earnings and profits of the controlled foreign corporation by the tested loss of such corporation.

"(d) QUALIFIED BUSINESS ASSET INVESTMENT.—For purposes of this section—

"(1) IN GENERAL.—The term 'qualified business asset investment' means, with respect to any controlled foreign corporation for any taxable year, the average of such corporation's aggregate adjusted bases as of the close of each quarter of such taxable year in specified tangible property—

"(A) used in a trade or business of the corporation, and

"(B) of a type with respect to which a deduction is allowable under section 167.

"(2) SPECIFIED TANGIBLE PROPERTY.—

"(A) IN GENERAL.—The term 'specified tangible property' means, except as provided in subparagraph (B), any tangible property used in the production of tested income.

"(B) Dual use property.—In the case of property used both in the production of tested income and income which is not tested income, such property shall be treated as specified tangible property in the same proportion that the gross income described in subsection (c)(1)(A) produced with respect to such property bears to the total gross income produced with respect to such property.

"(3) Determination of adjusted basis.—For purposes of this subsection, notwithstanding any provision of this title (or any other provision of law) which is enacted after the date of the enactment of this section, the adjusted basis in any property shall be determined—

"(A) by using the alternative depreciation system under section 168(g), and

"(B) by allocating the depreciation deduction with respect to such property ratably to each day during the period in the taxable year to which such depreciation relates.

"(3) Partnership property.—For purposes of this subsection, if a controlled foreign corporation holds an interest in a partnership at the close of such taxable year of the controlled foreign corporation, such controlled foreign corporation shall take into account under paragraph (1) the controlled foreign corporation's distributive share of the aggregate of the partnership's adjusted bases (determined as of such date in the hands of the partnership) in tangible property held by such partnership to the extent such property—

"(A) is used in the trade or business of the partnership,

"(B) is of a type with respect to which a deduction is allowable under section 167, and

"(C) is used in the production of tested income (determined with respect to such controlled foreign corporation's distributive share of income with respect to such property).

For purposes of this paragraph, the controlled foreign corporation's distributive share of the adjusted basis of any property shall be the controlled foreign corporation's distributive share of income with respect to such property.

"(4) REGULATIONS.—The Secretary shall issue such regulations or other guidance as the Secretary determines appropriate to prevent the avoidance of the purposes of this subsection, including regulations or other guidance which provide for the treatment of property if—

"(A) such property is transferred, or held, temporarily, or

"(B) the avoidance of the purposes of this paragraph is a factor in the transfer or holding of such property.

"(e) DETERMINATION OF PRO RATA SHARE, ETC.—For purposes of this section—

"(1) IN GENERAL.—The pro rata shares referred to in subsections (b), (c)(1)(A), and (c)(1)(B), respectively, shall be determined under the rules of section 951(a)(2) in the same manner as such section applies to subpart F income and shall be taken into account in the taxable year of the United States shareholder in which or with which the taxable year of the controlled foreign corporation ends.

"(2) TREATMENT AS UNITED STATES SHAREHOLDER.—A person shall be treated as a United States shareholder of a controlled foreign corporation for any taxable year of such person only if such person owns (within the meaning of section 958(a)) stock in such foreign corporation on the last day in the taxable year of such foreign corporation on which such foreign corporation is a controlled foreign corporation.

"(3) TREATMENT AS CONTROLLED FOREIGN CORPORATION.—A foreign corporation shall be treated as a controlled foreign corporation for any taxable year if such foreign corporation is a controlled foreign corporation at any time during such taxable year.

"(f) TREATMENT AS SUBPART F INCOME FOR CERTAIN PURPOSES.—

"(1) IN GENERAL.—

"(A) APPLICATION.—Except as provided in subparagraph (B), any global intangible low-taxed income included in gross income under subsection (a) shall be treated in the same manner as an amount included under section 951(a)(1)(A) for purposes of applying sections 168(h)(2)(B), 535(b)(10), 851(b), 904(h)(1), 959, 961, 962, 993(a)(1)(E), 996(f)(1), 1248(b)(1), 1248(d)(1), 6501(e)(1)(C), 6654(d)(2)(D), and 6655(e)(4).

"(B) EXCEPTION.—The Secretary shall provide rules for the application of subparagraph (A) to other provisions of this title in any case in which the determination of subpart F income is required to be made at the level of the controlled foreign corporation.

"(2) ALLOCATION OF GLOBAL INTANGIBLE LOW-TAXED INCOME TO CONTROLLED FOREIGN CORPORATIONS.—For purposes of the sections referred to in paragraph (1), with respect to any controlled foreign corporation any pro rata amount from which is taken into account in determining the global intangible low-taxed income included in gross income of a United States shareholder under subsection (a), the portion of such global intangible low-taxed income which is treated as being with respect to such controlled foreign corporation is—

"(A) in the case of a controlled foreign corporation with no tested income, zero, and

"(B) in the case of a controlled foreign corporation with tested income, the portion of such global intangible low-taxed income which bears the same ratio to such global intangible low-taxed income as—

"(i) such United States shareholder's pro rata amount of the tested income of such controlled foreign corporation, bears to "(ii) the aggregate amount described in subsection (c)(1)(A) with respect to such United States shareholder.".

(b) FOREIGN TAX CREDIT.—

(1) APPLICATION OF DEEMED PAID FOREIGN TAX CREDIT.—Section 960 is amended adding at the end the following new subsection:

"(d) DEEMED PAID CREDIT FOR TAXES PROPERLY ATTRIBUTABLE TO TESTED INCOME.—

"(1) IN GENERAL.—For purposes of subpart A of this part, if any amount is includible in the gross income of a domestic corporation under section 951A, such domestic corporation shall be deemed to have paid foreign income taxes equal to 80 percent of the product of—

"(A) such domestic corporation's inclusion percentage, multiplied by

"(B) the aggregate tested foreign income taxes paid or accrued by controlled foreign corporations.

"(2) INCLUSION PERCENTAGE.—For purposes of paragraph (1), the term 'inclusion percentage' means, with respect to any domestic corporation, the ratio (expressed as a percentage) of—

"(A) such corporation's global intangible low-taxed income (as defined in section 951A(b)), divided by

"(B) the aggregate amount described in section 951A(c)(1)(A) with respect to such corporation.

"(3) TESTED FOREIGN INCOME TAXES.—For purposes of paragraph (1), the term 'tested foreign income taxes' means, with respect to any domestic corporation which is a United States shareholder of a controlled foreign corporation, the foreign income taxes paid or accrued by such foreign corporation which are properly attributable to the tested income of such foreign corporation taken into account by such domestic corporation under section 951A.".

(2) APPLICATION OF FOREIGN TAX CREDIT LIMITATION.—

(A) SEPARATE BASKET FOR GLOBAL INTANGIBLE LOW-TAXED INCOME.—Section 904(d)(1) is amended by redesignating subparagraphs (A) and (B) as subparagraphs (B) and (C), respectively, and by inserting before subparagraph (B) (as so redesignated) the following new subparagraph:

"(A) any amount includible in gross income under section 951A (other than passive category income),".

(B) EXCLUSION FROM GENERAL CATEGORY INCOME.—Section 904(d)(2)(A)(ii) is amended by inserting "income described in paragraph (1)(A) and" before "passive category income".

(C) NO CARRYOVER OR CARRYBACK OF EXCESS TAXES.—Section 904(c) is amended by adding at the end the following: "This subsection shall not apply to taxes paid or accrued with respect to amounts described in subsection (d)(1)(A).".

(c) CLERICAL AMENDMENT.—The table of sections for subpart F of part III of subchapter N of chapter 1 is amended by inserting after the item relating to section 951 the following new item:

"Sec. 951A. Global intangible low-taxed income included in gross income of United States shareholders.".

(d) EFFECTIVE DATE.—The amendments made by this section shall apply to taxable years of foreign corporations beginning after December 31, 2017, and to taxable years of United States shareholders in which or with which such taxable years of foreign corporations end.

**SEC. 14202. DEDUCTION FOR FOREIGN-DERIVED INTANGIBLE INCOME AND GLOBAL INTANGIBLE LOW-TAXED INCOME.**

(a) IN GENERAL.—Part VIII of subchapter B of chapter 1 is amended by adding at the end the following new section:

**"SEC. 250. FOREIGN-DERIVED INTANGIBLE INCOME AND GLOBAL INTANGIBLE LOW-TAXED INCOME.**

"(a) ALLOWANCE OF DEDUCTION.—

"(1) IN GENERAL.—In the case of a domestic corporation for any taxable year, there shall be allowed as a deduction an amount equal to the sum of—

"(A) 37.5 percent of the foreign-derived intangible income of such domestic corporation for such taxable year, plus

"(B) 50 percent of—

"(i) the global intangible low-taxed income amount (if any) which is included in the gross income of such domestic corporation under section 951A for such taxable year, and

"(ii) the amount treated as a dividend received by such corporation under section 78 which is attributable to the amount de-

"(2) LIMITATION BASED ON TAXABLE INCOME.—

"(A) IN GENERAL.—If, for any taxable year—

"(i) the sum of the foreign-derived intangible income and the global intangible low-taxed income amount otherwise taken into account by the domestic corporation under paragraph (1), exceeds

"(ii) the taxable income of the domestic corporation (determined without regard to this section),

then the amount of the foreign-derived intangible income and the global intangible low-taxed income amount so taken into account shall be reduced as provided in subparagraph (B).

"(B) REDUCTION.—For purposes of subparagraph (A)—

"(i) foreign-derived intangible income shall be reduced by an amount which bears the same ratio to the excess described in subparagraph (A) as such foreign-derived intangible income bears to the sum described in subparagraph (A)(i), and "(ii) the global intangible low-taxed income amount shall be reduced by the remainder of such excess.

"(3) REDUCTION IN DEDUCTION FOR TAXABLE YEARS AFTER 2025.—In the case of any taxable year beginning after December 31, 2025, paragraph (1) shall be applied by substituting—

"(A) '21.875 percent' for '37.5 percent' in subparagraph (A), and

"(B) '37.5 percent' for '50 percent' in subparagraph (B).

"(b) FOREIGN-DERIVED INTANGIBLE INCOME.—For purposes of this section—

"(1) IN GENERAL.—The foreign-derived intangible income of any domestic corporation is the amount which bears the same ratio to the deemed intangible income of such corporation as—

"(A) the foreign-derived deduction eligible income of such corporation, bears to

"(B) the deduction eligible income of such corporation.

"(2) DEEMED INTANGIBLE INCOME.—For purposes of this subsection—

"(A) IN GENERAL.—The term 'deemed intangible income' means the excess (if any) of—

"(i) the deduction eligible income of the domestic corporation, over

"(ii) the deemed tangible income return of the corporation.

"(B) DEEMED TANGIBLE INCOME RETURN.—The term 'deemed tangible income return' means, with respect to any corporation, an amount equal to 10 percent of the corporation's qualified business asset investment (as defined in section 951A(d), determined by substituting 'deduction eligible income' for 'tested income' in paragraph (2) thereof and without regard to whether the corporation is a controlled foreign corporation).

"(3) DEDUCTION ELIGIBLE INCOME.—

"(A) IN GENERAL.—The term 'deduction eligible income' means, with respect to any domestic corporation, the excess (if any) of—

"(i) gross income of such corporation determined without regard to—

"(I) any amount included in the gross income of such corporation under section 951(a)(1),

"(II) the global intangible low-taxed income included in the gross income of such corporation under section 951A,

"(III) any financial services income (as defined in section 904(d)(2)(D)) of such corporation,

"(IV) any dividend received from a corporation which is a controlled foreign corporation of such domestic corporation,

"(V) any domestic oil and gas extraction income of such corporation, and

"(VI) any foreign branch income (as defined in section 904(d)(2)(J)), over

"(ii) the deductions (including taxes) properly allocable to such gross income.

"(B) DOMESTIC OIL AND GAS EXTRACTION INCOME.—For purposes of subparagraph (A), the term 'domestic oil and gas extraction income' means income described in section 907(c)(1), determined by substituting 'within the United States' for 'without the United States'.

"(4) FOREIGN-DERIVED DEDUCTION ELIGIBLE INCOME.—The term 'foreign-derived deduction eligible income' means, with respect to any taxpayer for any taxable year, any deduction eligible income of such taxpayer which is derived in connection with—

"(A) property—

"(i) which is sold by the taxpayer to any person who is not a United States person, and

"(ii) which the taxpayer establishes to the satisfaction of the Secretary is for a foreign use, or

"(B) services provided by the taxpayer which the taxpayer establishes to the satisfaction of the Secretary are provided to any person, or with respect to property, not located within the United States.

"(5) RULES RELATING TO FOREIGN USE PROPERTY OR SERVICES.—For purposes of this subsection—

"(A) FOREIGN USE.—The term 'foreign use' means any use, consumption, or disposition which is not within the United States.

"(B) PROPERTY OR SERVICES PROVIDED TO DOMESTIC INTERMEDIARIES.—

"(i) PROPERTY.—If a taxpayer sells property to another person (other than a related party) for further manufacture or other modification within the United States, such property shall not be treated as sold for a foreign use even if such other person subsequently uses such property for a foreign use.

"(ii) SERVICES.—If a taxpayer provides services to another person (other than a related party) located within the United States, such services shall not be treated as described in paragraph (4)(B) even if such other person uses such services in providing services which are so described.

"(C) SPECIAL RULES WITH RESPECT TO RELATED PARTY TRANSACTIONS.—

"(i) SALES TO RELATED PARTIES.—If property is sold to a related party who is not a United States person, such sale shall not be treated as for a foreign use unless—

"(I) such property is ultimately sold by a related party, or used by a related party in connection with property which is sold or the provision of services, to another person who is an unrelated party who is not a United States person, and

"(II) the taxpayer establishes to the satisfaction of the Secretary that such property is for a foreign use.

For purposes of this clause, a sale of property shall be treated as a sale of each of the components thereof.

"(ii) SERVICE PROVIDED TO RELATED PARTIES.—If a service is provided to a related party who is not located in the United States, such service shall not be treated described in subparagraph (A)(ii) unless the taxpayer established to the satisfaction of the Secretary that such service is not substantially similar to services provided by such related party to persons located within the United States.

"(D) RELATED PARTY.—For purposes of this paragraph, the term 'related party' means any member of an affiliated group as defined in section 1504(a), determined—

"(i) by substituting 'more than 50 percent' for 'at least 80 percent' each place it appears, and

"(ii) without regard to paragraphs (2) and (3) of section 1504(b).

Any person (other than a corporation) shall be treated as a member of such group if such person is controlled by members of such group (including any entity treated as a member of such group by reason of this sentence) or controls any such member. For purposes of the preceding sentence, control shall be determined under the rules of section 954(d)(3).

"(E) SOLD.—For purposes of this subsection, the terms 'sold', 'sells', and 'sale' shall include any lease, license, exchange, or other disposition.

"(c) REGULATIONS.—The Secretary shall prescribe such regulations or other guidance as may be necessary or appropriate to carry out the provisions of this section.".

(b) CONFORMING AMENDMENTS.—

(1) Section 172(d), as amended by this Act, is amended by adding at the end the following new paragraph:

"(9) DEDUCTION FOR FOREIGN-DERIVED INTANGIBLE INCOME.—The deduction under section 250 shall not be allowed.".

(2) Section 246(b)(1) is amended—

(A) by striking "and subsection (a) and (b) of section 245" the first place it appears and inserting ", subsection (a) and (b) of section 245, and section 250",

(B) by striking "and subsection (a) and (b) of section 245" the second place it appears and inserting "subsection (a) and (b) of section 245, and 250".

(3) Section 469(i)(3)(F)(iii) is amended by striking "and 222" and inserting "222, and 250".

(4) The table of sections for part VIII of subchapter B of chapter 1 is amended by adding at the end the following new item:

"Sec. 250. Foreign-derived intangible income and global intangible low-taxed income.".

(c) EFFECTIVE DATE.—The amendments made by this section shall apply to taxable years beginning after December 31, 2017.

## CHAPTER 2—OTHER MODIFICATIONS OF SUBPART F PROVISIONS

### SEC. 14211. ELIMINATION OF INCLUSION OF FOREIGN BASE COMPANY OIL RELATED INCOME.

(a) REPEAL.—Subsection (a) of section 954 is amended—

(1) by inserting "and" at the end of paragraph (2),

(2) by striking the comma at the end of paragraph (3) and inserting a period, and

(3) by striking paragraph (5).

(b) CONFORMING AMENDMENTS.—

(1) Section 952(c)(1)(B)(iii) is amended by striking subclause (I) and redesignating subclauses (II) through (V) as subclauses (I) through (IV), respectively.

(2) Section 954(b) is amended—

(A) by striking the second sentence of paragraph (4),

(B) by striking "the foreign base company services income, and the foreign base company oil related income" in paragraph (5) and inserting "and the foreign base company services income", and

(C) by striking paragraph (6).

(3) Section 954 is amended by striking subsection (g).

(c) EFFECTIVE DATE.—The amendments made by this section shall apply to taxable years of foreign corporations beginning after December 31, 2017, and to taxable years of United States shareholders with or within which such taxable years of foreign corporations end.

**SEC. 14212. REPEAL OF INCLUSION BASED ON WITHDRAWAL OF PREVIOUSLY EXCLUDED SUBPART F INCOME FROM QUALIFIED INVESTMENT.**

(a) IN GENERAL.—Subpart F of part III of subchapter N of chapter 1 is amended by striking section 955.

(b) CONFORMING AMENDMENTS.—

(1)(A) Section 951(a)(1)(A) is amended to read as follows:

"(A) his pro rata share (determined under paragraph (2)) of the corporation's subpart F income for such year, and".

(B) Section 851(b) is amended by striking "section 951(a)(1)(A)(i)" in the flush language at the end and inserting "section 951(a)(1)(A)".

(C) Section 952(c)(1)(B)(i) is amended by striking "section 951(a)(1)(A)(i)" and inserting "section 951(a)(1)(A)".

(D) Section 953(c)(1)(C) is amended by striking "section 951(a)(1)(A)(i)" and inserting "section 951(a)(1)(A)".

(2) Section 951(a) is amended by striking paragraph (3).

(3) Section 953(d)(4)(B)(iv)(II) is amended by striking "or amounts referred to in clause (ii) or (iii) of section 951(a)(1)(A)".

(4) Section 964(b) is amended by striking ", 955,".

(5) Section 970 is amended by striking subsection (b).

(6) The table of sections for subpart F of part III of subchapter N of chapter 1 is amended by striking the item relating to section 955.

(c) EFFECTIVE DATE.—The amendments made by this section shall apply to taxable years of foreign corporations beginning after December 31, 2017, and to taxable years of United States shareholders in which or with which such taxable years of foreign corporations end.

**SEC. 14213. MODIFICATION OF STOCK ATTRIBUTION RULES FOR DETERMINING STATUS AS A CONTROLLED FOREIGN CORPORATION.**

(a) IN GENERAL.—Section 958(b) is amended—

(1) by striking paragraph (4), and

(2) by striking "Paragraphs (1) and (4)" in the last sentence and inserting "Paragraph (1)".

(b) EFFECTIVE DATE.—The amendments made by this section shall apply to—

(1) the last taxable year of foreign corporations beginning before January 1, 2018, and each subsequent taxable year of such foreign corporations, and

(2) taxable years of United States shareholders in which or with which such taxable years of foreign corporations end.

**SEC. 14214. MODIFICATION OF DEFINITION OF UNITED STATES SHAREHOLDER.**

(a) IN GENERAL.—Section 951(b) is amended by inserting ", or 10 percent or more of the total value of shares of all classes of stock of such foreign corporation" after "such foreign corporation".

(b) EFFECTIVE DATE.—The amendment made by this section shall apply to taxable years of foreign corporations beginning after December 31, 2017, and to taxable years of United States shareholders with or within which such taxable years of foreign corporations end.

**SEC. 14215. ELIMINATION OF REQUIREMENT THAT CORPORATION MUST BE CONTROLLED FOR 30 DAYS BEFORE SUBPART F INCLUSIONS APPLY.**

(a) IN GENERAL.—Section 951(a)(1) is amended by striking "for an uninterrupted period of 30 days or more" and inserting "at any time".

(b) EFFECTIVE DATE.—The amendment made by this section shall apply to taxable years of foreign corporations beginning after December 31, 2017, and to taxable years of United States shareholders with or within which such taxable years of foreign corporations end.

## CHAPTER 3—PREVENTION OF BASE EROSION

**SEC. 14221. LIMITATIONS ON INCOME SHIFTING THROUGH INTANGIBLE PROPERTY TRANSFERS.**

(a) DEFINITION OF INTANGIBLE ASSET.—Section 936(h)(3)(B) is amended—

(1) by striking "or" at the end of clause (v),

(2) by striking clause (vi) and inserting the following:

"(vi) any goodwill, going concern value, or workforce in place (including its composition and terms and conditions (contractual or otherwise) of its employ-

"(vii) any other item the value or potential value of which is not attributable to tangible property or the services of any individual.", and

(3) by striking the flush language after clause (vii), as added by paragraph (2).

(b) CLARIFICATION OF ALLOWABLE VALUATION METHODS.—

(1) FOREIGN CORPORATIONS.—Section 367(d)(2) is amended by adding at the end the following new subparagraph:

"(D) REGULATORY AUTHORITY.—For purposes of the last sentence of subparagraph (A), the Secretary shall require—

"(i) the valuation of transfers of intangible property, including intangible property transferred with other property or services, on an aggregate basis, or

"(ii) the valuation of such a transfer on the basis of the realistic alternatives to such a transfer,

if the Secretary determines that such basis is the most reliable means of valuation of such transfers.".

(2) ALLOCATION AMONG TAXPAYERS.—Section 482 is amended by adding at the end the following: "For purposes of this section, the Secretary shall require the valuation of transfers of intangible property (including intangible property transferred with other property or services) on an aggregate basis or the valuation of such a transfer on the basis of the realistic alternatives to such a transfer, if the Secretary determines that such basis is the most reliable means of valuation of such transfers.".

(c) EFFECTIVE DATE.—

(1) IN GENERAL.—The amendments made by this section shall apply to transfers in taxable years beginning after December 31, 2017.

(2) NO INFERENCE.—Nothing in the amendment made by subsection (a) shall be construed to create any inference with respect to the application of section 936(h)(3) of the Internal Revenue Code of 1986, or the authority of the Secretary of the Treasury to provide regulations for such application, with respect to taxable years beginning before January 1, 2018.

**SEC. 14222. CERTAIN RELATED PARTY AMOUNTS PAID OR ACCRUED IN HYBRID TRANSACTIONS OR WITH HYBRID ENTITIES.**

(a) IN GENERAL.—Part IX of subchapter B of chapter 1 is amended by inserting after section 267 the following:

**"SEC. 267A. CERTAIN RELATED PARTY AMOUNTS PAID OR ACCRUED IN HYBRID TRANSACTIONS OR WITH HYBRID ENTITIES.**

"(a) IN GENERAL.—No deduction shall be allowed under this chapter for any disqualified related party amount paid or accrued pursuant to a hybrid transaction or by, or to, a hybrid entity.

"(b) DISQUALIFIED RELATED PARTY AMOUNT.—For purposes of this section—

"(1) DISQUALIFIED RELATED PARTY AMOUNT.—The term 'disqualified related party amount' means any interest or royalty paid or accrued to a related party to the extent that—

"(A) such amount is not included in the income of such related party under the tax law of the country of which such related party is a resident for tax purposes or is subject to tax, or

"(B) such related party is allowed a deduction with respect to such amount under the tax law of such country.

Such term shall not include any payment to the extent such payment is included in the gross income of a United States shareholder under section 951(a).

"(2) RELATED PARTY.—The term 'related party' means a related person as defined in section 954(d)(3), except that such section shall be applied with respect to the person making the payment described in paragraph (1) in lieu of the controlled foreign corporation otherwise referred to in such section.

"(c) HYBRID TRANSACTION.—For purposes of this section, the term 'hybrid transaction' means any transaction, series of transactions, agreement, or instrument one or more payments with respect to which are treated as interest or royalties for purposes of this chapter and which are not so treated for purposes the tax law of the foreign country of which the recipient of such payment is resident for tax purposes or is subject to tax.

"(d) HYBRID ENTITY.—For purposes of this section, the term 'hybrid entity' means any entity which is either—

"(1) treated as fiscally transparent for purposes of this chapter but not so treated for purposes of the tax law of the foreign country of which the entity is resident for tax purposes or is subject to tax, or

"(2) treated as fiscally transparent for purposes of such tax law but not so treated for purposes of this chapter.

"(e) REGULATIONS.—The Secretary shall issue such regulations or other guidance as may be necessary or appropriate to carry out the purposes of this section, including regulations or other guidance providing for—

"(1) rules for treating certain conduit arrangements which involve a hybrid transaction or a hybrid entity as subject to subsection (a),

"(2) rules for the application of this section to branches or domestic entities,

"(3) rules for treating certain structured transactions as subject to subsection (a),

"(4) rules for treating a tax preference as an exclusion from income for purposes of applying subsection (b)(1) if such tax preference has the effect of reducing the generally applicable statutory rate by 25 percent or more,

"(5) rules for treating the entire amount of interest or royalty paid or accrued to a related party as a disqualified related party amount if such amount is subject to a participation exemption system or other system which provides for the exclusion or deduction of a substantial portion of such amount,

"(6) rules for determining the tax residence of a foreign entity if the entity is otherwise considered a resident of more than one country or of no country,

"(7) exceptions from subsection (a) with respect to—

"(A) cases in which the disqualified related party amount is taxed under the laws of a foreign country other than the country of which the related party is a resident for tax purposes, and

"(B) other cases which the Secretary determines do not present a risk of eroding the Federal tax base,

"(8) requirements for record keeping and information reporting in addition to any requirements imposed by section 6038A.".

(b) Conforming Amendment.—The table of sections for part IX of subchapter B of chapter 1 is amended by inserting after the item relating to section 267 the following new item:

"Sec. 267A. Certain related party amounts paid or accrued in hybrid transactions or with hybrid entities.".

(c) EFFECTIVE DATE.—The amendments made by this section shall apply to taxable years beginning after December 31, 2017.

**SEC. 14223. SHAREHOLDERS OF SURROGATE FOREIGN CORPORATIONS NOT ELIGIBLE FOR REDUCED RATE ON DIVIDENDS.**

(a) IN GENERAL.—Section 1(h)(11)(C)(iii) is amended—

(1) by striking "shall not include any foreign corporation" and inserting "shall not include—

"(I) any foreign corporation",

(2) by striking the period at the end and inserting ", and", and

(3) by adding at the end the following new subclause:

"(II) any corporation which first becomes a surrogate foreign corporation (as defined in section 7874(a)(2)(B)) after the date of the enactment of this subclause, other than a foreign corporation which is treated as a domestic corporation under section 7874(b).".

(b) EFFECTIVE DATE.—The amendments made by this section shall apply to dividends received after the date of the enactment of this Act.

## Subpart C—Modifications Related to Foreign Tax Credit System

### SEC. 14301. REPEAL OF SECTION 902 INDIRECT FOREIGN TAX CREDITS; DETERMINATION OF SECTION 960 CREDIT ON CURRENT YEAR BASIS.

(a) REPEAL OF SECTION 902 INDIRECT FOREIGN TAX CREDITS.—Subpart A of part III of subchapter N of chapter 1 is amended by striking section 902.

(b) DETERMINATION OF SECTION 960 CREDIT ON CURRENT YEAR BASIS.—Section 960, as amended by section 14201, is amended—

(1) by striking subsection (c), by redesignating subsection (b) as subsection (c), by striking all that precedes subsection (c) (as so redesignated) and inserting the following:

**"SEC. 960. DEEMED PAID CREDIT FOR SUBPART F INCLUSIONS.**

"(a) IN GENERAL.—For purposes of subpart A of this part, if there is included in the gross income of a domestic corporation any item of income under section 951(a)(1) with respect to any controlled foreign corporation with respect to which such domestic corporation is a United States shareholder, such domestic corporation shall be deemed to have paid so much of such foreign corporation's foreign income taxes as are properly attributable to such item of income.

"(b) SPECIAL RULES FOR DISTRIBUTIONS FROM PREVIOUSLY TAXED EARNINGS AND PROFITS.—For purposes of subpart A of this part—

"(1) IN GENERAL.—If any portion of a distribution from a controlled foreign corporation to a domestic corporation which is a United States shareholder with respect to such controlled foreign corporation is excluded from gross income under section 959(a), such domestic corporation shall be deemed to have paid so much of such foreign corporation's foreign income taxes as—

"(A) are properly attributable to such portion, and

"(B) have not been deemed to have to been paid by such domestic corporation under this section for the taxable year or any prior taxable year.

"(2) TIERED CONTROLLED FOREIGN CORPORATIONS.—If section 959(b) applies to any portion of a distribution from a controlled foreign corporation to another controlled foreign corporation, such controlled foreign corporation shall be deemed to have paid so much of such other controlled foreign corporation's foreign income taxes as—

"(A) are properly attributable to such portion, and

"(B) have not been deemed to have been paid by a domestic corporation under this section for the taxable year or any prior taxable year.",

(2) and by adding after subsection (d) (as added by section 14201) the following new subsections:

"(e) FOREIGN INCOME TAXES.—The term 'foreign income taxes' means any income, war profits, or excess profits taxes paid or accrued to any foreign country or possession of the United States.

"(f) REGULATIONS.—The Secretary shall prescribe such regulations or other guidance as may be necessary or appropriate to carry out the provisions of this section.".

(c) CONFORMING AMENDMENTS.—

(1) Section 78 is amended to read as follows:

**"SEC. 78. GROSS UP FOR DEEMED PAID FOREIGN TAX CREDIT.**

"If a domestic corporation chooses to have the benefits of subpart A of part III of subchapter N (relating to foreign tax credit) for any taxable year, an amount equal to the taxes deemed to be paid by such corporation under subsections (a), (b), and (d) of section 960 (determined without regard to the phrase '80 percent of' in subsection (d)(1) thereof) for such taxable year shall be treated for purposes of this title (other than sections 245 and 245A) as a dividend received by such domestic corporation from the foreign corporation.".

(2) Paragraph (4) of section 245(a) is amended to read as follows:

"(4) POST-1986 UNDISTRIBUTED EARNINGS.—The term 'post-1986 undistributed earnings' means the amount of the earnings and profits of the foreign corporation (computed in accordance with sections 964(a) and 986) accumulated in taxable years beginning after December 31, 1986—

"(A) as of the close of the taxable year of the foreign corporation in which the dividend is distributed, and

"(B) without diminution by reason of dividends distributed during such taxable year.".

(3) Section 245(a)(10)(C) is amended by striking "902, 907, and 960" and inserting "907 and 960".

(4) Sections 535(b)(1) and 545(b)(1) are each amended by striking "section 902(a) or 960(a)(1)" and inserting "section 960".

(5) Section 814(f)(1) is amended—

(A) by striking subparagraph (B), and

(B) by striking all that precedes "No income" and inserting the following:

"(1) TREATMENT OF FOREIGN TAXES.—".

(6) Section 865(h)(1)(B) is amended by striking "902, 907," and inserting "907".

(7) Section 901(a) is amended by striking "sections 902 and 960" and inserting "section 960".

(8) Section 901(e)(2) is amended by striking "but is not limited to—" and all that follows through "that portion" and inserting "but is not limited to that portion".

(9) Section 901(f) is amended by striking "sections 902 and 960" and inserting "section 960".

(10) Section 901(j)(1)(A) is amended by striking "902 or".

(11) Section 901(j)(1)(B) is amended by striking "sections 902 and 960" and inserting "section 960".

(12) Section 901(k)(2) is amended by striking ", 902,".

(13) Section 901(k)(6) is amended by striking "902 or".

(14) Section 901(m)(1)(B) is amended to read as follows:

"(B) in the case of a foreign income tax paid by a foreign corporation, shall not be taken into account for purposes of section 960.".

(15) Section 904(d)(2)(E) is amended—

(A) by amending clause (i) to read as follows:

"(i) NONCONTROLLED 10-PERCENT OWNED FOREIGN CORPORATION.—The term 'noncontrolled 10-percent owned foreign corporation' means any foreign corporation which is—

"(I) a specified 10-percent owned foreign corporation (as defined in section 245A(b)), or

"(II) a passive foreign investment company (as defined in section 1297(a)) with respect to which the taxpayer meets the stock ownership requirements of section 902(a) (or, for purposes of applying paragraphs (3)

and (4), the requirements of section 902(b)).

A controlled foreign corporation shall not be treated as a noncontrolled 10-percent owned foreign corporation with respect to any distribution out of its earnings and profits for periods during which it was a controlled foreign corporation. Any reference to section 902 in this clause shall be treated as a reference to such section as in effect before its repeal.'', and

(B) by striking ''non-controlled section 902 corporation'' in clause (ii) and inserting ''noncontrolled 10-percent owned foreign corporation''.

(16) Section 904(d)(4) is amended—

(A) by striking ''noncontrolled section 902 corporation'' each place it appears and inserting ''noncontrolled 10-percent owned foreign corporation'',

(B) by striking ''NONCONTROLLED SECTION 902 CORPORATIONS'' in the heading thereof and inserting ''NONCONTROLLED 10-PERCENT OWNED FOREIGN CORPORATIONS''.

(17) Section 904(d)(6)(A) is amended by striking "902, 907," and inserting "907".

(18) Section 904(h)(10)(A) is amended by striking "sections 902, 907, and 960" and inserting "sections 907 and 960".

(19) Section 904(k) is amended to read as follows:

"(k) CROSS REFERENCES.—For increase of limitation under subsection (a) for taxes paid with respect to amounts received which were included in the gross income of the taxpayer for a prior taxable year as a United States shareholder with respect to a controlled foreign corporation, see section 960(c).".

(20) Section 905(c)(1) is amended by striking the last sentence.

(21) Section 905(c)(2)(B)(i) is amended to read as follows:

"(i) shall be taken into account for the taxable year to which such taxes relate, and".

(22) Section 906(a) is amended by striking "(or deemed, under section 902, paid or accrued during the taxable year)".

(23) Section 906(b) is amended by striking paragraphs (4) and (5).

(24) Section 907(b)(2)(B) is amended by striking "902 or".

(25) Section 907(c)(3)(A) is amended—

(A) by striking subparagraph (A) and inserting the following:

"(A) interest, to the extent the category of income of such interest is determined under section 904(d)(3),", and

(B) by striking "section 960(a)" in subparagraph (B) and inserting "section 960".

(26) Section 907(c)(5) is amended by striking "902 or".

(27) Section 907(f)(2)(B)(i) is amended by striking "902 or".

(28) Section 908(a) is amended by striking "902 or".

(29) Section 909(b) is amended—

(A) by striking "section 902 corporation" in the matter preceding paragraph (1) and inserting "specified 10-percent owned foreign corporation (as defined in section 245A(b) without regard to paragraph (2) thereof)",

(B) by striking "902 or" in paragraph (1),

(C) by striking "by such section 902 corporation" and all that follows in the matter following paragraph (2) and inserting "by such specified 10-percent owned foreign corporation or a domestic corporation which is a United States shareholder with respect to such specified 10-percent owned foreign corporation.", and

(D) by striking "SECTION 902 CORPORATIONS" in the heading thereof and inserting "SPECIFIED 10-PERCENT OWNED FOREIGN CORPORATIONS".

(30) Section 909(d) is amended by striking paragraph (5).

(31) Section 958(a)(1) is amended by striking "960(a)(1)" and inserting "960".

(32) Section 959(d) is amended by striking "Except as provided in section 960(a)(3), any" and inserting "Any".

(33) Section 959(e) is amended by striking "section 960(b)" and inserting "section 960(c)".

(34) Section 1291(g)(2)(A) is amended by striking "any distribution—" and all that follows through "but only if" and inserting "any distribution, any withholding tax imposed with respect to such distribution, but only if".

(35) Section 1293(f) is amended by striking "and" at the end of paragraph (1), by striking the period at the end of paragraph (2) and inserting ", and", and by adding at the end the following new paragraph:

"(3) a domestic corporation which owns (or is treated under section 1298(a) as owning) stock of a qualified electing fund shall be treated in the same manner as a United States shareholder of a controlled foreign corporation (and such qualified electing fund shall be treated in the same manner as such controlled foreign corporation) if such domestic corporation meets the stock ownership requirements of subsection (a) or (b) of section 902 (as in effect before its repeal) with respect to such qualified electing fund.".

(36) Section 6038(c)(1)(B) is amended by striking "sections 902 (relating to foreign tax credit for corporate stockholder in foreign corporation) and 960 (relating to special rules for foreign tax credit)" and inserting "section 960".

(37) Section 6038(c)(4) is amended by striking subparagraph (C).

(38) The table of sections for subpart A of part III of subchapter N of chapter 1 is amended by striking the item relating to section 902.

(39) The table of sections for subpart F of part III of subchapter N of chapter 1 is amended by striking the item relating to section 960 and inserting the following:

"Sec. 960. Deemed paid credit for subpart F inclusions.".

(d) EFFECTIVE DATE.—The amendments made by this section shall apply to taxable years of foreign corporations beginning after December 31, 2017, and to taxable years of United States shareholders in which or with which such taxable years of foreign corporations end.

**SEC. 14302. SEPARATE FOREIGN TAX CREDIT LIMITATION BASKET FOR FOREIGN BRANCH INCOME.**

(a) IN GENERAL.—Section 904(d)(1), as amended by section 14201, is amended by redesignating subparagraphs (B) and (C) as subparagraphs (C) and (D), respectively, and by inserting after subparagraph (A) the following new subparagraph:

"(B) foreign branch income,".

(b) FOREIGN BRANCH INCOME.—

(1) IN GENERAL.—Section 904(d)(2) is amended by inserting after subparagraph (I) the following new subparagraph:

"(i) IN GENERAL.—The term 'foreign branch income' means the business profits of such United States person which are attributable to 1 or more qualified business units (as defined in section 989(a)) in 1 or more foreign countries. For purposes of the preceding sentence, the amount of business profits attributable to a qualified business unit shall be determined under rules established by the Secretary.

"(ii) EXCEPTION.—Such term shall not include any income which is passive category income.".

(2) CONFORMING AMENDMENT.—Section 904(d)(2)(A)(ii), as amended by section 14201, is amended by striking "income described in paragraph (1)(A) and" and inserting "income described in paragraph (1)(A), foreign branch income, and".

(c) EFFECTIVE DATE.—The amendments made by this section shall apply to taxable years beginning after December 31, 2017.

**SEC. 14303. SOURCE OF INCOME FROM SALES OF INVENTORY DETERMINED SOLELY ON BASIS OF PRODUCTION ACTIVITIES.**

(a) IN GENERAL.—Section 863(b) is amended by adding at the end the following: "Gains, profits, and income from the sale or exchange of inventory property described in paragraph (2) shall be allocated and apportioned between sources within and without the United States solely on the basis of the production activities with respect to the property.".

(b) EFFECTIVE DATE.—The amendment made by this section shall apply to taxable years beginning after December 31, 2017.

**SEC. 14304. ELECTION TO INCREASE PERCENTAGE OF DOMESTIC TAXABLE INCOME OFFSET BY OVERALL DOMESTIC LOSS TREATED AS FOREIGN SOURCE.**

(a) IN GENERAL.—Section 904(g) is amended by adding at the end the following new paragraph:

"(5) ELECTION TO INCREASE PERCENTAGE OF TAXABLE INCOME TREATED AS FOREIGN SOURCE.—

"(A) IN GENERAL.—If any pre-2018 unused overall domestic loss is taken into account under paragraph (1) for any applicable taxable year, the taxpayer may elect to have such para-

percentage greater than 50 percent (but not greater than 100 percent) for 50 percent in subparagraph (B) thereof.

"(B) PRE-2018 UNUSED OVERALL DOMESTIC LOSS.—For purposes of this paragraph, the term 'pre-2018 unused overall domestic loss' means any overall domestic loss which—

"(i) arises in a qualified taxable year beginning before January 1, 2018, and

"(ii) has not been used under paragraph (1) for any taxable year beginning before such date.

"(C) APPLICABLE TAXABLE YEAR.—For purposes of this paragraph, the term 'applicable taxable year' means any taxable year of the taxpayer beginning after December 31, 2017, and before January 1, 2028.".

(b) EFFECTIVE DATE.—The amendment made by this section shall apply to taxable years beginning after December 31, 2017.

## PART II—INBOUND TRANSACTIONS

### SEC. 14401. BASE EROSION AND ANTI-ABUSE TAX.

(a) IMPOSITION OF TAX.—Subchapter A of chapter 1 is amended by adding at the end the following new part:

## "PART VII—BASE EROSION AND ANTI-ABUSE TAX



### "SEC. 59A. TAX ON BASE EROSION PAYMENTS OF TAXPAYERS WITH SUBSTANTIAL GROSS RECEIPTS.

"(a) IMPOSITION OF TAX.—There is hereby imposed on each applicable taxpayer for any taxable year a tax equal to the base erosion minimum tax amount for the taxable year. Such tax shall be in addition to any other tax imposed by this subtitle.

"(b) BASE EROSION MINIMUM TAX AMOUNT.—For purposes of this section—

"(1) IN GENERAL.—Except as provided in paragraphs (2) and (3), the term 'base erosion minimum tax amount' means, with respect to any applicable taxpayer for any taxable year, the excess (if any) of—

"(A) an amount equal to 10 percent (5 percent in the case of taxable years beginning in calendar year 2018) of the modified taxable income of such taxpayer for the taxable year, over

"(B) an amount equal to the regular tax liability (as defined in section 26(b)) of the taxpayer for the taxable year, reduced (but not below zero) by the excess (if any) of—

"(i) the credits allowed under this chapter against such regular tax liability, over

"(ii) the sum of—

"(I) the credit allowed under section 38 for the taxable year which is properly allocable to the research credit determined under section 41(a), plus

"(II) the portion of the applicable section 38 credits not in excess of 80 percent of the lesser of the amount of such credits or the base erosion minimum tax amount (determined without regard to this subclause).

"(2) MODIFICATIONS FOR TAXABLE YEARS BEGINNING AFTER 2025.—In the case of any taxable year beginning after December 31, 2025, paragraph (1) shall be applied—

"(A) by substituting '12.5 percent' for '10 percent' in subparagraph (A) thereof, and

"(B) by reducing (but not below zero) the regular tax liability (as defined in section

26(b)) for purposes of subparagraph (B) thereof by the aggregate amount of the credits allowed under this chapter against such regular tax liability rather than the excess described in such subparagraph.

"(3) INCREASED RATE FOR CERTAIN BANKS AND SECURITIES DEALERS.—

"(A) IN GENERAL.—In the case of a taxpayer described in subparagraph (B) who is an applicable taxpayer for any taxable year, the percentage otherwise in effect under paragraphs (1)(A) and (2)(A) shall each be increased by one percentage point.

"(B) TAXPAYER DESCRIBED.—A taxpayer is described in this subparagraph if such taxpayer is a member of an affiliated group (as defined in section 1504(a)(1)) which includes—

"(i) a bank (as defined in section 581), or

"(ii) a registered securities dealer under section 15(a) of the Securities Exchange Act of 1934.

"(4) APPLICABLE SECTION 38 CREDITS.—For purposes of paragraph (1)(B)(ii)(II), the term 'applicable section 38 credits' means the credit allowed under section 38 for the taxable year which is properly allocable to—

"(A) the low-income housing credit determined under section 42(a),

"(B) the renewable electricity production credit determined under section 45(a), and

"(C) the investment credit determined under section 46, but only to the extent properly allocable to the energy credit determined under section 48.

"(c) MODIFIED TAXABLE INCOME.—For purposes of this section—

"(1) IN GENERAL.—The term 'modified taxable income' means the taxable income of the taxpayer computed under this chapter for the taxable year, determined without regard to—

"(A) any base erosion tax benefit with respect to any base erosion payment, or

"(B) the base erosion percentage of any net operating loss deduction allowed under section 172 for the taxable year.

"(2) BASE EROSION TAX BENEFIT.—

"(A) IN GENERAL.—The term 'base erosion tax benefit' means—

"(i) any deduction described in subsection (d)(1) which is allowed under this chapter for the taxable year with respect to any base erosion payment,

"(ii) in the case of a base erosion payment described in subsection (d)(2), any deduction allowed under this chapter for the taxable year for depreciation (or amortization in lieu of depreciation) with respect to the property acquired with such payment,

"(iii) in the case of a base erosion payment described in subsection (d)(3)—

"(I) any reduction under section 803(a)(1)(B) in the gross amount of premiums and other consideration on insurance and annuity contracts for premiums and other consideration arising out of indemnity insurance, and

"(II) any deduction under section 832(b)(4)(A) from the amount of gross premiums written on insurance contracts during the taxable year for premiums paid for reinsurance, and "(iv) in the case of a base erosion payment described in subsection (d)(4), any reduction in gross receipts with respect to such payment in computing gross income of the taxpayer for the taxable year for purposes of this chapter.

"(B) TAX BENEFITS DISREGARDED IF TAX WITHHELD ON BASE EROSION PAYMENT.—

"(i) IN GENERAL.—Except as provided in clause (ii), any base erosion tax benefit attributable to any base erosion payment—

"(I) on which tax is imposed by section 871 or 881, and

"(II) with respect to which tax has been deducted and withheld under section 1441 or 1442,

shall not be taken into account in computing modified taxable income under paragraph (1)(A) or the base erosion percentage under paragraph (4).

"(ii) EXCEPTION.—The amount not taken into account in computing modified taxable income by reason of clause (i) shall be reduced under rules similar to the rules under section 163(j)(5)(B) (as in effect before the date of the enactment of the Tax Cuts and Jobs Act).

"(3) SPECIAL RULES FOR DETERMINING INTEREST FOR WHICH DEDUCTION ALLOWED.—For purposes of applying paragraph (1), in the case of a taxpayer to which section 163(j) applies for the taxable year, the reduction in the amount of interest for which a deduction is allowed by reason of such subsection shall be treated as allocable first to interest paid or accrued to persons who are not related parties with respect to the taxpayer and then to such related parties.

"(4) BASE EROSION PERCENTAGE.—For purposes of paragraph (1)(B)—

"(A) IN GENERAL.—The term 'base erosion percentage' means, for any taxable year, the percentage determined by dividing—

"(i) the aggregate amount of base erosion tax benefits of the taxpayer for the taxable year, by

"(ii) the sum of—

"(I) the aggregate amount of the deductions (including deductions described in clauses (i) and (ii) of paragraph (2)(A)) allowable to the taxpayer under this chapter for the taxable year, plus

"(II) the base erosion tax benefits described in clauses (iii) and (iv) of paragraph (2)(A) allowable to the taxpayer for the taxable year.

"(B) CERTAIN ITEMS NOT TAKEN INTO ACCOUNT.—The amount under subparagraph (A)(ii) shall be determined by not taking into account—

"(i) any deduction allowed under section 172, 245A, or 250 for the taxable year,

"(ii) any deduction for amounts paid or accrued for services to which the exception under subsection (d)(5) applies, and

"(iii) any deduction for qualified derivative payments which are not treated as a base erosion payment by reason of subsection (h).

"(d) BASE EROSION PAYMENT.—For purposes of this section—

"(1) IN GENERAL.—The term 'base erosion payment' means any amount paid or accrued by the taxpayer to a foreign person which is a related party of the taxpayer and with respect to which a deduction is allowable under this chapter.

"(2) PURCHASE OF DEPRECIABLE PROPERTY.—Such term shall also include any amount paid or accrued by the taxpayer to a foreign person which is a related party of the taxpayer in connection with the acquisition by the taxpayer from such person of property of a character subject to the allowance for depreciation (or amortization in lieu of depreciation).

"(3) REINSURANCE PAYMENTS.—Such term shall also include any premium or other consideration paid or accrued by the taxpayer to a foreign person which is a related party of the taxpayer for any reinsurance payments which are taken into account under sections 803(a)(1)(B) or 832(b)(4)(A).

"(4) CERTAIN PAYMENTS TO EXPATRIATED ENTITIES.—

"(A) IN GENERAL.—Such term shall also include any amount paid or accrued by the taxpayer with respect to a person described in subparagraph (B) which results in a reduction of the gross receipts of the taxpayer.

"(B) PERSON DESCRIBED.—A person is described in this subparagraph if such person is a—

"(i) surrogate foreign corporation which is a related party of the taxpayer, but only if such person first became a surrogate foreign corporation after November 9, 2017, or

"(ii) foreign person which is a member of the same expanded affiliated group as the surrogate foreign corporation.

"(C) DEFINITIONS.—For purposes of this paragraph—

"(i) SURROGATE FOREIGN CORPORATION.—The term 'surrogate foreign corporation' has the meaning given such term by section 7874(a)(2)(B) but does not include a foreign corporation treated as a domestic corporation under section 7874(b).

"(ii) EXPANDED AFFILIATED GROUP.—The term 'expanded affiliated group' has the meaning given such term by section 7874(c)(1).

"(5) EXCEPTION FOR CERTAIN AMOUNTS WITH RESPECT TO SERVICES.—Paragraph (1) shall not apply to any amount paid or accrued by a taxpayer for services if—

"(A) such services are services which meet the requirements for eligibility for use of the services cost method under section 482 (determined without regard to the requirement that the services not contribute significantly to fundamental risks of business success or failure), and

"(B) such amount constitutes the total services cost with no markup component.

"(e) APPLICABLE TAXPAYER.—For purposes of this section—

"(1) IN GENERAL.—The term 'applicable taxpayer' means, with respect to any taxable year, a taxpayer—

"(A) which is a corporation other than a regulated investment company, a real estate investment trust, or an S corporation,

"(B) the average annual gross receipts of which for the 3-taxable-year period ending with the preceding taxable year are at least $500,000,000, and

"(C) the base erosion percentage (as determined under subsection (c)(4)) of which for the taxable year is 3 percent (2 percent in the case of a taxpayer described in subsection (b)(3)(B)) or higher.

"(2) GROSS RECEIPTS.—

"(A) SPECIAL RULE FOR FOREIGN PERSONS.—In the case of a foreign person the gross receipts of which are taken into account for purposes of paragraph (1)(B), only gross receipts which are taken into account in determining income which is effectively connected with the conduct of a trade or business within the United States shall be taken into account. In the case of a taxpayer which is a foreign person, the preceding sentence shall not apply to the gross receipts of any United States person which are aggregated with the taxpayer's gross receipts by reason of paragraph (3).

"(B) OTHER RULES MADE APPLICABLE.—Rules similar to the rules of subparagraphs (B), (C), and (D) of section 448(c)(3) shall apply in determining gross receipts for purposes of this section.

"(3) AGGREGATION RULES.—All persons treated as a single employer under subsection (a) of section 52 shall be treated as 1 person for purposes of this subsection and subsection (c)(4), except that in applying section 1563 for purposes of section 52, the exception for foreign corporations under section 1563(b)(2)(C) shall be disregarded.

"(f) FOREIGN PERSON.—For purposes of this section, the term 'foreign person' has the meaning given such term by section 6038A(c)(3).

"(g) RELATED PARTY.—For purposes of this section—

"(1) IN GENERAL.—The term 'related party' means, with respect to any applicable taxpayer—

"(A) any 25-percent owner of the taxpayer,

"(B) any person who is related (within the meaning of section 267(b) or 707(b)(1)) to the taxpayer or any 25-percent owner of the taxpayer, and

"(C) any other person who is related (within the meaning of section 482) to the taxpayer.

"(2) 25-PERCENT OWNER.—The term '25-percent owner' means, with respect to any corporation, any person who owns at least 25 percent of—

"(A) the total voting power of all classes of stock of a corporation entitled to vote, or

"(B) the total value of all classes of stock of such corporation.

"(3) SECTION 318 TO APPLY.—Section 318 shall apply for purposes of paragraphs (1) and (2), except that—

"(A) '10 percent' shall be substituted for '50 percent' in section 318(a)(2)(C), and

"(B) subparagraphs (A), (B), and (C) of section 318(a)(3) shall not be applied so as to consider a United States person as owning stock which is owned by a person who is not a United States person.

"(h) EXCEPTION FOR CERTAIN PAYMENTS MADE IN THE ORDINARY COURSE OF TRADE OR BUSINESS.—For purposes of this section—

"(1) IN GENERAL.—Except as provided in paragraph (3), any qualified derivative payment shall not be treated as a base erosion payment.

"(2) QUALIFIED DERIVATIVE PAYMENT.—

"(A) IN GENERAL.—The term 'qualified derivative payment' means any payment made by a taxpayer pursuant to a derivative with respect to which the taxpayer—

"(i) recognizes gain or loss as if such derivative were sold for its fair market value on the last business day of the taxable year (and such additional times as required by this title or the taxpayer's method of accounting),

"(ii) treats any gain or loss so recognized as ordinary, and

"(iii) treats the character of all items of income, deduction, gain, or loss with respect to a payment pursuant to the derivative as ordinary.

"(B) REPORTING REQUIREMENT.—No payments shall be treated as qualified derivative payments under subparagraph (A) for any taxable year unless the taxpayer includes in the information required to be reported under section 6038B(b)(2) with respect to such taxable year such information as is necessary to identify the payments to be so treated and such other information as the Secretary determines necessary to carry out the provisions of this subsection.

"(3) EXCEPTIONS FOR PAYMENTS OTHERWISE TREATED AS BASE EROSION PAYMENTS.—This subsection shall not apply to any qualified derivative payment if—

"(A) the payment would be treated as a base erosion payment if it were not made pursuant to a derivative, including any interest, royalty, or service payment, or

"(B) in the case of a contract which has derivative and nonderivative components, the payment is properly allocable to the nonderivative component.

"(4) DERIVATIVE DEFINED.—For purposes of this subsection—

"(A) IN GENERAL.—The term 'derivative' means any contract (including any option, forward contract, futures contract, short position, swap, or similar contract) the value of which, or any payment or other transfer with respect to which, is (directly or indirectly) determined by reference to one or more of the following:

"(i) Any share of stock in a corporation.

"(ii) Any evidence of indebtedness.

"(iii) Any commodity which is actively traded.

"(iv) Any currency.

"(v) Any rate, price, amount, index, formula, or algorithm.

Such term shall not include any item described in clauses (i) through (v).

"(B) TREATMENT OF AMERICAN DEPOSITORY RECEIPTS AND SIMILAR INSTRUMENTS.—Except as otherwise provided by the Secretary, for purposes of this part, American depository receipts (and similar instruments) with respect to shares of stock in foreign corporations shall be treated as shares of stock in such foreign corporations.

"(C) EXCEPTION FOR CERTAIN CONTRACTS.—Such term shall not include any insurance, annuity, or endowment contract issued by an insurance company to which subchapter L applies (or issued by any foreign corporation to which such subchapter would apply if such foreign corporation were a domestic corporation).

"(i) REGULATIONS.—The Secretary shall prescribe such regulations or other guidance as may be necessary or appropriate to carry out the provisions of this section, including regulations—

"(1) providing for such adjustments to the application of this section as are necessary to prevent the avoidance of the purposes of this section, including through—

"(A) the use of unrelated persons, conduit transactions, or other intermediaries, or

"(B) transactions or arrangements designed, in whole or in part—

"(i) to characterize payments otherwise subject to this section as payments not subject to this section, or

"(ii) to substitute payments not subject to this section for payments otherwise subject to this section and

"(2) for the application of subsection (g), including rules to prevent the avoidance of the exceptions under subsection (g)(3).".

(b) REPORTING REQUIREMENTS AND PENALTIES.—

(1) IN GENERAL.—Subsection (b) of section 6038A is amended to read as follows:

"(b) REQUIRED INFORMATION.—

"(1) IN GENERAL.—For purposes of subsection (a), the information described in this subsection is such information as the Secretary prescribes by regulations relating to—

"(A) the name, principal place of business, nature of business, and country or countries in which organized or resident, of each person which—

"(i) is a related party to the reporting corporation, and

"(ii) had any transaction with the reporting corporation during its taxable year,

"(B) the manner in which the reporting corporation is related to each person referred to in subparagraph (A), and

"(C) transactions between the reporting corporation and each foreign person which is a related party to the reporting corporation.

"(2) ADDITIONAL INFORMATION REGARDING BASE EROSION PAYMENTS.—For purposes of subsection (a) and section 6038C, if the reporting corporation or the foreign corporation to whom section 6038C applies is an applicable taxpayer, the information described in this subsection shall include—

"(A) such information as the Secretary determines necessary to determine the base erosion minimum tax amount, base erosion payments, and base erosion tax benefits of the taxpayer for purposes of section 59A for the taxable year, and

"(B) such other information as the Secretary determines necessary to carry out such section.

For purposes of this paragraph, any term used in this paragraph which is also used in section 59A shall have the same meaning as when used in such section.".

(2) INCREASE IN PENALTY.—Paragraphs (1) and (2) of section 6038A(d) are each amended by striking "$10,000" and inserting "$25,000".

(c) DISALLOWANCE OF CREDITS AGAINST BASE EROSION TAX.—Paragraph (2) of section 26(b) is amended by inserting after subparagraph (A) the following new subparagraph:

"(B) section 59A (relating to base erosion and anti-abuse tax),".

(d) CONFORMING AMENDMENTS.—

(1) The table of parts for subchapter A of chapter 1 is amended by adding after the item relating to part VI the following new item:

"PART VII. BASE EROSION AND ANTI-ABUSE TAX".

(2) Paragraph (1) of section 882(a), as amended by this Act, is amended by inserting " or 59A," after "section 11,".

(3) Subparagraph (A) of section 6425(c)(1), as amended by section 13001, is amended to read as follows:

"(A) the sum of—

"(i) the tax imposed by section 11, or subchapter L of chapter 1, whichever is applicable, plus

"(ii) the tax imposed by section 59A, over".

(4)(A) Subparagraph (A) of section 6655(g)(1), as amended by sections 12001 and 13001, is amended by striking "plus" at the end of clause (i), by redesignating clause (ii) as clause (iii), and by inserting after clause (i) the following new clause:

"(ii) the tax imposed by section 59A, plus".

(B) Subparagraphs (A)(i) and (B)(i) of section 6655(e)(2), as amended by sections 12001 and 13001, are each amended by inserting "and modified taxable income" after "taxable income".

(C) Subparagraph (B) of section 6655(e)(2) is amended by adding at the end the following new clause:

"(iii) MODIFIED TAXABLE INCOME.—The term 'modified taxable income' has the meaning given such term by section 59A(c)(1).".

(e) EFFECTIVE DATE.—The amendments made by this section shall apply to base erosion payments (as defined in section 59A(d) of the Internal Revenue Code of 1986, as added by this section) paid or accrued in taxable years beginning after December 31, 2017.

## PART III—OTHER PROVISIONS

### SEC. 14501. RESTRICTION ON INSURANCE BUSINESS EXCEPTION TO PASSIVE FOREIGN INVESTMENT COMPANY RULES.

(a) IN GENERAL.—Section 1297(b)(2)(B) is amended to read as follows:

"(B) derived in the active conduct of an insurance business by a qualifying insurance corporation (as defined in subsection (f)),".

(b) QUALIFYING INSURANCE CORPORATION DEFINED.—Section 1297 is amended by adding at the end the following new subsection:

"(f) QUALIFYING INSURANCE CORPORATION.—For purposes of subsection (b)(2)(B)—

"(1) IN GENERAL.—The term 'qualifying insurance corporation' means, with respect to any taxable year, a foreign corporation—

"(A) which would be subject to tax under subchapter L if such corporation were a domestic corporation, and

"(B) the applicable insurance liabilities of which constitute more than 25 percent of its total assets, determined on the basis of such liabilities and assets as reported on the corporation's applicable financial statement for the last year ending with or within the taxable year.

"(2) ALTERNATIVE FACTS AND CIRCUMSTANCES TEST FOR CERTAIN CORPORATIONS.—If a corporation fails to qualify as a qualified insurance corporation under paragraph (1) solely because the percentage determined under paragraph (1)(B) is 25 percent or less, a United States person that owns stock in such corporation may elect to treat such stock as stock of a qualifying insurance corporation if—

"(A) the percentage so determined for the corporation is at least 10 percent, and

"(B) under regulations provided by the Secretary, based on the applicable facts and circumstances—

"(i) the corporation is predominantly engaged in an insurance business, and

"(ii) such failure is due solely to runoff-related or rating-related circumstances involving such insurance business.

"(3) APPLICABLE INSURANCE LIABILITIES.—For purposes of this subsection—

"(A) IN GENERAL.—The term 'applicable insurance liabilities' means, with respect to any life or property and casualty insurance business—

"(i) loss and loss adjustment expenses, and

"(ii) reserves (other than deficiency, contingency, or unearned premium reserves) for life and health insurance risks and life and health insurance claims with respect to contracts providing coverage for mortality or morbidity risks.

"(B) LIMITATIONS ON AMOUNT OF LIABILITIES.—Any amount determined under clause (i) or (ii) of subparagraph (A) shall not exceed the lesser of such amount—

"(i) as reported to the applicable insurance regulatory body in the applicable financial statement described in paragraph (4)(A) (or, if less, the amount required by applicable law or regulation), or

"(ii) as determined under regulations prescribed by the Secretary.

"(4) OTHER DEFINITIONS AND RULES.—For purposes of this subsection—

"(A) APPLICABLE FINANCIAL STATEMENT.—The term 'applicable financial statement' means a statement for financial reporting purposes which—

"(i) is made on the basis of generally accepted accounting principles,

"(ii) is made on the basis of international financial reporting standards, but only if there is no statement that meets the requirement of clause (i), or

"(iii) except as otherwise provided by the Secretary in regulations, is the annual statement which is required to be filed with the applicable insurance regulatory body, but only if there is no statement which meets the requirements of clause (i) or (ii).

"(B) APPLICABLE INSURANCE REGULATORY BODY.—The term 'applicable insurance regulatory body' means, with respect to any insurance business, the entity established by law to license, authorize, or regulate such business and to which the statement described in subparagraph (A) is provided.".

(c) EFFECTIVE DATE.—The amendments made by this section shall apply to taxable years beginning after December 31, 2017.

**SEC. 14502. REPEAL OF FAIR MARKET VALUE METHOD OF INTEREST EXPENSE APPORTIONMENT.**

(a) IN GENERAL.—Paragraph (2) of section 864(e) is amended to read as follows:

"(2) GROSS INCOME AND FAIR MARKET VALUE METHODS MAY NOT BE USED FOR INTEREST.—All allocations and apportionments of interest expense shall be determined using the adjusted bases of assets rather than on the basis of the fair market value of the assets or gross income.".

(b) EFFECTIVE DATE.—The amendment made by this section shall apply to taxable years beginning after December 31, 2017.

# TITLE II

**SEC. 20001. OIL AND GAS PROGRAM.**

(a) DEFINITIONS.—In this section:

(1) COASTAL PLAIN.—The term "Coastal Plain" means the area identified as the 1002 Area on the plates prepared by the United States Geological Survey entitled "ANWR Map – Plate 1" and "ANWR Map – Plate 2", dated October 24, 2017, and on file with the United States Geological Survey

and the Office of the Solicitor of the Department of the Interior.

(2) SECRETARY.—The term "Secretary" means the Secretary of the Interior, acting through the Bureau of Land Management.

(b) OIL AND GAS PROGRAM.—

(1) IN GENERAL.—Section 1003 of the Alaska National Interest Lands Conservation Act (16 U.S.C. 3143) shall not apply to the Coastal Plain.

(2) ESTABLISHMENT.—

(A) IN GENERAL.—The Secretary shall establish and administer a competitive oil and gas program for the leasing, development, production, and transportation of oil and gas in and from the Coastal Plain.

(B) PURPOSES.—Section 303(2)(B) of the Alaska National Interest Lands Conservation Act (Public Law 96–487; 94 Stat. 2390) is amended—

(i) in clause (iii), by striking "and" at the end;

(ii) in clause (iv), by striking the period at the end and inserting "; and"; and

(iii) by adding at the end the following:

"(v) to provide for an oil and gas program on the Coastal Plain.".

(3) MANAGEMENT.—Except as otherwise provided in this section, the Secretary shall manage the oil and gas program on the Coastal Plain in a manner similar to the administration of lease sales under the Naval Petroleum Reserves Production Act of 1976 (42 U.S.C. 6501 et seq.) (including regulations).

(4) ROYALTIES.—Notwithstanding the Mineral Leasing Act (30 U.S.C. 181 et seq.), the royalty rate for leases issued pursuant to this section shall be 16.67 percent.

(5) RECEIPTS.—Notwithstanding the Mineral Leasing Act (30 U.S.C. 181 et seq.), of the amount of adjusted bonus, rental, and royalty receipts derived from the oil and gas program and operations on Federal land authorized under this section—

(A) 50 percent shall be paid to the State of Alaska; and

(B) the balance shall be deposited into the Treasury as miscellaneous receipts.

(c) 2 LEASE SALES WITHIN 10 YEARS.—

(1) REQUIREMENT.—

(A) IN GENERAL.—Subject to subparagraph (B), the Secretary shall conduct not fewer than 2 lease sales area-wide under the oil and gas program under this section by not later than 10 years after the date of enactment of this Act.

(B) SALE ACREAGES; SCHEDULE.—

(i) ACREAGES.—The Secretary shall offer for lease under the oil and gas program under this section—

(I) not fewer than 400,000 acres area-wide in each lease sale; and

(II) those areas that have the highest potential for the discovery of hydrocarbons.

(ii) SCHEDULE.—The Secretary shall offer—

(I) the initial lease sale under the oil and gas program under this section not later than 4 years after the date of enactment of this Act; and

(II) a second lease sale under the oil and gas program under this section not later than 7 years after the date of enactment of this Act.

(2) RIGHTS-OF-WAY.—The Secretary shall issue any rights-of-way or easements across the Coastal Plain for the exploration, development, production, or transportation necessary to carry out this section.

(3) SURFACE DEVELOPMENT.—In administering this section, the Secretary shall authorize up to 2,000 surface acres of Federal land on the Coastal Plain to be covered by production and support facilities (including airstrips and any area covered by gravel berms or piers for support of pipelines) during the term of the leases under the oil and gas program under this section.

**SEC. 20002. LIMITATIONS ON AMOUNT OF DISTRIBUTED QUALIFIED OUTER CONTINENTAL SHELF REVENUES.**

Section 105(f)(1) of the Gulf of Mexico Energy Security Act of 2006 (43 U.S.C. 1331 note; Public Law 109–432) is amended by striking "exceed $500,000,000 for each of fiscal years 2016 through 2055." and inserting the following: "exceed—

"(A) $500,000,000 for each of fiscal years 2016 through 2019;

"(B) $650,000,000 for each of fiscal years 2020 and 2021; and

"(C) $500,000,000 for each of fiscal years 2022 through 2055.".

**SEC. 20003. STRATEGIC PETROLEUM RESERVE DRAWDOWN AND SALE.**

(a) DRAWDOWN AND SALE.—

(1) IN GENERAL.—Notwithstanding section 161 of the Energy Policy and Conservation Act (42 U.S.C. 6241), except as provided in subsections (b) and (c), the Secretary of Energy shall draw down and sell from the Strategic Petroleum Reserve 7,000,000 barrels of crude oil during the period of fiscal years 2026 through 2027.

(2) DEPOSIT OF AMOUNTS RECEIVED FROM SALE.—Amounts received from a sale under paragraph (1) shall be deposited in the general fund of the Treasury during the fiscal year in which the sale occurs.

(b) EMERGENCY PROTECTION.—The Secretary of Energy shall not draw down and sell crude oil under subsection (a) in a quantity that would limit the authority to sell petroleum products under subsection (h) of section 161 of the Energy Policy and Conservation Act (42 U.S.C. 6241) in the full quantity authorized by that subsection.

(c) LIMITATION.—The Secretary of Energy shall not drawdown or conduct sales of crude oil under subsection

(a) after the date on which a total of $600,000,000 has been deposited in the general fund of the Treasury from sales authorized under that subsection.

# H.R. 1

| *Managers on the part of the* HOUSE | *Managers on the part of the* SENATE |
|---|---|
| From the Committee on Ways and Means, for consideration of the House bill and the Senate amendment, and modifications committed to conference: | |
| Mr. Brady of Texas | |
| Mr. Nunes | |
| Mr. Roskam | |
| Mrs. Black | |
| Mrs. Noem | |
| Mr. Neal | |
| Mr. Levin | |

# H.R. 1—Continued

| *Managers on the part of the* HOUSE | *Managers on the part of the* SENATE |
|---|---|
| Mr. Doggett | |
| | |
| | |
| | |
| | |
| | |
| | |
| | |

| *Managers on the part of the* HOUSE | *Managers on the part of the* SENATE |
|---|---|
| From the Committee on Energy and Commerce, for consideration of sec. 20003 of the Senate amendment, and modifications committed to conference: | |
| Mr. Upton | |
| Mr. Shimkus | |
| Ms. Castor of Florida | |
| | |
| | |
| | |

# H.R. 1—Continued

| *Managers on the part of the* HOUSE | *Managers on the part of the* SENATE |
|---|---|
| From the Committee on Natural Resources, for consideration of secs. 20001 and 20002 of the Senate amendment, and modifications committed to conference: | |
| Mr. Bishop of Utah | |
| Mr. Young of Alaska | |
| Mr. Grijalva | |
| | |
| | |
| | |
| | |